Dealers,
Healers,
Brutes
& Saviors

Dealers, Healers, & Brutes & Saviors

Eight Winning Styles
for Solving
Giant Business Crises

GERALD C. MEYERS & SUSAN MEYERS

John Wiley & Sons, Inc.

New York • Chichester • Weinheim • Brisbane • Singapore • Toronto

This publication is designed to provide accurate and authoritative information in
regard to the subject matter covered. It is sold with the understanding that the
publisher is not engaged in rendering professional services. If legal, accounting,
medical, psychological or any other expert assistance is required, the services of a
competent professional person should be sought.

PHOTO CREDITS: Page 98: Christopher Jacobs Productions; Page 158: credit—
UAW Solidarity; Page 180 (top): Carroll-Haig Studios; Page 194 (bottom): © Carolyn
Caddes, 1997. Pages 20, 40, 54, 64, 76, 88, 108, 144, 180 (bottom), 210, 244: Ken
Andrea of Carnegie Mellon University.

ISBN 0-471-34782-5

Printed in the United States of America.

10 9 8 7 6 5 4 3 2 1

This book is for
Barbara, Andy, and Nancy
and for
Jonathan and Jacob

CONTENTS

ACKNOWLEDGMENTS

We want to thank the executives who appear in this book for their cooperation and remarkable candor. They are:

James B. Adamson	Chairman and CEO, Advantica Restaurant Group, Inc.
Vaughn L. Beals	Former Chairman and CEO, Harley-Davidson Motor Company
Peter I. Bijur	Chairman and CEO, Texaco, Inc.
Dennis L. Carter	Vice President, Marketing, Intel Corporation
Alfred A. Checchi	Former Co-Chairman, Northwest Airlines, Inc.
Robert L. Crandall	Former Chairman and CEO, American Airlines, Inc.
Steven F. Goldstone	Chairman and CEO, Nabisco Holdings Group
Gerald Greenwald	Former Chairman and CEO, United Airlines, Inc.
Andrew S. Grove	Chairman, Intel Corporation
Floyd Hall	Chairman and CEO, Kmart Corporation
Richard A. Hazleton	Chairman and Former CEO, Dow Corning Corporation

Thomas G. Labrecque	Former Chairman and CEO, The Chase Manhattan Corporation
Craig R. Lentzsch	President and CEO, Greyhound Lines, Inc.
Keith R. McKennon	Former Chairman and CEO, Dow Corning Corporation
Robert S. "Steve" Miller	Former CEO, Morrison Knudsen and CEO, Waste Management, Inc.
Peter J. Pestillo	Vice Chairman and Chief of Staff, Ford Motor Company
Henry B. Schacht	Former Chairman and CEO, Lucent Technologies Inc.
Richard A. Snell	Chairman and CEO, Federal-Mogul Corporation
Richard F. Teerlink	Former CEO, Chairman of the Board of Directors, Harley-Davidson Motor Company
Frank J. Vega	President and CEO, Detroit Newspapers
Stephen M. Wolf	Chairman, USAirways, Inc.
Stephen P. Yokich	President, International Union, United Automobile Workers of America
Jerome B. York	Vice Chairman, Tracinda Corporation
Samuel Zell	Chairman and President, Equity Group Investments

We are grateful for the support of several university deans, associate deans, and department heads at the University of Michigan Business School and Carnegie Mellon University, Graduate School of Industrial Administration. Thanks to B. Joseph White, Ilker Baybars, Susan Ashford, Jane Dutton, Robert S. Sullivan, Elizabeth E. Bailey, and Douglas M. Dunn. Also to Edward A. Snyder at the University of Virginia Darden School for bringing the real world into the classroom.

We thank the late George Leland Bach, the first dean at GSIA, and the late Richard M. Cyert, president of Carnegie Mellon University, for their friendship and insights into business and government behavior.

We want to acknowledge Ann Grekila and Joanne Ripple, associates who for more than fifteen years skillfully juggled secretarial details.

To all the graduate students at the University of Michigan Business School and the Graduate School of Industrial Administration at Carnegie Mellon University, who brought these stories to life in the classroom. Also to the teaching assistants who dug out much of the research for this book. They kept the dialogue challenging.

We thank our literary agent, Sheree Bykofsky, for recognizing the promise of our ideas. We are also grateful to our very able editor, Renana Meyers, for her cheerfulness and steady encouragement.

Thanks to Kim Davis, Julie Leitman, Alice Lucey, Serine Steakley, and Mandy Smith, whose steady faith and friendship helped to keep this book on course.

A special thanks to Thomas B. Jacob, Miriam Jacob, Maureen and James Simmons, Andrew Meyers and Nancy Smith, all family members who cheered us on. We are also thankful to Barbara Meyers and Jonathan Simmons. You kept us going from beginning to end. We owe you our gratitude.

PREFACE

>——◆——<

The twin turbines of the shiny Gulfstream IV whined to a halt. The cockpit door heaved back, and the metal steps of the private jet folded down. I was standing at the bottom of those steps, ready to shake hands with one of the best-known, best-paid business executives in America.

I had read plenty about RJR Nabisco chairman and CEO Steve Goldstone, but we had never met. Goldstone had just survived a pressure-cooker of a year. His company's flagship product, cigarettes, was under withering fire from angry consumers, ambitious lawyers, and the Food and Drug Administration. Goldstone was deep into extremely delicate negotiations in hopes of forging a Congressional compromise settling dozens of potentially ruinous lawsuits against his industry.

Goldstone had flown to Pittsburgh that day in May 1997 to spend the afternoon with my graduate business students at Carnegie Mellon University. I was expecting to greet a tobacco company cartoon, a chain-smoking, tough-talking smoothie, maybe Joe Camel himself in a gray flannel suit. All morning I had worried that my students would treat him with contempt and cynicism, and that a smug Goldstone would respond with dry, lawyerly indifference.

But Steve stepped off that plane smiling and greeted me with a witty remark. We shook hands and headed for our limo. Our conversation all the way to campus was respectful and stimulating. As I briefed Steve about the day ahead I saw in his face only curiosity and an eagerness to mix it up. Here was a lively, sensitive man who defied all of my expectations. I couldn't wait to get him in front of my students.

For fifteen years I've orchestrated frank, no-holds-barred sessions between my graduate business students and America's best business leaders. One week it's Goldstone getting off the plane; the next week it's American Airlines CEO Bob Crandall; the following week it's Texaco CEO Peter Bijur; then financial expert Steve Miller. Most of these executives treat my students like real people and relish the candid give-and-take. Many drape themselves over the podium, draining soft drinks and cracking jokes. Their informal demeanor says "Go ahead, ask me anything!" We do. Most of the time they give back real, unrehearsed answers.

They also shatter stereotypes. We've been stunned by how three-dimensional these business leaders are, no matter how lofty their achievements have been. There hasn't been an angel, a demon, or a cardboard cutout in the whole bunch. They speak of their apprehensions and miscalculations. They show warmth, anger, and about half the time, humility. Crandall rolled up his shirtsleeves and exhibited a great, unexpected sense of fun. Northwest Airlines former co-CEO Al Checchi, whose name is usually followed by a statement of his net worth, repeatedly returned to issues of civic responsibility. Ford chief of staff Pete Pestillo, a master negotiator, seemed shy.

The cumulative experience of spending one-on-one and classroom time with these top business managers provided me with something extraordinary: a firsthand exposure to their inside stories. The chance to ask important, often irreverent questions. A gritty understanding of how such executives make decisions; why they make mistakes; what powerful forces prey on them; what they value; what they are willing to sacrifice to stay on top; and what they'll fight for to the bitter end. Hundreds of CEOs walked me behind the scenes, lawyers and public relations people mercifully stripped away. I heard incredible tales of narcissism, greed, ambition, deceit, and dishonesty, all woven together into a cloth of creativity, productiveness, progress, generosity, and kindness.

After visits by nearly 300 top managers, I naturally began to think about ways to classify these business leaders as a breed. A former Fortune 100 CEO for years myself, I thought I was well-qualified to judge horseflesh. So I searched for common threads, for a list of universal qualities that I could bring to my graduate students and say, "Here it is, ladies and gentlemen, here's the stuff of leadership, one, two, three."

But a funny thing happened on the way to my list. What I realized from these firsthand encounters was that leadership in a crunch has no stock personality, no standard approach. I saw that the best business leadership occurs when the right conditions meet up with the right person—the man or woman with the problem-solving style best suited to the circumstances. And, as I thought more deeply about this, something else interesting happened. I realized that the business leaders visiting my classroom fell naturally into seven or so groupings. Each group had an identifiable style befitting a particular kind of crisis. It seemed useful to view these people as types, not stereotypes, and these groupings offered a shorthand way of classifying their approaches.

Most companies suffer from incrementalism. The boss makes a little change here or there, and over time the company morphs into a new creature, with fins to make the beast swim or feathers to make it fly. Small changes are safe and even prudent much of the time. The trouble is that over time they fail to add up, or accrete in unproductive ways and carry a company into an unplanned direction. Incrementalism is the easiest thing to do, and it's what most companies do most of the time. Of course, not every company conflict merits a major shake-up. But a crisis does.

The executives in this book are the classroom visitors I just can't forget. They met their crises head-on. They didn't just move small sections around—they took their companies apart. They used jackhammers, not pickaxes. They spread out the pieces, kept what was good, killed what was bad, and then rebuilt, sometimes in radical new ways. Their solutions on occasion were counterintuitive. They defied expectations. They succeeded despite objections from whiners, do-gooders, and naysayers. In summary, they didn't just solve their problems; their solutions were transforming.

These people are behind some of the biggest business stories of the decade. All of them have shared generously of their experiences, insights, personal triumphs, regrets (if any), and advice. These business leaders understand that dirty deals get done; that people drive from their egos rather than from their brains; that there isn't a meritocracy alive out there. But leaders like Goldstone and Crandall also champion creativity, productivity, and progress. Their management styles, and their stories, offer lessons that I hope to pass on to others—particularly to rising young executives.

Many exceptional business leaders do not appear here. Some of those left out are women and some are members of minority groups. They deserve special mention in a book about defying the odds and cracking the status quo. Women executives, in particular, seldom accept invitations to address my students. This may speak to the extra pressure they feel on the job, or to outside demands on their time, or even to my failure to convey their importance as role models for my female graduate students. In the years ahead I intend to attract more top female executives to my classroom. I hope that some of these successful businesspeople will be former students from my classes.

In the meantime, the parade of private jets continues to deliver the best of the business galaxy to my classroom. Some of these executives will certainly join the top ranks of those in this book. They will have to be exceptional to match this remarkable group.

—Gerald C. Meyers

Dealers, Healers, Brutes & Saviors

Unorthodox Operators
Taming Big Labor

Unorthodox Operators:

⇨ Know when and how to break tradition
⇨ Stimulate change with all its messy disruptions as a means to a better end
⇨ Bear tremendous risk without cracking
⇨ Understand that creative solutions are threatening but proceed anyway
⇨ May force a company into a crisis to get a big result

Strong, well-organized labor can quickly cripple a miscalculating company. Any company bent on progress with a minimum of labor interference must keep its workforce watered and well-fed, and keep labor relations in apple-pie order.

But big labor and big business share a rich and nasty history. The relationship is historically and by nature adversarial. Stakes on both sides are always high, and emotions typically boil over, even when heated by the smallest flame. Both sides commonly expect the worst from the other and are already gnashing their teeth by the time they sit down at the bargaining table. It takes exceptional leadership to bring a company through a big labor confrontation unbloodied.

Sometimes the best approach to an old problem is to break formula, particularly when the circumstances are right. Executives Frank Vega, Peter J. Pestillo, and Gerald Greenwald astutely recognized a changed labor environment, then tackled labor problems in unorthodox ways. These executives boldly challenged entrenched, highly political industrial unions that were holding nooses around their companies' necks. Each broke ground using a different approach: one by matching himself to the needs of an historic labor experiment, another by outfoxing the enemy, and a third by—some would say—defiantly pouring gasoline on the flames.

The accused arsonist: Detroit Newspaper Agency CEO Vega. Vega sent this message to his company's unions: Hellfire and damnation, do it my way! A warrior, Vega busted his mighty unions with gusto and changed the newspapering labor landscape.

The fox: Ford Motor Company vice chairman and chief of staff Pestillo. Pestillo led negotiations with the United Auto Workers after sending this valentine: I love you, I love what you can do for me, so let's do it your way. A shrewd behind-the-scenes operator, Pestillo devised a labor agreement that brilliantly contained Ford's costs while punishing competitors.

The chameleon: United Airlines chairman Greenwald, who conveyed this supersincere message: Fellows, I'm sure we can work it out somehow. Greenwald, in a pathbreaking role, went on to bring labor peace at United and produce a nice profit.

Historical circumstances in the last two decades opened the door for executives like Vega, Pestillo, and Greenwald. The modern labor movement, born during the Industrial Revolution, had offered workers a way to bargain collectively for better wages and working conditions. Americans viewed organized labor suspiciously in its early years, but embraced it after the Depression. By the late 1940s and early 1950s, unions could claim as members about one in three U.S. workers. But early in the 1980s, after a quarter-century of political strength and relative peace, labor lost its momentum. President Ronald Reagan, once a Screen Actors Guild president and the only union member to serve in the White House, signaled the end of an era in 1981 by firing striking air traffic controllers, permanently. Strikes and work stoppages fell to 50-year lows. Union membership fell to less than 15 percent of the total work force. The public withdrew its knee-jerk support, and astute managers recognized that the time was ripe for new tactics.

Unorthodox problem solving in business, even under the best of circumstances, requires an iron stomach. Creative solutions in this world are often highly suspect. Big companies are far more comfortable living by boilerplate rules, no matter how stiff or stale. Most executives don't like to take chances. They live day by day, putting out fires and trying to please stakeholders. But sometimes circumstances require a big result, and that's when companies want someone competent and creative calling the shots.

Unorthodox operators are mavericks who are marked by their drive and talent. They welcome change, with all its messy disruption and rattling uncertainty, as a means to a better end. These leaders have the conviction and courage to see their efforts through no matter how many threats or derailments they may encounter. Unorthodox operators are risk-takers. They know that a wrong move can dismember their company, but they bear that risk without cracking.

These leaders succeed only with the undiluted confidence of higher-ups. Executives running public companies are typically responsible to shareholders through a board of directors, and sometimes a CEO. Second-guessing superiors will finish off a fresh effort, good or bad, before it has a chance. Detractors and naysayers are always out in full force during a company shake-up, and the media will publicize every perceived blunder. Without unqualified support, unorthodox leadership will be torpedoed or spitballed to death.

Nontraditional approaches to labor work best in companies that are in grave need of cost reforms, either via cost reductions or by growing without additional cost increases. These companies typically have considerable momentum in the wrong direction. They lost their way because they lacked a master plan. Companies like these cry out for radical change, and they can benefit enormously from a crisis, even if they need a leader to spur the company into one.

Labor-intensive organizations have the most to gain (or lose) in a labor conflict. The compensation, work requirements, health care, pensions, and peace of mind of tens of thousands of people will be affected, for better or worse, by the outcome. A poorly matched approach or lousy timing might take years to correct. Some companies never fully recover from an ill-advised disruption or work stoppage. On the other hand, the rewards of an unorthodox approach can be rich. A successful shake-up can unlock enormous profitability.

Vega, Pestillo, and Greenwald's approaches are instructive because they called these subtle shots so well. They had the timing, the backing, the skills, and the guts to challenge old thinking, and their solutions have become business landmarks.

Frank Vega

Frank Vega at the
Detroit Newspaper Agency

*"Most people don't know what they're here for. . . .
I know I was put here to deal with the Detroit strike."*

Frank Vega, CEO of the Detroit Newspaper Agency, never wanted to come to Detroit, or to play hero or bad guy. In Detroit, however, Vega is both. For years he strapped on a gun for work and traveled with a body-guard. His life has been threatened more times than he cares to count. Many Detroiters would like to see Frank Vega come to a nasty end. Others would run through walls for him.

In 1997 Vega busted the mighty Detroit Newspaper Agency's unions, with gusto. Before that the papers—the *Detroit News* and the *Detroit Free Press*—were losers in one of the richest markets in the country, held hostage by labor rules from a bygone era. Now the union is dead, both papers are making money for the first time, and Vega is an industry legend. Newspaper giants Knight Ridder and Gannett love him for single-handedly sending a message that management is in charge again; that Vega or someone like him can come in and cut a greedy union down to size—even in a huge, chanting, brotherhood of a town like Detroit.

Vega, 49, is a fast talker, a chain-smoker, a golf fanatic. He wears a suit and tie only when there is no other way out. His blunt conversation is studded with four-letter words no matter who's listening. Vega can stay in a chair but he looks happier in motion. His office is decorated with a practice putting strip and a statue of Darth Vader. He's a curious blend of executive sophistication and defiant street smarts. A CEO without boardroom pretensions. A bulldog with manners. A gunslinger.

UNION ROOTS

His roots are union. The son of steelworkers, and the oldest of four children, Vega grew up without luxuries, living with his divorced mother in Florida. His newspaper career began at 13 as a carrier for the *Tampa Tribune,* and he became Tampa's best salesboy. Vega practically flunked out of college, and he'll tell you that up front with no apology. He returned to take a job at the *Tampa Times* and began climbing the ranks. "I remember delivering the paper the day [President] Kennedy was shot," Vega says, explaining why newspapering called to him. "I related to the paper daily. It was exciting to put out a new product every day. I was always a good sales guy and I felt newspapers had a future. I felt I could do this the rest of my career and enjoy it."

Vega moved among an impressive series of newspapering jobs in Tampa, Philadelphia, Oakland, and New York. He spent a stretch with Al Neuharth, whom Vega calls "one of my mentors," setting up a national distribution plan for the fledgling *USA Today*. In time he was back on home turf in Florida, running a group of papers for Gannett. Vega, in his own words, was fat and happy. He was playing loads of golf. Then, in 1991, Gannett sent him on a reconnaissance mission. The giant newspaper chain was distressed about its *Detroit News* and the Knight-Ridder-owned *Detroit Free Press,* two longtime rival newspapers that were stumbling along under a joint operating agreement. The JOA, in place for a year, was not making good progress on its bottom line. What Vega saw in Detroit, he says, was "the biggest, most inefficient paper in the country." Vega filed his report with Gannett. He suggested ways to whip Detroit into shape, provided a list of people to do the job, and then went home.

"They left me alone for six weeks," he recalls. "I thought I'd gotten away with it. Then they called me. Said, 'We have a favor to ask; we want you to go to back to Detroit.' " Vega smiles wryly. "I said that's a big favor."

COMPETE OR COLLAPSE

Gannett and Knight-Ridder Inc. are the two largest newspaper chains in the United States. The Detroit JOA, the largest joint operating agreement in the country, was granted to preserve Detroit as a two-paper town, but it was also expected to save piles of money. Instead, both papers grew sicker. Circulation deteriorated. Revenues stagnated. Costs rose, the anticipated efficiencies from joint operations never materialized, and profits fell below the industry standard. The technology revolution was passing Detroit by. A printing plant that had been renovated for $22 million operated at only 50 percent efficiency, with 35 percent more personnel than the industry standard. For decades preceding the JOA, unions had whipsawed one paper against the other for concession after concession. Vega calls what he saw featherbedding at its worst. "There are universal truths in this business," he explains. "The number of people it takes to man a piece of equipment, how many people per page, and so forth. Detroit was manning in many cases three or four times higher than anywhere else in the country."

The Detroit Newspaper Agency (DNA), jointly owned by Gannett and Knight-Ridder and acting as business agent for the *News* and *Free Press*, had troubles extending beyond operations. Advertisers were upset about rate increases. Readers were increasingly distressed by the blurring distinctions between the two papers, even though they were both fiercely independent, retained separate editorial departments, and their editorial pages camped at opposite ends of the political spectrum. Vega knew that management had to offer advertisers better value and get a grip on its readership. But as Vega saw it, union restrictions and high cost structures were making it impossible for the Detroit newspapers to compete.

The Detroit newspaper crisis fit like a bad puzzle piece into the larger, national newspapering picture. Newspapering, a mature industry, had been stagnant for decades. A proliferation of alternatives, including news magazines, 24-hour news channels, and the Internet, had slowed growth. Consolidation was the trend. Many papers had merged just to stay alive. The industry was striving to improve profitability by lowering costs and raising revenues. Advances in printing technology had helped many papers enjoy huge cost savings over the previous decade because staffing needs grew so much lighter. New technology could also track customer demographics and offer advertisers—who represent 80 percent of newspaper revenues—a better market. Many papers were offering advertisers these better values, and increasing ad sales, by doing just this.

But not Detroit.

SHOWDOWN TIME

Crises are not all bad. They can be productive, and they are sometimes worth creating in the name of progress. The management at the Detroit newspapers probably understood that slow evolutionary change would never produce results fast enough to ensure survival. Vega unquestionably was sent to Detroit to whip efficiencies out the Detroit papers as reasonably fast as he could, and he knew his job from day one.

It is entirely likely that the Detroit management—and the huge newspaper chains it answered to—intentionally precipitated a period of rapid, radical change, even though chaos, productivity losses, and hostility would surely result, and even though employees might revolt. Metropolitan Council of Newspaper Unions Chair Al Derey, who led the union effort, asserted from the get-go that DNA's agenda was to undermine bargaining and to provoke an ineffective strike. A Federal labor judge has since ruled as much. The ruling is crawling through the courts on appeal.

Vega hates this accusation. He's out of his chair, across the room. He's disappointed that this has come up, he says, smiling but shaking his head. "We didn't push the strike," he insists. "We were willing to go three or four contracts to get this place right." The unions were "full of themselves," Vega continues contemptuously. Their bottom-line issues were membership, dues, and power. "Unions have become big business. They're supposed to represent the little guy, but they don't." All through this defense, Vega smiles. "Union leadership was dumb," he finishes. This is not a complaint. Vega looks ready to jump up and do a jig.

The undisputed facts: Talks in the spring of 1995 went extremely badly. Management called for downsizing, belt-tightening, and updated labor arrangements. Labor lashed back that the goal was union-busting and said management was refusing to bargain with them seriously after years of employee sacrifices. Each side accused the other of incompetence and greed.

Heated rhetoric became fighting words. On July 13, 1995, six unions, representing nearly every nonmanagement employee, including 2,500 reporters, editors, photographers, composing room staff, photoengravers, mailers, printers, and drivers, walked off their jobs. The strike was about money, about control, about culture and turf. Perhaps management was spoiling for a fight; if so, the unions would give them one.

The showdown was destined to last 20 bitter months, spill blood, cause millions of dollars in property damage, rip a hole in the Detroit community, and press Frank Vega's leadership to the wall. In the end it would also change the Detroit newspapers forever. "What the unions did by going on strike was hand me 12 years of negotiations," Vega states. "If they had stayed in the plant they could have killed me. They could have gotten what they wanted much more efficiently by being the enemy within." Instead, they handed Frank Vega the meanest fight—and the biggest prize—of his career.

"WE'RE GOING TO BRING YOU GUYS DOWN!"

Vega handled the strike from the beginning with a calculated tenacity. Other big U.S. newspaper executives had faced their own labor donny-brooks, but none of them went on the attack quite like Frank Vega did. Vega's unorthodox approach to breaking union rule: smash-mouth diplomacy. Union busting at the CEO level is customarily a laborious, premeditated engagement, full of careful chess moves. Vega charged in like a bull.

He smelled the strike, he says, long before the walkout. "We usually negotiate with four to six people, but this time the Teamsters brought in 40 people. One guy kept asking, 'Are we going to get free gloves? Are we going to get free gloves?' He asked every meeting. Another wanted bigger commissions, another wanted something else. There were 40 different agendas," Vega says. "We realized that it was not going the way it needed to go." The night before the strike, Vega says, negotiations dead-locked. "They were pushing us right to the edge. Their lawyer stood up and said, 'We're going to bring you guys down!' Everybody cheered." That same evening, Vega says, two union representatives brought in a counterproposal. It was terrible, Vega says, and was even missing a boil-erplate management rights clause. Vega says he caught the eye of a union rep, someone he says he knew well and liked. "I guess you know we're going on strike tomorrow," Vega recalls saying. The rep looked back at him. Then he teared up. "He said, 'I may never work here again,'" Vega remembers. "He understood the moment."

"IF I'VE GOT A REPUTATION. . . ."

Vega knew he had to act quickly and decisively. One of the first things he did was move his entire office away from windows so nothing would be thrown at him through the glass. Papers, computers, his desk, trin-kets—all were carried piece by piece in 30 minutes to a windowless room deep in the *Detroit News* building.

Vega makes decisions with swift conviction. "If I've got a reputation," he says, "it's for making decisions." Starting that first night, and straight through the strike, Vega made hundreds of them, one slammed up against the next, under intense pressure. There was no time for ambivalence or rumination. Decision making like this is often criticized as shooting from the hip. It requires excellent instincts. Vega was a superb marksman working from a well-planned campaign.

The strike plan, an extraordinarily thorough document, dated back to contract talks in 1992. "Unions are always threatening," Vega says. "They say, 'We'll strike you and close your ass down.' We had to be prepared. . . . And people say that we created a strike because we were so well prepared for it. That irritates the hell out of me. It's like living in Florida and knowing about hurricanes. You buy flashlights, tape up windows, bring in extra water because you know hurricanes are possible. You don't just sit there and wait."

STAYING AHEAD OF TROUBLE

What distinguished this strike plan from any other at Detroit Newspapers, or from any other newspaper management strike plan anywhere, was its comprehensive detail. Nothing was left to chance. From the first night of the strike on, Vega had operations mapped out. A massive security force was in place. Local police had been alerted months before. About 500 temporary workers waited in local motels. Food services were mobilized, and mattresses and cots were ready for workers trapped in buildings. Even so, the first night was bedlam. Nearly 3,000 people surrounded the building and no one got in or out.

As the strike progressed, Vega organized 1,000 newspaper carriers, 500 cell phones, 500 beepers, and a fleet of rental cars. Knight-Ridder and Gannett flew in substitute pressmen and journalists from around the country, and an outside firm took the place of striking Teamsters. Pit crews repaired thousands of slashed tires and replaced hundreds of shattered windshields. Vega says he had contingency plans for his contingency plans. "Toilet paper," Vega says. "We could have been locked in this building for three months and never run out of toilet paper." The cost was enormous, but the payoff was priceless: The struck newspapers didn't miss a single day of publication. Every published issue was a show of guts and determination.

GET THE PAPER OUT

A powerful beacon in Vega's brain said Get the paper out, get the paper out, get the paper out, and every action he took supported this goal. Early on, newspaper quality was terrible. Instead of publishing two thick, ad-stocked dailies, the plants were running off a thin joint edition crammed with wire service reports and short on local news. Vega didn't get distracted. "There's always a starting point," he says. "You progress." An intense sense of purpose is common to highly successful people, but Vega's drive was near-messianic. "Most people don't know what they're here for," he says. "I knew I was put here to deal with this Detroit strike."

Labor responded to Vega's success with outrage. For a time, hundreds of picketers surrounded company offices, printing plants, and distribution centers night and day. The unions mounted a circulation and advertising boycott, in effect trying to chase off their own readers. Strikers pelted police with rocks, and police in riot gear fired back with pepper spray. DNA's security guards were widely accused of roughing up strikers. Newsboxes were stuffed with pipe bombs. Thousands of vehicles were vandalized, and a delivery truck was firebombed. "Local hospitals treated a lot of stitches, bruises, and cuts," Vega summarizes. Labor called any violence on the part of strikers provoked. The newspapers refused to accept the blame.

At summer's end, both sides claimed victory and preserved a measure of bravado. A sign in the *Detroit News* newsroom read, "Twice the work, half the staff, and none of the whining." Picketers responded with their own sign: "Twice the trash, half the truth, and none of the ethics." In truth, both sides were hurting. Contract talks were frozen, with both sides far apart on complex issues. Labor had been unable to shut down operations or whip up unequivocal community support. Management was distressed because business was off. The strike continued, costing Gannett and Knight-Ridder buckets of money.

FLY AIR VEGA

Still, management had the stronger hand. A *Free Press* ultimatum ordering editorial staff members back to work and threatening permanent replacements if they didn't return strengthened the trickle of guild employees crossing the picket line. Circulation was off, but not alarmingly so. An army of replacement workers was turning out thicker, more familiar-looking papers which soon resumed separate editions, and the best-known sportswriter at the *Free Press,* Mitch Albom, was at his desk again.

The unions were deeply frustrated. They had counted heavily on Detroit's deep labor roots and the powerful legacies of local labor leaders like Walter P. Reuther and Jimmy Hoffa to clinch victory. So, two months into the strike, labor organized what it hoped would be a decisive show of strength. What followed, Vega says, was a huge psychological turning point, but not the one labor had aimed for.

On Labor Day weekend in 1995, a flood of people set out to shut down DNA's Sterling Heights printing plant. "The unions got everybody and their half-cousin out," says Vega. Protesters shouted, banged on things with their signs, and blocked off exits so as to trap distributor trucks inside. The unions felt they had a just cause and demonstrated as fiercely as they felt.

Vega stayed focused. Sometime after midnight, he began airlifting newspapers out of the plant, right over the heads of the angry strikers. The Sikorsky choppers could carry only 12,000 newspapers per flight—not enough to make a real dent in distribution—but they achieved a huge symbolic victory. It was a tremendous show of power, stamina, deep pockets, and determination—and entirely unorthodox. Vega says he watched the operation from a nearby overpass. "They were totally demoralized," he says of the strikers. "I knew they were thinking, 'Shit, how are we going to stop helicopters?' We didn't move that many papers, but they realized we would do anything we had to in order to get those papers out." The operation was christened "Air Vega." When the sun rose the next morning, "I knew one thing," Vega says. "They couldn't stop us."

IMAGE MANAGEMENT

By October, management had the undisputed edge. Advertisers were returning, if at discount rates. Nearly half of the Newspaper Guild members had crossed the picket line, and the papers were publishing daily. But the damage was hard to dismiss. Circulation was about 24 percent below prestrike numbers. Long-term costs from advertising losses were still accruing. In the Detroit community, the newspapers were the subject of hard feelings and diminished goodwill. From this point on, Vega says, much of the challenge was mental.

Vega doesn't excavate through many psychological layers when discussing the strike. He's an instinctive leader who manages from the gut, not the brain or heart. Even so, he had a remarkable understanding of how his mission had shifted. Vega sensed that he had to keep his people focused and energized beyond the early emergency strike period. Many nonstriking employees were harassed on their way to work, then discovered their cars vandalized in the company lot at the end of the day. The emotional pressures were intense. For months they had suffered the company's battle in very personal, demoralizing ways.

Vega worked hard to keep employees invested. He wanted them to feel they had a stake in saving the company, that they were fighting the good fight and much appreciated for it. Car-insurance deductibles, for example, were automatically paid off for nonstriking employees. "Everybody here knew they were a spoke in the wheel," Vega says. "Everyone knew what they had to do, and understood the importance of their contribution." He mentions Tom Wolfe's book *The Right Stuff*, in which even the janitor knew his mission. "If someone asked that janitor, 'What's your job?' of course his job is to clean toilets, but he says, 'To go to the moon!' Our mission here was to keep these papers alive. That was the mission of our janitors, too."

For weeks Vega practically lived in his office building. Instead of holing up in his CEO suite, he walked around constantly, talking to people, showing up in the printing plant on weekends, and crossing the picket line when necessary. Sometimes, Vega says, he would sneak back into the crowd of strikers at night. This is not unorthodox behavior for a labor relations manager, but at the CEO level it is never done. Vega was energized by the risk. It speaks volumes about him. He showed that he was not some frightened, elite executive type watching everyone else bare their neck on the front line.

Vega understood the importance of cultivating a powerful image to bolster employees inside the company and to intimidate strikers outside. Vega admits that there were many moments when he wasn't sure what to do, or wasn't certain he was doing the right thing. Still, he had to build confidence. To this end, he masterfully spun a handful of negatives into positives. For example, throughout the strike, Vega was the object of tremendous rage. He was the face on the company, the commander to destroy. Death threats, harassing phone calls, and intimidating letters poured in. To reinforce his evil image, the union dubbed him "Darth Vega," borrowing the name of an evil *Star Wars* character. Management typically takes the high road in such confrontations, particularly when the public is watching, preferring to promote a good-guy image. Vega could have fought off the nickname. Instead, he adopted it. T-shirts were printed up that read, "Darth Vega, may the DNA be with you!" A destructive hailstorm battered Detroit on the first day of the strike. "People said, 'How does Vega do it?'" Vega recalls. "Of course I had nothing to do with it, but you play it. It builds confidence . . . you play to that aura, that mantle."

RESISTING SENTIMENT

Vega also understood that he had to resist his sentiments—be they angry or sympathetic. He knew strikers personally who had a new baby at home or who had money troubles. He'd been raised in a union family. "I knew I'd been brought to Detroit in part because of that," he says. Vega is comfortable with union activity and culture. He also showed himself to be comfortable killing one. "Unions are a cult in Detroit," he defends.

Cult or not, in his early Detroit years, Vega sometimes hit the links or a bar with someone union. He thinks union leadership didn't like that closeness, especially when management and labor relations soured. "We still have people here outside," he says, jacking his thumb toward the window of his downtown Detroit office. It is exactly three years to the day since the strike began. Vega still sees an occasional picket. "There hasn't been a day in the last four years that I don't say, 'Those poor sons of bitches.' They were earning $70,000 a year without a college degree. That's gone." Vega goes back to savaging unions as big business. "They're not about protecting the little guy," he says. "You feel sorry for 'em out there," he finishes, gesturing at the window again. "I can feel sorry, but I can't let conscience or sorrow cloud the issues."

SATISFYING STAKEHOLDERS

By the spring of 1996, nine months in, strikers were still calling for a management surrender. The unions were waiting on a clutch of lawsuits aimed at stopping or reversing DNA's progress. They were also publishing their own newspaper. But the courts were creeping slowly, and the striker paper, *The Sunday Journal,* was beginning to look like a financial disaster. Strained union leaders offered a return to work but insisted on amnesty for all fired strikers. Vega's answer: No chance.

As Vega and DNA management saw it, the strike was all but over. A reader flipping through papers might not even realize that a strike was still in progress. Losses were staggering, but management claimed that on balance the strike had left the papers way ahead. Production was rolling along smoothly, with 600 to 700 fewer employees than before the strike. Marketing was more responsive. Readers were getting better papers. Owner Knight-Ridder announced its second-best earnings in five years. Gannett announced all-time record earnings. Vega denounced what was left of the strike as a war of attrition, and time certainly seemed to be on the newspapers' side.

DNA's success was bolstered because, for the most part, the company addressed stakeholders' needs well, particularly during the early strike months. Vega had to satisfy several vital audiences—readers, the community at large, advertisers, owners, and employees. Vega took care of the employees on a daily basis. Other stakeholders required different kinds of attention. Vega feels he might have done a better job here. "Part of being a leader," he says, "is that you're never f-ing satisfied." Some things went well enough. Beginning early on in the strike, Vega stayed in touch with major advertisers to keep them informed. Heavy hitters were telephoned and reassured daily. Vega, *Free Press* publisher Heath Meriwether, and *News* publisher Robert Giles at times used their own publications as platforms to reach readers, a mixed effort. The DNA also used other media outlets to cultivate public support.

"What's most important in controlling your strike?" Vega asks. "Public perception. But in Detroit, it's difficult. Twenty-five percent of the people are union here and are against you, anyway." By Vega's own estimate, he miscalculated the importance of community support and fell short in communicating with the public. Strike violence was inevitable, Vega believes, but the extent to which the Detroit community took the strike to heart caught him off guard.

Vega also had to reassure company owners. He says Gannett and Knight-Ridder never told him how to run his strike. "They did say one thing," he recalls. " 'Don't sell the future.' " He also remembers at least one discussion about money. "We lost about $100 million in '95," he says. "In September '95 alone we lost about $30 million—that's about a million a day. They said, 'What are you going to do about that?' I said I would cut that number in half in October, in half in November, and in half again in December. When I said it, I wasn't really sure how to do it, but I knew it was the right answer." Vega's reassurances bought him time. He delivered, and on schedule.

RECONSTRUCTION

Management and labor were still at an impasse on the strike's first anniversary. Vega knew by this juncture that he could run his business profitably on a smaller payroll. The papers published a full-page "Message to the Community" signed by Giles, Meriwether, and Vega. Noting the anniversary, they stated that "we don't feel it's an occasion to celebrate." After 65 bargaining sessions, they wrote, a settlement was no closer. Unions and supporters still "throw star nails, break windows, damage news racks and steal newspapers, block entrances to our facilities and yell racial and sexual slurs. They've even targeted employees at their homes." In the meantime, two "vigorous and separate" newspapers were being published. Vega and his associates pledged to keep negotiating, and they thanked supporters. The unions were in a bad spot. Violence had cost them a chunk of community support. The strain on union families by this time was immense. Many strikers had crossed the picket line or taken new jobs.

By February 1997, twenty months in, national labor leaders were urging the Detroit locals to return to work unconditionally. The strike had drained the International Brotherhood of Teamsters and the National Newspaper Guild of hundreds of thousands of dollars in strike pay. Local labor finally gave in—but in a twist, vowed to press on with reader and advertiser boycotts until they got a signed contract. Former strikers also challenged the legitimacy of thousands of permanent replacement workers. The newspapers offered to reinstate former strikers as positions came open. Labor's response: Go to hell. Metropolitan Council of Newspaper Unions' Chief Al Derey called the dispute a heroic fight against "corporate giants that don't have souls." Rhetoric aside, the newspapers declared the strike history and celebrated victory.

Private concerns about standing lawsuits, ongoing community strife, or lost advertising were not voiced in public.

POSTSTRIKE NEWSPAPERING

Vega understood that his work wasn't done just because the crisis had cooled. But certainly his job description had changed. "There was so much adrenaline during the strike," he says. "We were coming out of the chaos and intensity. There was a real letdown after the strike. It's hard to get people out of a crisis mentality into day-to-day operations again. People can feel that if they're not dealing with a crisis, it's boring." Once it was thrilling to squeak out a newspaper under fire, Vega explains. "Now, someone's job might be, is the color on this page accurate?"

Vega's new charge—refocusing employees—was complicated by the composition of his reconstituted workforce. In any single department at either paper he might have employees who had never struck, some who had crossed picket lines, others hired during the strike, and former strikers back on the payroll. It was a combustible mix, with unequal parts of loyalty and raw hostility.

Vega was determined to run DNA as a new organization. He had to effectively deploy his new workforce while tending to daily operations. Both papers still had to publish every day. To kill off postcrisis complacency and preserve new hard-won efficiencies, Vega built a number of motivating programs and task forces into the daily fabric. Vega says he was vigilant about keeping employees from sliding back into old performance habits. "People hate and resent change," he says. "People gravitate back to the old way." After the revolution, Vega wasn't about to let anyone regress.

"Things have changed here," Vega says. "The unions had us by the neck. We will never be intimidated here again. We have improved every measurable aspect of how we operate here, and we will never settle for less again. It's a new operation here and we won't be derailed."

AN ERA PASSED

What is the legacy of the Detroit strike? It may be too early for a precise assessment. National Labor Relations Board (NLRB) suits still stand.

Hundreds of former employees await a final ruling that will determine whether they are reinstated, with back pay. Although the strike is legally over, the boycott continues, and many employees work on without a contract, under imposed conditions. Just past the strike's three-year anniversary, circulation was still down 28 percent. Overall revenues were still down, too—one account says by at least $120 million. And DNA may never regain the goodwill of much of the Detroit community.

Even so, Vega calls the strike a whopping management success. "This was the first time a newspaper was totally successful in putting out papers during a strike," he says. "This was the first strike where distribution [problems were] overcome. And the odds were astronomically against us in getting those papers out." When all is said and done, Vega believes, this is where the strike was won.

Operations in Detroit are now far more efficient. Prestrike, Vega's organization never ran presses faster than 40,000 copies per hour. Three years poststrike they were running at 60,000. Detroit is still very much a two-newspaper town, and by many measures both papers are better products now. "[The *News*] went from being Gannett's worst operation to being closer to the top," Vega summarizes. "We're no longer the caboose of the newspaper organization." Gannett and Knight-Ridder had to eat the strike, but both chains are now earning record profits.

Labor lost in Detroit. This doesn't settle all future newspaper strikes, but with the available technology, a deep-pockets company like Gannett or Knight-Ridder, and management warriors like Vega, newspaper strikes have become much riskier ventures. "Once we went out and continued to publish, it sent a shot across the bow of every paper in America," publisher Meriwether says. Gannett and Knight-Ridder now have a model for strike-busting. When they want to subdue another newspaper union they can dust off a tested battle plan—and organized labor knows this, too. Some believe Frank Vega fought off the last big urban newspaper strike of our time.

TAKING STOCK

Vega readily admits that labor miscalculations greatly assisted his cause. He enjoys recalling how labor misjudged management's resolve; how labor never cobbled together a cohesive strategy; how poor tactics cost them public support and divided their own membership. The unions also misunderstood the inevitability of the new technology, Vega says, and never grew into the new era.

The unions were dumb, says Vega. That's his opinion. Luck—or an opponent's poor moves—can certainly be an ingredient of success. What's more certain in Vega's case is that he was smart, terribly smart, about beating his company's life-threatening crisis. Vega is distinctly different from the usual organization man. His tolerance for pain and risk are exceptional. He enjoys a fight for the sport it offers and seldom second-guesses himself. He has a small conscience and little empathy for those who get in the way. Vega inspired an army of ordinary people to risk even their own safety for the sake of their employer. "They knew they could follow him over the hill," says *Free Press* publisher Meriwether. "They knew Frank was not someone who was going to cave."

"It was the most exhilarating time of my life," recalls Vega. "Nothing in my career has ever tested my stamina, my intelligence, my ability to motivate people, or my leadership as the early weeks of that strike."

At this writing Frank Vega is still in Detroit. He describes his CEO duties now as "kind of easy." Vega knows how to goof off and is not ashamed to do it. He golfs. Often. Asked for a precise estimate, Vega guesses he spent 100 days on the links last year. He's got his handicap down to eight. Vega has worked himself out of a job—it's one of the penalties of accomplishment. Out on the golf course, Vega says, he wonders about his next mission. He's sure it will come to him. "People have always told me, since I was 15, that I've been in life in the right place at the right time," he says. It's a telling comment, coming from a CEO who used to strap on a gun for work.

Peter J. Pestillo

Peter J. Pestillo at
Ford Motor Company

"All labor relations are law, economics, politics, and theater."

The American automotive industry has a legendary, storm-struck relationship with labor, in particular with the United Auto Workers. Ford hit rock bottom with the UAW in 1937 during the "Battle of the Overpass," when management hired and armed strikebreakers who severely beat several employees organizing a Dearborn, Michigan, plant. Every third year, as contracts are renegotiated, the specter of that violence hangs over the bargaining table.

But Ford's labor relations have improved sharply since 1980, when Peter J. Pestillo arrived there. Pestillo is a radical departure from his predecessors at Ford or any other automaker. He has cultivated a peaceful, trusting relationship with the UAW that short-circuits conflict and saves Ford billions in production losses. There is also a second, subtler angle to Pestillo: He is an expert at playing the UAW off against Ford's rivals. Labor relations used to be a headache at Ford. Now it is one of the company's most powerful competitive weapons.

Pestillo is a quiet strategist who plays his cards close to the vest and avoids public view. In groups Pestillo is rather stiff, but he can use personal diplomacy like a stiletto when he so chooses. He has a sharp-as-steel understanding of union dynamics and has won the unlikely trust of UAW leaders because he understands their motivations so well. Best-known for his deft, disciplined work behind the scenes and extremely influential despite his low profile, Pestillo has had a strong hand in shaping the entire auto industry, and a range of industries beyond.

BREAKING WITH THE PAST

Pestillo was an automotive industry outsider when he joined Ford. The son of a union machinist, he spent a summer after high school working for a ball bearing company and paying dues to the UAW. Pestillo went to Fairfield University, then worked his way through law school at Georgetown University. At General Electric he watched labor relations tank in 1969 and 1970 during a 101-day strike. Pestillo then moved on to B.F. Goodrich, where he helped make peace with United Rubber Workers to end a decade of strikes. He arrived at Ford in 1980. In 1998, Pestillo became vice chairman and chief of staff, but he remains Ford's chief labor strategist. "I can't seem to get away," he cracks.

Ford was "absolutely in a ditch" when he hired on, Pestillo says. Cash-starved and weakened by a recession, Ford was fighting soft sales and lacked a fuel-efficient, front-wheel-drive car to challenge imports. Top executives were marshaling resources to introduce the Taurus sedan and dreading upcoming contract talks. Pestillo negotiated a contract both sides could live with that boiled down to more overtime instead of more workers. This formula would keep Ford lean and flexible in coming years, and the UAW liked it because they didn't want anyone on the street.

Pestillo recalls prompting a productive dialogue back then by, in his words, raising the right issues. "Rather than argue about wage cuts, I argued about quality," he clarifies. "You can't get unions to rally around productivity, but you can get them to rally around quality. Phil Caldwell [then president of Ford] was very good at negotiating. Quality issues gave us something to talk about. Then, when you get talking, you can talk about almost anything."

UAW labor leaders liked Pestillo's nonadversarial manner and came away impressed. Subsequent dealings with Pestillo pleased them, too. In 1987, he signed a deal protecting employment for UAW workers who might otherwise face layoffs. Ford had few employees in this category and no planned layoffs, but GM was poised to release tens of thousands of workers and had to abide by the deal, too. On Ford's behalf, Pestillo agreed to many more benefits and job security safeguards. These agreements were part of pattern contract negotiations and cost GM dearly when it was trying like heck to become more efficient.

CULTIVATING A RELATIONSHIP

Pestillo's negotiation skills were well-respected by 1996, but contract talks that year and a subsequent UAW strike against a key Ford supplier became career-defining events.

The UAW in 1996 approached negotiations in a state of high distress. Membership was on the slide, down from 1.5 million in the late 1970s to just below 800,000. There were many reasons for the decline, including automotive industry outsourcing, a split-off of Canadian auto workers, automation, and job transfers over borders north and south. Foreign automakers and their nonunion U.S. plants had also taken bites out of membership. The UAW was losing clout, and labor leaders fretted about their organization's long-term viability. Their top concern going into contract talks in 1996 was job security.

American automakers in 1996 had their own worries. They were struggling to stay competitive with Japanese transplants like Toyota, Honda, Nissan, and Mitsubishi. U.S. carmakers were paying wages and benefits that were up to $15 an hour higher than these nonunionized transplants. Transplants benefited from a younger work pool carefully selected to fit company-serving profiles, and as a result, Japanese automakers enjoyed an advantage of as much as $1,000 per vehicle compared to their costly American competitors.

U.S. automakers knew their best competitive strategy was to gradually trim employment while constructing more efficient facilities. Workforce reductions were especially critical at GM, a company choking on excess workers. About half of the UAW's Big Three membership worked for GM, which made more of its own parts than American competitors. GM went into contract talks in 1996 desperate to get down to fighting weight.

When the time came in 1996 for UAW President Stephen Yokich to select an automaker to lead contract talks, Yokich picked Ford. Yokich knew he could get the best terms there—terms that would become a template for talks with other automakers. Over the years, Pestillo had cultivated a startling, unlikely relationship with Yokich. Call them pals. Yokich had been a guest in Pestillo's luxury box at Detroit Lions games. The two men had golfed together, dined together, gone boating together, and traveled together to overseas auto shows.

Though they have been on opposite sides of the table professionally, Pestillo and Yokich appreciate each other privately. "We're personal friends and colleagues," Pestillo says. "We share common views on lots of things. And we're careful. If we're eating out, we don't talk business." This is a friendship built on common ground, several parts golf and companionship, and the rest an equal interest in the bottom line. Only Pestillo and Yokich know the exact mixture, and in the end it doesn't much matter. What does matter is the way Pestillo has turned a traditionally adversarial relationship into something approaching cooperation. As a result, Ford has the best labor relations in the industry.

PLAYING THE ANGLES

The 1996 contract that Pestillo and Yokich negotiated stunned auto industry and labor experts. Ford guaranteed union jobs at 95 percent of the company's then-current hourly work force. This gave Yokich exactly what he wanted. It offered tremendous job security and buried the threat of a membership die-out by setting a core employment level. Job-level guarantees like this were unheard of in the auto industry, and in almost any other industry as well.

In exchange, Pestillo got huge future savings at Ford by nailing down the right to pay a lower wage to new in-house parts supply workers. This two-tier wage system was an extraordinary union concession that abandoned a long-abiding policy of equal wages for all workers. Ford's commitment to minimum employment levels wasn't troubling to Pestillo, particularly since jobs lost to productivity gains were exempted. Ford had downsized sharply in the 1980s and then grown on truck sales in the 1990s. It was riding three years of solid sales and rising market share.

But Pestillo and Ford had another angle to celebrate: For arch-rival GM, the contract was a disaster. GM had the highest labor costs in the North American auto industry. It desperately needed to cut its work-force by between 40,000 and 70,000 jobs. A minimum employment clause suited a company with growing market share, like Ford, but GM was losing share. Now its hands were tied when it came to reducing labor. GM would have to shed workers through productivity increases, a much slower route.

Ford workers ratified the three-year contract overwhelmingly. Some 66,000 UAW employees at cash-rich Chrysler also signed. The deal left Pestillo and Yokich grinning and GM stewing. Ford's rival refused to go along without a fight. Yokich turned on the pressure by threatening strikes at important component plants. GM faced potential losses of $50 million a day. Management signed.

STRATEGIC PEACEMAKING

Before the ink on the 1996 contract could dry, Pestillo demonstrated his unorthodox approach again, this time with a parts supplier. In February 1997 the UAW struck Johnson Controls, Inc., a seat supplier where workers were organizing. Johnson Controls refused to recognize the UAW as a bargaining agent, and it offered Ford a supply of seats built by nonunion hands while it put down its UAW dispute. Ford needed these seats for some of its hottest products, including the Expedition, a sport utility vehicle that already had a three-month waiting list.

But Pestillo did something radical: He refused the strikebreaker-built seats, even though he knew Ford might have to suspend production and idle thousands of employees; even though he knew the shutdown could cost Ford $1.5 million a day in lost profits. Pestillo was willing to pay this price to preserve labor peace and his strategic relationship with Yokich. It was unprecedented for an automaker to side with its union against a supplier. Parts suppliers were stunned, then angry. The largely nonunion U.S. supplier industry was furious at Ford for dictating their labor relations, particularly because they were already under pressure from the Big Three to cut costs.

Pestillo stuck to his guns and ignored the outrage, as well as the criticism of auto industry insiders. As the Johnson strike dragged on, Ford turned to an alternate seat supplier, Lear Corp., which also happened to be a major Johnson Controls competitor. Stung twice, Johnson Controls caved in to the UAW. The seat supplier agreed to wage concessions and a unionized plant. UAW leaders celebrated, then vowed to repeat such tactics if necessary at other suppliers as they looked forward to future negotiations.

Pestillo handed UAW leaders a huge political victory, something they needed, something Pestillo understood. He also dangled the possibility that Ford would not block UAW efforts to unionize supplier plants, meaning the UAW might pressure suppliers with impunity. If Ford would turn down nonunion parts, labor leaders could tell union-resistant suppliers to go to hell. Behind this UAW-friendly action, Pestillo had done his own calculating. He hoped that strengthening the UAW in this way might, in time, help it organize Japanese transplants and raise costs for those competitors.

Later that same year, in 1997, Ford posted after-tax profits of $2.53 billion in its second quarter, the highest quarterly earnings ever by an automaker. It was reported as among the highest corporate earnings in any quarter, by any company in U.S. history.

SHAPING SUCCESS

The 1996 contract and the Johnson Controls strike were career moments for Pestillo, but he has aimed Ford at prosperity in broader ways, too.

Pestillo supported his bosses, first Phil Caldwell, then Don Peterson, Red Poling, Alex Trotman, and currently Jacques Nasser, in shaping a policy based on the idea that excess capacity in slack times was a far greater threat to profitability than lost sales during boom periods. So, while competitors ran more plants to capture a larger market share, Ford instead let volume push it to the wall. Instead of adding employees, Ford maximized overtime. This run-lean strategy paid off particularly well during the recession that tailed the Persian Gulf War. While GM was forced to idle workers while continuing to pay full wages, Ford simply cut back overtime. The United Auto Workers likes Ford's lean operation, too. They press often for higher wages, and Ford can afford them because it is not saddled, as are other manufacturers, with excessive, fixed costs.

RETHINKING THE EXPECTED

Pestillo has brilliantly rethought Ford's labor relations. He knows that management and labor both seek security, and he has exploited this commonality. Pestillo has also befriended union powerbrokers and top-level labor insiders, particularly international leaders like Yokich and local potentates. In this way, Pestillo has handed Ford a critical competitive weapon. Conspiracy theorists who accuse Ford of beating the competition by wrapping its arm around the UAW are not far off.

Pestillo prefers a low profile. It is both a personal preference and what he feels the job demands. "I don't like to be on the front page," he says. "Cults of personality don't take root. I try to make my successes institutional rather than personal. The press ultimately runs you down—that's where the story is."

Is Ford ready to support UAW attempts to organize at another nonunion parts supplier? "Johnson Controls was a unique set of facts," Pestillo hedges. "It didn't require much of a decision." Maybe Ford would support another strike. Maybe not. Ford will decide on a case-by-case basis, Pestillo says. "Do I foster organization? No," Pestillo says. "Strained neutrality? Yes."

Pestillo has managed to fit well under the autocratic oversight of the Ford family and has survived many shake-ups over the years. The Fords, Pestillo says, are not a major influence on labor relations these days, although they played an active role in the period that passed with Henry Ford II. "Henry Ford II was a better student of labor relations than he is given credit for," Pestillo says, "but from 1987 forward, you can't find a real active family presence." William C. Ford, great grandson of Henry Ford I and currently Ford's nonexecutive chairman of the board, remains involved and Pestillo has supported him at the bargaining table. Although no longer directing labor policy at Ford, the Ford family is clearly keeping very well informed.

Pestillo says his labor relations approach "hasn't changed at all" in his two decades at Ford. "My principal obligation is to communicate and persuade," he says. "We don't win big fights, as GM has learned. Even if you're right, you lose." Why does he think GM's labor relations have gone south? "Too many guys in charge at different times," Pestillo answers. GM doesn't understand unions as political institutions, he adds. "We recognize union leaders as politicians and we try to satisfy their needs. And the needs of their people, too." By way of example, Pestillo describes how Ford closed down one plant, then moved many of those laid-off employees into new positions at another plant.

"All labor relations are law, economics, politics, and theater," Pestillo rattles off. "If you botch theater, politics, and law, you can't make it up in economics."

Other words of wisdom? "People stay people, wherever you operate."

Also: "Labor is 11 percent of the private workforce, and their potential for mischief is colossal."

Pestillo says he'd like to be known for doing an effective job, period. He remains a Phil Caldwell fan, and he admires Bill Clinton the politician. "He's a master at working a room, at finding an edge," Pestillo says. "Much of what *we* do is politics, too." He brushes off any CEO ambitions. Until recently he was Ford's chief of staff, an improbable job description for an auto industry executive. "It's an imprecise title," Pestillo muses. Now Pestillo is chair and CEO of Visteon, the $17.8 billion Ford components manufacturing spin-off. Visteon has become Ford's number one labor relations challenge.

Thanks to Pestillo, Ford has not suffered a single strike in the United States since 1986. It is by far the most efficient American automaker. The company maintained peace during 1999 contract negotiations, coming through admirably under very trying conditions. At times Ford has actually touted its UAW alliance to promote sales, bragging over loudspeakers to 70,000 people at Detroit Lions football games that Ford is on the UAW's team (the Ford family owns the Detroit Lions). This may not sell more cars, but it is the public tip of a behind-the-scenes labor strategy at Ford that is worth billions.

Gerald Greenwald

Gerald Greenwald at United Airlines

*"I want to be known as the guy who made the concept
of ESOP a legitimate option."*

Gerry Greenwald is a very unlikely guy to run America's largest airline.

Greenwald is not a razzle-dazzle, go-go money man or charismatic risk-taker. Instead he is low-key, self-deprecating, a good listener. Though he seldom speaks off the cuff, he can be impressively articulate. He projects a smart but modest presence, even in front of a crowd. His appetite for public acclaim is pea-sized compared to that of most high-level CEOs. Warm, friendly, intellectually inclined, Greenwald comes across more like a college president than an airline chief.

All this gentle affability is deceptive. Greenwald has the heart of a pragmatist, not a romantic. He plays the subordinate role superbly, even when he knows he holds the reins. At Chrysler he let Lee Iacocca take all the credit, in part because he understood Iacocca, but also because Greenwald is no ego-feeding glory seeker. Power seeker, yes, compensation seeker, oh yes, but spotlight seeker, no. Greenwald works best in stealthy, behind-the-scenes positions, which explains why he was extremely well-suited to lead United Airlines' ESOP (Employee Stock Ownership Plan) experiment.

"I want to be known as the guy who made the concept of ESOP a legitimate option for companies trying to build themselves into more profitable, better places to work," Greenwald says. "I hope it will become a more acceptable option because of what employees have proven at UAL."

A BEAST OF A JOB

The son of a Russian immigrant wholesale grocer, Greenwald grew up in St. Louis. He pored over economics textbooks at Princeton, then signed on at Ford in 1957 and became president of Ford of Venezuela. Lee Iacocca sold him on joining Chrysler in its darkest days, in the late 1970s. As chief financial negotiator he helped face down the bankruptcy threat and prospered, as did Chrysler. He became Iacocca's heir apparent, but Greenwald was always in Iacocca's big shadow, and his domineering boss showed no sign of ever departing. Finally, in 1990, he could take it no more. Greenwald and other top executives, including CFO Robert S. (Steve) Miller and President Harold Sperlich, quit.

Greenwald's departure that spring was sweetened by a job offer. He signed up, at labor's request, to lead a buyout attempt at UAL (the holding company for United Airlines). Three months later the buyout was dead, but Greenwald collected a fat fee anyway (about $9 million). Iacocca once cracked that it had been a dandy summer job. Greenwald hired on to run corporate buyouts at Dillon, Read & Co., then in 1992 became president and co-chief-executive at Olympia & York Developments Ltd., Edgar Bronfman's troubled Canadian real estate concern. Greenwald was trying to breathe life into another troubled company, struggling Czech truckmaker Tatra Koprivnice, when United's unions came calling again. This time they had a buyout that worked.

Greenwald had accepted a beastly job. United was damaged goods, and labor relations stank. United had emerged from deregulation the largest U.S. air carrier and had banked on its sheer size to supply a competitive edge. But deregulation revolutionized the marketplace. Low-cost carriers and start-ups gobbled up market share. Many of United's rivals cut the fat or tightened up to stay competitive. United began to look very vulnerable.

In the 1980s, CEO Richard J. Ferris slashed costs and cut his workforce. When he asked his pilots to accept a two-tier wage system, they walked out for 29 days. Ferris made a star-crossed stab at combining United Airlines, Westin Hilton hotels, and Hertz to create Allegis, a traveler's one-stop shopping conglomerate. The strategy so weakened UAL that it became the object of several hostile takeover attempts. Ferris was eliminated in a 1987 proxy fight. UAL heaved a sigh of relief and returned to its core business.

United's disheartened unions attempted and failed several takeovers of their own before the Gulf War in 1990 shot out the lights for the entire industry. The big airlines squabbled over a diminished group of increasingly price-sensitive customers, and were often trumped by small, lean carriers like Southwest Airlines. In 1992, United posted a sickening $538 million loss, as compared to AMR, American Airline's parent company, which lost $25 million. Buyout and takeover rumors sent the company's stock price soaring.

Chairman Stephen Wolf laid it on the line. Without drastic changes, he said, United faced bankruptcy. Labor leaders knew Wolf was right, but the unions detested Wolf's cost-cutting style, distrusted his aloofness, and wanted him out. In 1993, pilots and machinists agreed: They would grant company-saving concessions, but only to prevent layoffs, and only if they were granted a majority stake in the company—and then only if they could handpick their own CEO.

A GREAT EXPERIMENT

The deal was signed. UAL directors sold their pilots' and machinists' unions a 55 percent chunk of the company in exchange for enormous wage and work-rule concessions over a six-year period. Labor got 2 of 12 board seats, with an additional seat set aside for nonowner employees. UAL directors also extracted the right to create a new, separate "airline within an airline" to compete with low-cost challengers.

United Airlines in one fell swoop became the largest employee-owned company in the United States. Labor leaders hailed the new model as a superior labor-management arrangement. In reality, it was a great experiment with no real precedent. UAL predicted the buyout would hurt the company for about two years, then improve earnings for more than a decade. About $5.2 billion was expected to flow from labor cost reductions and another $3 billion from new short-haul carrier earnings.

Greenwald was pressed into service. He had no airline experience. It was also his first job as chief executive officer of a major U.S. corporation. He immediately received a huge compensation package and something more remarkable: the cautious trust of United's new employee-owners. The unions liked Greenwald's conciliatory style. They believed he would avoid ruthless cost cutting and keep his promises.

Greenwald was eager. He arrived at United with two superskills—his financial acumen and a deep sympathy for the human side of negotiations. His first assignment was to unite his workforce, a tricky task since more than half of United's 76,000 employees, including flight attendants and reservationists, were not part of the ESOP. Owners or otherwise, everyone's paycheck had taken a hit, and many people were angry. Some new employee-owners were upset because they thought they had overpaid for their shares. After years of uncertainty, United's workforce was disastrously fragmented and demoralized. Even the company name was a bad joke.

Greenwald had to persuade the unions to set aside their parochial interests and engage in the business of building a more efficient airline. Employees needed to unite around the idea of ownership. Greenwald began traveling the company, listening to grievances and coaching workers to take charge. His down-to-earth approach surprised employees—they'd never had access to the top of the company before. They'd never seen a CEO roll up his sleeves and listen to all comers: pilots, mechanics, anyone with a gripe or suggestion. Greenwald's personal contact with United employees broke down the thick, pockmarked wall between management and labor. It enhanced his credibility, allowed him to directly address concerns, and gave him opportunities to explain his vision.

CHAMELEON

Asked to describe his management style at this time, Greenwald thinks a long time, then answers in a single word: "Chameleon." "The best leaders and managers tailor their style to suit specific situations," Greenwald states. "They need to be what is needed at the time and place." At Chrylser, Greenwald offers by way of example, cash was pouring out the door and the company was overpopulated to support profits. "What Chrysler needed then was an S.O.B. It was a ruthless way, and I didn't feel good about it, but there was no choice. The focus was on survival. We couldn't meet Friday's payroll."

He chose a different approach at United. "UAL had a bad history," Greenwald says. "It was managed as a severe command and control company. It was a service business that couldn't seize its opportunities. I needed to be a leader and build consensus. I pushed authority to lower levels to get people to make their own decisions. No more 'I need to ask my supervisor' stuff."

To soften UAL's corporate culture—and to encourage employees to make more decisions for themselves—Greenwald ditched many old company rules. He gave pilots more freedom to set their own air speed. He got rid of a rule requiring female employees to wear shoes with an inch-and-half heel when walking through the airport. Greenwald wanted employees to feel and act like decision makers, to understand they could decide the company's future.

Beyond fortifying his workforce, the new CEO had other urgent tasks. Institutional investors were jittery about future performance and board independence. Flight attendants needed coaxing into the ownership fold. Greenwald wanted to form task forces with employee involvement to assess operations. He also needed to hire a number-two man with airline industry experience.

UNORTHODOX GIVE-AND-TAKE

UAL's new "airline within an airline" also needed launching, and Greenwald moved on this quickly. In July 1994 United announced a shuttle designed to compete with Southwest Airlines in a market it had surrendered years before. Some questioned the timing and wisdom of attacking a strong niche competitor on its own turf. United was doomed if it overshot its resources, they said, particularly if it had to ask a fragile workforce for more concessions. UAL was $4 billion in debt, but Greenwald and his board believed the shuttle was part of the solution. They pushed ahead.

United also set off on a pricey expansion. While other airlines downsized, Greenwald added thousands of new employees. He increased shuttle flights and built costly new hangars. A new jumbo jet order rolled in. Greenwald's goal in all this was to improve service and beat Southwest. Doubters again questioned United's debt-carrying position, but Greenwald said the expansion was necessary after years of cuts and declining service.

Greenwald also looked into buying another airline, not so unorthodox, but in a remarkable turnabout he killed the plan when UAL employees objected. The buyout target was US Air. Greenwald took a serious look at the purchase in 1995 and included employee-owners in the decision making, a radical approach. When employees expressed reservations over what seemed a logical combination, Greenwald dropped the merger. "Employees in both companies weren't ready for it," Greenwald explains. "United people took the view of 'Don't shake us up,' and USAir [now US Airways] people said, 'Why should we sacrifice?' " Greenwald says he believed strongly in the merger from a business standpoint. "It would have been a great combination," he says. Even so, he walked away.

There was another unusual give-and-take between Greenwald and labor in 1996, when pilots' and machinists' unions rejected proposed wage increases as miserly. By this date Greenwald's leadership was bearing fruit. Operating income was way up. UAL's stock price had more than doubled since mid-1994, sick time and worker's compensation claims were way down, and operating revenue per worker was climbing faster than at American or Delta. Greenwald expressed his frustration with union demands. The unions fired back invective. A very traditional-looking labor-management rift opened, toppling some of the hard-won cooperation Greenwald had sweated over. Management saw the danger and relented. It amounted to a snapback: Greenwald agreed that wages would be restored in the year 2000 to 1994 levels. This was an extremely unorthodox capitulation, but Greenwald understood that the ESOP was on the line and chose to preserve goodwill.

IMPERFECT SUCCESS

The ESOP arrangement, an imperfect but undeniable success, flourished in the late 1990s with help from the robust U.S. economy. Prospering Americans flew more and came back from cut-price carriers. United's shuttle investment has paid off handsomely. The company now carries less debt, has a younger fleet, and is enjoying an extended period of unparalleled prosperity. "We've had 22 quarters of successively improving profitability," Greenwald said in November 1998, "and still counting."

Macroeconomics helped at United, but Greenwald deserves much credit for the airline's prosperity. His personal approach won labor's trust. That trust allowed a suspicious, splintered workforce to stop battling management and pull together during a critical period. Greenwald expertly handled the human side of UAL's crisis equation with his intuitive negotiation skills.

The surprise is that all the while under that nice-guy exterior, a pragmatist was hard at work. While making nice to the unions, Greenwald quietly tightened the screws over the years on manpower, fuel, and flight services. Greenwald also knowingly installed a tough, not always popular, second-in-command, John A. Edwardson, who became a lightning rod for employee discontent. Greenwald let him do the dirty work: controlling costs, knocking down union requests, watching the bottom line. Meanwhile, Greenwald, if not loved, maintained his good guy image. He is a master at accomplishing unpopular, unpleasant tasks without alienating his constituents, and this is part of how he did it at United.

Greenwald is a model of modern management, certainly of airline management. Instead of the grizzled, swaggering, leather-flightjacket-and-goggles type that dominated the industry until recently (think Frank Borman at Eastern), he was the first nonairline-trained and non-confrontational CEO in the business, followed later by Leo Mullin at Delta. Times have changed in this industry, from the early days when flying was a risky novelty, to the substantial and glamorous middle years, to the present, when air travel is recognized as a commodity business run with high technology and managed by equally sophisticated top executives.

EXTENDING THE OWNERSHIP CULTURE

Greenwald vows that when he is through at United he will never work full-time again. His cooperative, relationship-oriented style has a wearing underside. "I get upset with myself too easily," he confides. "I go out running for a physical comedown. I like skiing a lot—you cannot think about anything else when going downhill fast." Greenwald plans to head home to Colorado, to ski and just relax. Good friend Bill Hambrecht says he knows Greenwald better than that. A major business crisis will kick up somewhere, Hambrecht says. Greenwald will get a phone call. His retirement will go *pffftt*.

The ESOP at United, timed to expire in 2000, will take more to recharge. The radical power shift that saved United worked as an emergency device, but a renewal would raise dilemmas for employee-owners about how to buy new shares, how to maintain majority share, how to include new hires, and how to cash out employees who want to sell. A second go-round of concessions sounds preposterous.

Greenwald calls the ESOP "a very good idea but not a panacea." It prevented layoffs and preserved United as a big carrier, he summarizes. Operating costs were lowered. Employees grew into new decision making roles. But ESOP arrangements are risky, Greenwald continues. They require better planning and a quicker response to downturns to avoid a labor struggle. In 1998, when United suffered an enormous falloff in Asian business, the company absorbed the blow by catching it early and responding immediately. "Deep layoffs at United would be trouble," Greenwald says.

Still, Greenwald expresses no regrets about his role at United and still sounds excited as an intellectual and as a pragmatist about the historic labor experiment he led. "The ESOP is still a good idea," Greenwald states. "I'm looking forward to extending the ownership culture. Maybe we should be extending the ESOP."

At United, however, the ESOP arrangement has begun to crumble. Contract negotiations in 1996 left a lingering rift between management and labor. Employee-owners have expressed frustration that they can't cash in ESOP shares until retirement. Greenwald was disappointed when his unions rejected Edwardson, his capable but tough-minded heir apparent. New CEO James E. Goodwin is a knowledgeable industry insider, but duplicating Greenwald's talent and temperament will be difficult. UAL stockholders are holding their breath.

CHAPTER 2

Peacemakers
Finding a Solution

Peacemakers:

⇨ Lead like Churchill, not like Patton
⇨ Never lose sight of the human side of business
⇨ Seldom come from the corner office
⇨ Encourage others who can't stomach change or conflict
⇨ Frequently baffle the media

Some business leaders specialize in making peace, not war.

Peacemakers have a calming effect. They help dizzy or overwrought adversaries find common ground. They guide each side through the process of smoothing out their differences. Some peacemakers hitch willing but out-of-synch parties, others rescue deteriorating partnerships. The job has variations, but the result is always the same—productive working harmony, sometimes for the very first time.

Peacemakers abhor dictatorial management and seek consensus instinctively. These managers are comfortable with change and can grease the skids for jittery participants. Peacemakers think structurally and constructively without losing sight of the human side of the equation. They understand human nature, tolerate disagreement well, and provide clear direction without issuing edicts. These executives always perform under intense pressure from within their organizations and from outside stakeholders. Agitated parties may be ready to yank a company apart, or may have started the demolition work already. The job of engineering an acceptable solution often requires the skills of a symphony conductor.

Peacemakers behave more like Winston Churchill than George Patton. They play to win by the end of the season. They don't have to hit a home run every time at bat. They don't take mighty swings and risk a whiff. Instead, they put the ball in play, move the runner along, and clinch the pennant by doing things right play by play. Peacemakers build for the cumulative effect, and this is no mean feat. It can be tough to sell the virtues of patience when everyone wants a quick fix.

Top executives seldom make natural peacemakers. They are typically too hardheaded and ego-driven. The aggression and confidence that drive most top executives is precisely what makes them so successful, and is by no means a liability. Still, most CEOs would blow a peacemaking opportunity. This is about leadership on the quiet. It's a cool, stealthy approach.

Peacemakers are not flashy performers. Their victories are commonly obscured by more sensational events and higher-profile executives. Ask if they enjoy working behind the scenes and they respond mildly, indifferently. They just don't miss the scrutiny that comes with the spotlight. Staying low—and in some cases, staying invisible—can be enormously helpful when it comes to getting the job done, most importantly because it can avoid arousing the opposition.

The results of a successful peacemaking campaign sometimes sneak up on a company in the best way.

For this reason, the media often has difficulty with peacemaking leadership. It can't get a grip on the maneuvering. It can't find the story. Peacemakers don't shout, beat drums, or wave banners. They don't seek out an audience and they don't trumpet their strategies.

This territory is well-known to Texaco CEO Peter Bijur, former Lucent Technologies chairman Henry Schacht, and former Chase Manhattan Bank president Thomas Labrecque. Bijur reunited Texaco after top executives were captured on tape and accused of making disparaging remarks about minorities. Schacht and able first lieutenant Dick McGinn remolded a stodgy, utility-minded workforce into the telecommunications powerhouse that today is Lucent Technologies. Labrecque helped his bank through a gut-wrenching merger by playing a brilliant second fiddle.

Successful peacemakers reshape their organizations so that they can move forward on a solid footing with a unified objective. Their stock in trade is a calm, steady hand on the wheel, guided by an internal compass that few can see at the outset.

Somehow they know the road, where to go, how to get there, and who they can rely upon for help. In the spiritual world, they would be known as prophets.

Peter I. Bijur

Peter I. Bijur at Texaco

"You can't pay people enough to do what I had to do."

Before he became Texaco's new CEO, there were nights when Peter Bijur said he didn't sleep well. Bijur would lie awake, studying the shadows, brooding. The question eating him was this: If I become CEO, what at am I going to do if there's a disaster?

Bijur got his promotion. Texaco got its disaster. Some said later that America's third-largest oil company in 1996 was in fact a disaster waiting to happen. Texaco's catastrophe did not bubble up around a wrecked oil tanker or a drilling explosion—this crisis was of the human sort, triggered by a disgruntled employee, a damning tape, a set of media-savvy attorneys, and a front-page *New York Times* article alleging bigotry that is now a permanent piece of the Texaco story. Bijur is the CEO who made peace to save Texaco.

Bijur is a product of the Texaco culture but not part of the oil industry's old guard. He's forceful, but he's also flexible and open-minded. His management style is inclusive: When trouble strikes, Bijur doesn't barricade himself in his office but instead purposefully seeks out contrary perspectives to sharpen his decision making. Tall and balding, down-to-earth and earnest, Bijur can get frosted at criticism but he has a rare, very valuable capacity to back off, reengage, and then charge back fresher and smarter.

Bijur was born in New York, studied marketing at Columbia University, and in 1966 took his MBA straight to Texaco. At age 42 he became the company's youngest vice president ever. Bijur deftly handled the sale of about $1 billion in Getty Oil assets after a Texaco takeover. He ran Texaco's international divisions, at different times guiding production assets in the North Sea and the Saudi-Kuwaiti neutral zone. Thirty-two years into his Texaco career, Bijur became CEO. He had four months to enjoy his ascent before trouble struck.

SECRET TAPE

Texaco in 1996 was a much-respected company. Its oil exploration and production operations placed it among the "seven sisters" of the global oil industry. The company was largely regarded as a generous Southern-styled employer that spent a bundle on advertising and on cultivating its public image, sponsoring, for example, live New York Metropolitan Opera broadcasts.

Like the rest of the industry, Texaco in the 1990s had been sculpted by more than two decades of economic pressure brought on by OPEC and falling oil prices. In 1987, Pennzoil filed an $11 billion lawsuit against Texaco for pushing into a Pennzoil deal to acquire Getty Oil. Texaco declared bankruptcy to avoid liquidation and eventually agreed to a multibillion-dollar settlement, then fought off a hostile takeover attempt by Carl Icahn. Management emerged rattled but still in control.

Changing market conditions during this same period forced a restructuring. Texaco shed $7 billion in assets, stripped away layers of management, and laid off many of its 19,000 employees. Wall Street applauded the restructuring, but downsized employees took it hard. Some griped; others hired attorneys. Restructuring was neither a cause nor an effect of discrimination, but when all of the pink slips had been passed out, minority employment at Texaco was down from 10 percent in 1984 to 8 percent in 1996.

White employees had been downsized, too. One of them was Richard Lundwall, a 30-year employee who had started at Texaco pumping gas and worked his way into a personnel position in the finance department. In 1995, just a week before Christmas, Lundwall learned he would lose his job. He was indignant, then enraged. Three months later, lying in a hospital recovering from kidney surgery, Lundwall remembered something: his tapes.

Lundwall had secretly recorded conversations at work for years, sometimes as a memory aid for typing up meeting minutes, sometimes for protection. Most of these tapes he tossed into boxes and forgot about. But in 1994, Lundwall had carried his hidden microcassette recorder into a meeting and captured Texaco executives—himself included—exchanging derogatory remarks about minorities. Meeting participants had also plotted aloud to shred documents demanded in *Roberts v. Texaco,* a racial discrimination lawsuit filed against Texaco earlier in the year.

Lundwall has offered conflicting explanations for what he did next.

He has said at different times that he wanted to do the right thing; that he wanted justice; and even that he hoped to file his own age discrimination lawsuit. For reasons that only Richard Lundwall fully understands, he delivered the tape from this 1994 meeting to attorneys Cyrus Mehri and Michael Hausfeld. Hausfeld, an activist Washington lawyer, had won tens of millions from Texaco in 1992 in a dispute over a leaky storage tank and earned a multimillion-dollar fee. When Lundwall called with the tape, Hausfeld and Mehri's firm was representing the six black plaintiffs in *Roberts v. Texaco.*

PUBLIC HUMILIATION

Roberts v. Texaco, a class-action lawsuit, alleged that Texaco operated on the good-old-boy system and retaliated against any employee who dared to object. Texaco maintained a secret database for "high potential" employees, plaintiffs claimed. Qualified whites were rewarded, the suit alleged, and qualified blacks didn't count. If the $530 million lawsuit went to trial, a sympathetic jury could award as much as $300,000 in additional compensatory damages to each of the 1,400 potential claimants.

Texaco had flatly denied these charges for two years and refused to settle, even though it might have done so relatively cheaply and headed off a showdown. Bijur says that at the time it made more sense to fight back. Shell Oil and BP Oil had also faced bias suits. "Texaco was cooperating, providing data; we were in discussion with attorneys," Bijur says. "We were defending ourselves in court because we didn't believe Texaco had a racially charged atmosphere. We had diversity programs under way because we believed it was good business to do that; we were hiring minorities; we had objectives and goals; and we were really making quite good progress. So we defended ourselves."

Texaco's attorneys didn't know about Lundwall's tapes. They also grossly underestimated Hausfeld, who has a masterful understanding of the media and knew just what to do with Lundwall's recordings. Hausfield's law firm made a quick transcript. Two days later, while Bijur was golfing in Augusta, Georgia, he got a phone call from his public relations manager. "He said, 'You're not going to believe this, but there's going to be an article in tomorrow morning's *New York Times* about some tape recordings made by a Texaco employee and it's not going to be very pretty!' " Bijur recalls. Lundwall? "I had heard his name," Texaco's CEO says, "but I wouldn't have recognized him if I'd seen him." Bijur flew to New York. He read the article around midnight when the *Times'* first edition hit the newstands. Seven hours later, the rest of the world read it over breakfast.

The date: November 4, 1996. The byline: Kurt Eichenwald, a name Bijur still says with a tight jaw. Eichenwald described senior Texaco officials caught on tape allegedly discussing plans to shred documents detailing discriminatory hiring practices. But there was worse—much worse. Officers at the all-white, all-male Texaco meeting had allegedly referred to minority employees as "black jelly beans" and "f-ing niggers." Banter about Christmas, Hanukkah, and Kwanzaa celebrations allegedly included more racist remarks. The substance and tone of the conversation appeared blatantly offensive, and no one at the meeting had objected.

The article unleashed a cyclone. No U.S. oil company could claim to be even close to cutting edge on diversity issues, but now Texaco was in the spotlight and its shortcomings were front-page news. Embarrassing statistics followed. None of Texaco's top executives were minorities. Only 23 of 2,029 senior managers were black. In June 1996, five months before the tape's appearance, an Equal Employment Opportunity Commission (EEOC) examination of Texaco's records in the course of determining the merits of *Roberts v. Texaco* had concluded that Texaco failed to promote blacks as readily as whites in certain salary categories. Bijur's company did have a black director, University of Texas at Dallas president Franklyn Jenifer, but workforce numbers still lagged behind industry standards.

FIRESTORM

The scandal widened immediately. Federal prosecutors launched a criminal investigation into whether Texaco executives had illegally destroyed documents. Every big newspaper covered the story and most printed accusatory op-ed pieces. Leadership Conference of Civil Rights executive director Wade Henderson called the tapes "the functional equivalent of the Rodney King video for employment discrimination."

Jay Leno milked the scandal on late-night television. Americans sat in their living rooms, laughing derisively. "Texaco became a household word connected with racism," Bijur says grimly.

Texaco overnight faced the threat of a widespread shareholder revolt. For example, New York State Comptroller H. Carl McCall warned Bijur that the allegations, if proven, indicated a "corporate culture of disrespect" that might warrant selling off millions of shares of state-owned Texaco stock. Falling share prices had already reduced the overall value of Texaco by more than a billion dollars.

Bijur realized that his company faced possible financial ruin. The oil industry wasn't famous for its forthright relationship with the public. Exxon executives were memorably defensive after the 1989 Valdez accident in Alaska. Shell Oil mishandled an attack by environmentalists when it pushed through plans to sink a drilling rig in the North Sea. Bijur had to blaze a new trail.

The first thing he did was gather a group of trusted advisors around a conference table. "We tried to plot what to do," he remembers. "We knew we needed the tapes, and we knew we needed to say something but we didn't know what to say. We met morning and afternoon and around the clock." A war room was set up with banks of televisions to track the story. Another room was added shortly afterward, this one ringed with computers and employees answering the more than 30,000 messages that would eventually pour into Bijur's office, many threatening to stop doing business with his company altogether.

Bijur felt stymied in the days just after the scandal struck. "We couldn't even get the tapes to listen to," he says. "And a firestorm was swirling around my company." Bijur waited all day Monday, all day Tuesday, and half the day Wednesday before he felt he could fully respond to the allegations, he says, because he didn't have the facts. Two and a half days of waiting in the furnace of a public perception crisis is forever. Bijur finally couldn't wait any more. Tapes or no tapes, he had to get out front.

"SKUNKED"

Bijur publicly denied any systematic efforts at Texaco to discriminate against minorities, expressed shame and outrage over the reported remarks, and vowed that if the alleged misconduct were confirmed, heads would roll. Texaco employees watched an outraged and apologetic Bijur on videotape restating the company's code of conduct. An immediate review of every diversity and equal employment opportunity began. A prominent outside lawyer, A. Leon Higgenbotham, was assigned to work within Texaco to ensure that company practices were fair and respectful. Texaco also hired an outside lawyer to investigate the tape incident. "Wherever the truth leads," Bijur told a reporter at that time, "that is where we'll go."

On November 6, Bijur finally heard the tapes firsthand. "They were terribly scratchy, we could barely make out anything at all," Bijur says. Lundwall had done his secret taping on a microrecorder hidden in his suit pocket. Parts of the conversation were inaudible, other portions were difficult to decipher. Even so, Bijur heard enough. "On some tapes, very offensive discussions were going on," he says. Bijur called a news conference and suspended with pay two high-ranking Texaco executives, J. David Keough and Peter Meade, then cut off benefits to Lundwall, already laid off, and retired Texaco treasurer Robert Ulrich. That night he appeared on *Nightline*. Bijur hadn't slept for days and he looked it. Still, he came across as contrite and sincere. Many praised Bijur for his forthrightness at this point, but others branded it slick public relations.

Bijur went home from his *Nightline* appearance distraught. Earlier that day he had learned for the first time about 30 sealed affidavits collected over two years by plaintiffs' attorneys, each one from a black Texaco employee, each complaining about incidents of alleged intolerance. Some claimed that in addition to being passed over for promotions they had been subjected to racist remarks, including references to Aunt Jemima, orangutans, and porch monkeys.

Before Lundwall's tapes appeared, Bijur says, Texaco believed it would win its lawsuit. Even after Lundwall's tapes appeared, Bijur felt there was hope. "We had excellent arguments," he says. "We had statistics showing how African-Americans in our company were being compensated, we had statistics showing promotion experiences for African-Americans, and our lawyers felt we were going to win that case." Now a judgment against Texaco seemed probable. "We had the lawsuit pending, the smoking gun of the tapes with the epithet, and we were going to be hit next Sunday with 30 more affidavits, and *The New*

York Times was going to put an article out," Bijur says, describing his reaction back then. "And now we're really skunked."

NEW TRANSCRIPTION

A short time later, Bijur received a separately ordered, digitized analysis of Lundwall's tapes. The results were stunning. After outside investigators had removed background noise and digitally enhanced the recording, the most offensive racial slurs were absent. The word "niggers" appeared instead to be "Nicklas," as in St. Nick. "Black jelly beans" appeared to come from language used in a diversity training workshop. The most inflammatory language on the tape—every syllable of it widely reported—had never been spoken at all.

Bijur stayed contrite and controlled in public. Racial epithets aside, he stated, the tone of the taped conversation remained unacceptable. His outrage is more evident now. The plaintiff's transcripts were "just flat wrong," he says, and if the tapes had been properly digitized from the outset and if the media had behaved responsibly, the issue would have been destruction of documents, not institutional bigotry. "There would never have been a discussion of the racial issue," he says. "It would have appeared in the bowels of the press." If Bijur believes that the taped conversation was offensive even without the reported racial epithets, then should the difference between the two transcriptions much matter? "Fact: There's a lot of difference between using a racial epithet and saying people are getting jobs and maybe not deserving them," he says coldly. "I didn't like the tone of that meeting, but they didn't use those incendiary words."

As the days ticked by, Texaco continued to face a menacing lawsuit and a morally outraged public. The corrected transcription didn't much register with the public—the damage was done. Most whites expressed shock about the derogatory comments, but blacks said the remarks confirmed what they knew already, that racism is alive and well in American business. Civil rights leaders were especially vocal on this point. In response, Bijur attempted some one-on-one peacemaking. He sat down with civil rights advocates, including National Association for the Advancement of Colored People's then-president Kweisi Mfume and Reverends Jesse Jackson and Al Sharpton. The meeting backfired. Jackson walked out calling for a boycott and threatening pickets unless Texaco settled its suit. National civil rights leaders said they planned to make an example out of the oil company. A separate group of San Diego clergy and business leaders joined the boycott chorus and told customers to cut up their Texaco credit cards.

"WE COULD HAVE GOTTEN KILLED"

Bijur saw that Texaco was going down unless he took decisive action, even if the charges didn't square with what he believed were the facts. So Bijur in mid-December offered to settle *Roberts v. Texaco*. It was the only honorable thing to do, Bijur said publicly, but in his heart Bijur felt he had no alternative. "We could have stonewalled for a while but we would have been killed, for example, in the stock market," he says. Or in court. Bijur remains sensitive to criticism that he settled too readily. "The truth is, the plaintiffs put me in a position to come up with something by this time or the offer was off," he clarifies. "I could have called their bluff, but also we could have gotten killed. I needed to stop it." Then Bijur speaks like a peacemaker: "I felt by settling we could move the agenda from conflict to healing. Once the lawsuit was settled, we could start the healing process."

Texaco offered the largest settlement in a racial discrimination lawsuit in U.S. history. The cash payout alone totaled a mammoth $115 million. It wasn't a crippling sum over five years for a company with annual revenues exceeding $46 billion, but it wasn't the most important part of the settlement, either.

Bijur pledged sweeping changes at Texaco. The company would step up recruiting efforts and raise black and female employment levels. Managers who hired and promoted women and minorities would be rewarded. Texaco would do more business with minority-owned banks, advertisers, vendors, and contractors. Most significantly, however, Texaco would permit an unprecedented level of external scrutiny. A seven-member "Equality and Tolerance Task Force" would shape personnel policy and report directly to the board. Their recommendations were mandatory unless Texaco could convince a federal judge that they were unsound business practices or technically unrealistic.

Bijur had fiercely resisted ceding such authority. "I fought it as hard as I could," he says. "Statistically, I had evidence that we should not be subjected to that. But we were facing an $800 million penalty in court, and the jury was going to hear a tape, and on that tape was going to be an intolerant tone and attitude, and whether I could have gotten that tape changed in time to remove the incendiary language, I didn't know, but I did know one thing: I didn't want to go to court because we were going to lose."

In January 1997, while the settlement awaited approval, the EEOC moved in. EEOC officials had threatened along the way to intervene, but now the agency dropped its threat in exchange for the right to oversee Texaco's employment efforts for the next five years. Texaco would report annually to the agency on its hiring and promotion of racial minorities, providing details about each applicant for each position. The EEOC would be allowed to examine internal records and interview employees and applicants, and could sue if Texaco failed to perform. Whatever Bijur thought of the arrangement, he consented without public complaint.

PEACE EFFORTS

In March 1997 the settlement was approved. Although the class-action lawsuit was never certified, the settlement went to about 1,400 people who received an average lump sum of about $80,000 each. A few got as much as $150,000. Black employees also received an 11 percent raise. All totaled, Texaco paid $26 million in salary increases, $35 million for the five-year task force, and $115 million to the plaintiffs, some $29 million of which went to Hausfeld and company.

Bijur practically banned discussion of the settlement. "I spent an enormous amount of my personal time flying around the country meeting with employees, in Los Angeles, Midland, Texas, you name it, I was there—and we have operations all over the United States," Bijur says of that time. "I said, 'Now look, we agreed to pay this, we're going to pay it because its part of the settlement, and,' " he pauses here, then says emphatically, " 'You're going to forget it. *You're going to forget it.* If I find a single one of you making a comment to another Texaco employee saying 'Oh, you got a lot of money, you going to buy a Cadillac?' Or if a black employee says to a white employee, 'Too bad you didn't get the money,' I'll fire you. *I'll fire you.*" Bijur issued this ultimatum to root out divisiveness. "You know what?" he adds. "It worked." Bijur sounds a little amazed. "A lot of people said, 'Hey, it's not fair.' Life is not fair."

Mfume and Jackson called the settlement a good first step. They called off the boycott and dropped plans to press for a stock divestiture. Civil rights leaders called Texaco's new diversity efforts a model for business. However, civil rights groups didn't entirely let go of the opportunity that was Texaco. The scandal had given them a rallying point, and a victory, and raised a broad public debate about discrimination issues that they could build upon. "The civil rights leadership turned around and became supportive, not totally, but generally supportive," Bijur says of the settlement aftermath.

TURNAROUND

Texaco was credited with making a sharp turnaround. Wall Street liked the settlement, the story fell off the front page, and Jay Leno stopped talking about black jelly beans. The circumstances are notable: Neither side had proven its position. No impartial judge or jury sifted the evidence. Nobody ever determined with any certainty whether blacks had been systematically discriminated against at Texaco, nor was it ruled out. No one ever determined whether Texaco had been grossly misrepresented by the plaintiffs' counsel or the media, but nobody ruled that out, either. Texaco didn't admit guilt in any legal sense in its historic settlement. Even so, the public understood it that way.

In January 1997 Texaco dismissed one executive caught on the tape, permanently suspended another, and cut off benefits to two more for engaging in improper conduct. "I fired those employees not because they broke the law, but because they violated Texaco's corporate code of conduct," Bijur says. Lundwall stayed in the news, facing obstruction of justice charges that might have resulted in up to 10 years in prison and as much as $250,000 in fines. But Lundwall and Ulrich, caught on tape together allegedly plotting to shred documents, were acquitted in May 1998.

Bijur doesn't call Lundwall a whistleblower. Then what was he? Texaco was going through an era of significant downsizing, Bijur says, and Lundwall, 54, was afraid he would lose his job. Lundwall made surreptitious recordings hoping he could catch something incriminating about age discrimination, Bijur says. "In his mind, when someone came around with pink slips and it was his turn, he could say, 'I have tapes

talking about age discrimination and I don't think you want to do this.' "
Bijur believes Lundwall never intended to help the plaintiffs in *Roberts
v. Texaco.* "He was looking out for himself."

MIRROR OF SOCIETY

Texaco has made exemplary progress on race issues. It has met or
exceeded minority hiring and promotion goals. It has also dramatically
increased the amount of business transacted with minority-owned companies. Thousands of employees have attended diversity workshops,
and Texaco now "bends over backwards to treat people with respect,"
Bijur says. "I believe this company has truly changed. We're much more
inclusive. We think all the time about how we're treating our people.
Something like this can really focus you." Late in 1998, Texaco cut about
5 percent of its workforce in response to low oil prices. It's a safe bet that
the layoffs were scrutinized up, down, and sideways to be certain that
they were not—nor could even remotely appear to be—discriminatory.

Bijur continues to distrust the media. He feels he was "caught on the
horns of a dilemma" back in November 1996, when his company was
headline news. "The press is biased one way or another on any issue, but
they have an agenda and you will learn from them what they want you
to learn," he says. "Secondly, I, as chief executive officer in a company
about whom the press is writing, have no standing. As soon as I say
something it looks like I'm being defensive. You've already been told
one thing by the press, and you tend to believe that because it's already
out there. . . . If I put out information that is true, it doesn't get picked
up. For example," Bijur explains, "when we had the tapes digitized and
found out that the epithet which caused this firestorm was never said,
do you know where that appeared? Way back in the bowels of the
paper." Texaco is a major player on the world scene. Members of the
media continue to knock on Bijur's door. "We just have to give them the
facts and hope they're responsible," he summarizes.

Bijur still fends off accusations that Texaco once fostered a racist
environment. "Is Texaco racist?" he asks. "Do we have a toxic environment, as Jesse Jackson asked me? We are a mirror image of society.
In society there is racism, in Texaco there is racism. There is racism in
every organization in this country. Do I think it's any worse at Texaco?

I absolutely do not. I know a lot of people at Texaco—I don't know all 27,000, but in 32 years you get to know a lot of people—and I can honestly say that I've never been at a meeting where I heard the n-word."

"You can always do more and we will continue to do more because we are committed to rooting out intolerance," Bijur concludes. "But I can't change peoples' attitudes. I can change their behavior, but attitudes are ingrained. I can control what you say in the workplace but I can't control what you think."

DECISIONS FROM THE GUT

If forced to live through Texaco's crisis again, Bijur says he would do nothing differently. "I would handle it exactly same way. I don't think the company could have handled it better." Ultimately, he says, he followed his gut, through every terrible day until the crisis cooled. "You can't pay people enough to do what I had to do," he says. Bijur felt he had "27,000 souls, 250,000 shareholders and their families, and all of our customers, service station dealers, and people around the world dependent upon my decisions. I knew if I screwed this up, the company might not be here tomorrow."

Bijur has worked hard to turn Texaco's disaster into an opportunity. Supporters praise him for a speedy, sincere-sounding apology and a comprehensive, hands-on follow-up. Texaco has become a model of equal opportunity, they say, and Bijur demonstrated some outstanding crisis management, the sort that would have served Exxon well during its Valdez disaster.

The opinion is not unanimous, however. Critics say that Texaco deserved what it got after stonewalling for two years instead of dealing forthrightly with a racial discrimination lawsuit. Some wonder whether Texaco has correctly diagnosed its problems, or is taking the right actions to correct them. A few say Texaco has gone overboard and worry that a workplace focus on diversity may do more harm than good. Texaco's solution raises important questions about what can reasonably be expected from any business trying to change racist attitudes. "Generally, diversity is good for business," Bijur says, "but I can't judge what other companies can or should be doing. What we've done here is right for us."

CARRYING ON

Bijur's office is furnished with oriental carpets and an assortment of memorabilia. He also keeps several lumps of coal on his desk as a kind of reminder of the company's energy-producing roots. His management style is a "collaborative team-based approach where at the end of the day I get all the information and make a decision," he says. "It's different from command and control. I try to surround myself with the best people." He strives to keep Texaco's vision well-defined and to ensure that the people running the company follow that vision and agree with it.

Lundwall and his tapes, Bijur says, were a "complete bolt out of the blue," although Texaco was "very well aware" of diversity issues. With his firsthand knowledge of how quickly a controlled situation can explode, is Bijur living on a sharp new set of pins and needles? "I've been with this company for 33 years, we operate in 150-plus countries in the world, and on some days there is a personnel crisis, some days a crisis with a platform, or a gasoline tanker truck spill, or an environmental incident. We are very, very good as an industry at managing crises. Some are bigger than others, some are more public than others. A crisis is a crisis is a crisis, and we're an industry used to dealing with them."

A job like this calls for an occasional escape. Bijur puts distance between himself and his desk by climbing into a Cessna 182. "I go up on weekends," Bijur says. "I buzz around." He's been flying for more than 30 years and describes it as "very intellectually stimulating." There is something else about this pastime, he says, that he also enjoys: "You're totally in control of your own destiny."

Bijur's solution at Texaco was simple in concept but demanding in execution. Peace was the goal, no matter what the price. With the whole business world watching, under intense legal, political, and financial pressure, Bijur carried his company through its moment of crisis and beyond, and he very much deserves credit for it.

Henry Schacht

Henry Schacht at
Lucent Technologies

*"We talked Lucent, Lucent, Lucent. You were not not
allowed to talk about anything else."*

Henry Schacht proves that a giant ego is not required for outstanding business leadership. Schacht's transferable skills are also enviable. He jumped from running an old-line company like Cummins Engine to leading Lucent Technologies, a cutting-edge telecommunications manufacturer that has been on a fantastic growth streak since going public.

When Schacht joined Lucent the company was a question mark, shot through with uncertainty and in search of an identity. Schacht's team-building approach steered an organization with a plodding utility mentality into becoming an aggressive, entrepreneurial enterprise. He established a sense of possibility at Lucent. "That was my mission," Schacht says, "to lift people's expectations."

Schacht is a study in modesty. A slim, light-haired, bespectacled man, he even questioned whether he belonged in this book. He is an exceptionally able thinker whose penetration and focus make him a spectacular problem solver. He also excels at helping other people focus, almost by taking himself out of the equation. A conversation with Schacht leaves you thinking about ideas, not about the personality or ego behind them. Schacht isn't out to dazzle, but to connect and produce. There is something masterfully neutral about him.

He says his upbringing was "the least unusual you could possibly have." Schacht was raised by his mother in Erie, Pennsylvania, and attended Yale on a scholarship. He worked for a year at the American Brake Shoe Company, then went into the service in the late 1950s. "I was in Vietnam before anyone knew there was a Vietnam," he says. "I was in Saigon long before any shooting—one of 11 naval officers in the whole country." Stateside again, he earned his MBA at Harvard.

TURNAROUND AT CUMMINS

When Cummins Engine owner Irwin Miller hired Schacht he expected big things, but he couldn't know that Schacht would rocket through the ranks so quickly. Cummins was a sedate manufacturer of a dull line of diesel engines in Columbus, Indiana. A person either fits in or perishes in a small company town like Columbus. It takes skill to navigate a company town and still take in the needs of far-flung customers all over the planet, and Schacht did that.

But Schacht did more. He transformed Cummins into an efficient, competitive, and very profitable company. The old manufacturing operation was always being tested by a crisis of some sort, including fickle customers, competition from giants like Caterpillar and later Penske, and regulators who hated diesel for its smoke and soot. Middle Eastern fuel cutoffs hurt, too. But the firm's biggest battle was against the Japanese, who threatened to eliminate Cummins with their better, less expensive products. Schacht forced Cummins to suck in its gut and cut prices. Subsequent cost reductions and layoffs created a small-town shockwave. Schacht's peacekeeping genius kept operations together while Cummins reengineered its products and made workforce adjustments. The turnaround came under very trying circumstances. In 1995, after 18 years at Cummins, Schacht retired—for a few months. Then AT&T CEO Robert Allen came calling.

MONOPOLIES DON'T NEED TO LISTEN

AT&T through the early 1980s was the largest, costliest, most inbred monopoly in the United States. The company was founded 1885 and by 1934 owned four out of every five telephones in the country. After World War II, AT&T grew ever fatter and less responsive to consumer wishes. Monopolies don't need to listen to customers. CEO Charles Brown presided over AT&T's deterioration in the 1970s, followed by Kenneth Olsen, another Bell old-timer intent on preserving the status quo.

Politicians and regulators came down hard. The Justice Department in 1984 forced AT&T to divest its local telephone operations and they became the Regional Bell Operating Companies. AT&T held on to its phone equipment and long-distance service businesses. But late in the 1980s the telecommunications industry exploded, and traditional boundaries between industries and products began to disappear. AT&T struggled to keep up. In an effort to broaden its offerings, AT&T acquired computer maker NCR, a costly mistake. Still, by the mid-1990s, AT&T was an $80 billion company galumphing along behind the telecommunications revolution.

So in 1995, Allen announced a second—but this time voluntary—split. His decision was prompted by fresh federal legislation permitting local and long-distance companies to compete in each other's markets. AT&T's biggest customers, the "Baby Bells," were increasingly hesitant to buy phone equipment from what they saw as a future competitor. They believed AT&T wasn't offering them the most timely or best-quality products because it had a conflict of interest. Schacht calls Allen's split-up decision uncomplicated. "Competition between the operating companies [the Baby Bells] and AT&T was certain to grow," he says. "AT&T's public business [equipment sales] had begun to atrophy, and the rest of the business was starved for cash."

HENRY AND RICH

AT&T split into three independent companies: the $51 billion "new" AT&T Corporation, a telephone company; the $8 billion NCR Corporation, which made highly specialized computers; and the then-yet-unnamed Lucent Technologies, a $22 billion research and equipment manufacturing business.

Lucent, in turn, was made up of two parts. Its hardware side, which made phones, computers, switches, and other telecommunications equipment, was an inefficient, loosely organized bundle of disparate factories in many sizes and locations that had previously been known as Western Electric. AT&T had always run this piece of the company like a captive supplier. Costs were covered by price hikes, no matter how high or how often they might come. Lucent's other side, Bell Laboratories, was a renowned research facility famous for inventing the semiconductor, the laser, the cellular phone, and solar batteries. Bell Labs was a haven for Nobel Prize winners and eggheads whose innovations hadn't necessarily translated into commercial development. It was a scientific paradise, where researchers worked in isolation, oblivious to the bottom line, with the best brains and zero business acumen.

Richard A. McGinn, the 27-year AT&T veteran who had run these businesses under AT&T, had personally drawn up their spin-off arrangements. Employees felt an allegiance to McGinn, and he was considered a shoo-in for the top job at Lucent. Allen judged the circumstances differently. He saw McGinn as a management heavyweight who certainly knew the business backwards and forwards but lacked exposure to Wall Street, the press, the competition, suppliers, and all of the challenges stakeholders present. Allen went to AT&T's board and proposed Schacht for the top job. Schacht, an AT&T board member himself, accepted. McGinn became president.

Resentment and rivalry might have destroyed the Schacht-McGinn relationship, and Lucent would have paid the price, but Schacht insisted from day one that he and McGinn share equal command. "I made it clear to everyone that I was not his boss," Schacht says. "We were going to have a partnership in launching this company." Schacht also let everyone know that there was no race for CEO, and that the only way McGinn wouldn't get the job was if he were hit by a truck. They were Henry and Rich, a team. This powersharing relationship mirrored a partnership between Schacht and James Henderson, a top Cummins executive who succeeded Schacht as CEO. It was a far cry from the top-down hierarchical structure at the old AT&T. Former AT&T employees must have thought they were hallucinating.

FORMIDABLE CHALLENGES

The intense work of transforming AT&T's plodding research and technology arm into a cutting-edge telecommunications firm began. Lucent faced formidable challenges. Employees needed a new sense of identity and a much more entrepreneurial culture. Some 23,000 of 125,000 jobs were slated for elimination, which threatened to strangle morale. The telecommunications industry was a highly competitive market, and although Lucent was starting life as the world's largest maker of telephone equipment, it had reason to be nervous. AT&T would buy at least $3 billion worth of equipment from Lucent over the next three years, but after that Lucent could expect no preferential treatment. On the other side, Baby Bells ready to try other markets needed to load up on equipment but suspected Lucent's old AT&T ties. Lucent had inherited $3.8 billion in debt from AT&T and its costs were the highest in the industry. Equipment demands were climbing overseas, but Lucent was a weak international player compared to companies like Motorola or Nokia. "There was a strong opinion that we would find the going extremely difficult," Schacht summarizes.

Schacht and his team tackled identity issues immediately. Lucent hadn't brought in anyone from the outside—top management consisted of 17 people, young and old, all from AT&T. "We had to decide, what kind of company do we want to be?" Schacht says. "Why that company? How do we convince 125,000 people to behave that way, if it's different than what they're accustomed to?"

Schacht and McGinn began to transform the old AT&T army into a new workforce. "We had groups that operated quite independently, with little horizontal linkage and no lateral connection," he explains. And with no allegiance to Lucent. All day every Monday for six months, Schacht and McGinn met with the top 20 people in the company. "We talked Lucent, Lucent, Lucent," Schacht says. "You were not allowed to talk about anything else." Halfway through the year Schacht and McGinn switched gears and began meeting with other employees and talking about values and the company's new mission statement.

The response to that mission statement was telling. The statement defined Lucent as a high-performance company delivering superior shareholder value. "But we had a huge pushback on that, about whether delivering superior stakeholder value ought to be the mission of a corporation," Schacht says. "It astonished all of us." The old AT&T mentality was still alive, Schacht explains. "AT&T was about employment security, about putting the cost in and getting the guaranteed returns. We had an awful lot of talking to do about risks and rewards." Schacht and his team overhauled Lucent's compensation system, then offered stock options to every employee, hoping to make them feel like owners.

GOOD LUCK, SHREWD DECISIONS

Schacht also worked to build up the business. The new company name and logo were an early effort in this direction. The moniker "Lucent," which suggests clarity and light, was selected from among 700 candidates. The new logo, a bright red circle painted in a single brushstroke, was designed to convey creativity and innovation. The circle was chosen by Carleton S. Fiorina, who has since become president and chief executive of computer giant Hewlett-Packard, and only the third woman to lead a Fortune 500 company.

Lucent's initial public offering was a whopping success. In September 1996, the company sold 112 million shares at $27 each, netting $3 billion in the largest IPO to that point in American history. The remaining 80 percent of the company went later to AT&T shareholders. Lucent joined Motorola, Alcatel of France, and Siemens of Germany as a leading global phone company. New contracts and new products followed on quickly.

Some of Lucent's early success was extremely good luck, and Schacht says so himself. The telecommunications boom created an enormous explosion in second-line growth, and demand for older Lucent products, specifically circuit switches, surged. "When you need to make a radical management change, you need to hope for the wind at your back rather than in your face," Schacht says. "In our first year there was a very strong wind at our back." Consumers demanded Lucent's most developed, highest-margin systems. "Demand went out of sight," Schacht says. He smiles. "It's nice to be lucky."

But it wasn't all luck. Shrewd decision making also propelled Lucent's success. "We wanted to be a high-performance growth company," Schacht says. "We declared that. We said that's what we're going to shoot for. From October '95 on, everything was designed to make the company look and behave that way." The high-performance growth concept was repeated over and over to Lucent's 125,000 employees. "At least 50 percent of our people were scared stiff," he remembers. "They had spent 127 years of history in a company that was a warm blanket, and we had to create feelings of expectation, excitement, and a belief in the necessity of change." Lucent had to move faster, take more risks, and behave more entrepreneurially, Schacht says. "This was a very conservative, somewhat older workforce, and we had to do this with 125,000 people for whom this was not a way of life."

TRANSFORMATION

To meet performance and growth goals, Schacht and his team boosted R&D spending after benchmarking against Motorola and Hewlett-Packard. They also discovered as they ran the numbers that return on assets was low. "We weren't too happy about that," Schacht says. "It came out of that monopoly position. The heritage was, if you spent money, you got a guaranteed rate of return. There had never been a mention of analysis, cost effectiveness, or the customer."

To reestablish relationships with old AT&T customers, Schacht paid calls on the CEOs at all the Baby Bells. "I went one-on-one at McGinn's insistence," he says. "The only question they asked was, 'How often do you see Bob Allen?' They didn't believe it was really going to be a clean break." Lucent campaigned to convince these multibillion-dollar customers that its AT&T allegiance was finished.

Lucent headquarters relocated to Murray Hill, New Jersey, home of Bell Labs. AT&T's distinguished research arm had made legendary contributions to computer networking and software, but its 25,000 employees showed little interest in commercializing research. "During the monopoly period, the labs thought of themselves as publicly funded," Schacht states. "We said, 'No more!'" Schacht and McGinn began to spend chunks of time in the laboratory and quickly linked a far greater proportion of Bell Labs' research directly into development. Bell Labs had been filing an average of a patent a day under AT&T, but by the end of Lucent's first year, daily filings had more than tripled.

Schacht's objective at Lucent was double-digit sales growth. "Nobody had paid attention to sales growth in this company before," he says. "Nobody had to." Lucent's team also aimed for "superior shareholder value." By April 1997, management's hard work was bearing fruit. The telecommunications equipment market was growing by 10 to 12 percent annually, and Lucent was in a position to capitalize on it. Costs were down, major contracts were coming in, and sales were strong. Some sales were propelled by pent-up demand after the spin-off, but new equipment was also selling, and then there was the dam-busting demand created by second-line growth. Lucent's workforce was two-thirds of the way through massive job cuts and upbeat. Share prices had doubled since the IPO, and soon they would triple.

In October 1997, at the end of Lucent's first full year following the IPO, Schacht announced his retirement, and McGinn took over. The partnership, practically unheard of and predicted by many to fail, succeeded exactly according to plan. "The toughest thing for a manager to do is get out of the way when the time comes," Schacht says. "It's not easy but it's absolutely important." Schacht calls his departure his most difficult moment at Lucent.

MISSIONARY

Schacht sounds like a missionary when he describes his accomplishments at Lucent. He got people working together, he says. He offered intelligent guidance but not orders. He lifted sights, he says, created a sense of common purpose, and helped people set goals and reach for big results.

The best managers choose an approach to suit individual conditions, Schacht says, while preserving their own personal values. "There are very few really good managers who hold true to their value systems and make no compromise except to adapt the tactical side of their approach to the circumstances." This is the standard Schacht strives for himself.

Schacht still harbors a very strong allegiance to AT&T and comes out swinging when the subject turns to Allen, whose defenders haven't been lining up of late. Allen was the brain behind the spin-off that created Lucent, Schacht says. "Give Bob Allen credit for the split. The value was not obvious, but Bob saw it."

Schacht led Cummins through a tough turnaround to prosperity, then left Lucent growing with market values soaring. Will there be a third success story, and a fourth? "I never expected there to be a second, but I never say never," he responds. "I don't worry about the next thing," he adds. "I'll find ways to contribute." Schacht and his wife are currently soaking up the New York metropolitan area. He plays tennis when possible, he says, "with great enthusiasm and modest ability."

LUCENT'S NEXT CHALLENGE

Lucent's next challenge is to satisfy a new generation of buyers in a fast-cycle industry and stay ahead of a growing field of competitors that includes Cisco Systems and 3Com Corp. Customers now are demanding networks that can carry voice, data, and images at very high speeds. Lucent dominates the North American circuit switch market but is preparing to compete if and when packet networks become the standard. In recent years it has made a number of packet-related acquisitions, including Ascend Communications Inc. Where are customers headed next? "I don't know," Schacht says. "I don't think anyone knows, including the customers. This is as opaque a set of circumstances as I've ever seen, and I do not believe the end game is either known or visible."

Schacht is capable of fighting a good war, but he is better suited to peacemaking. He whipped his company into shape and selflessly cultivated a successor. When Schacht stepped down, adored by Lucent shareholders (whose investments quadrupled during his tenure), he left behind a fantastically profitable, customer-responsive company, still on the rise.

Schacht would protest that he didn't do it alone. He's right, and McGinn and the rest of the Lucent team deserve fair credit. Still, Schacht's spirit guided Lucent's success, and when the great book on telecommunications history is written, no one will look up from the last page and ask, "Henry who?"

Thomas G. Labrecque

Thomas G. Labrecque
at Chase Manhattan Bank

*"Lots of people said it couldn't be done, that I couldn't have
an impact in that position. They were wrong."*

Most peacemakers are rock-steady, and Tom Labrecque at Chase Manhattan Bank is no exception. He found his career challenge right where
he began and never left home. Labrecque was an accomplished peacemaker in a tumultuous industry. His role in a company-defining merger
defied all convention.

Labrecque is not a seat-of-the-pants type. He is a tall, athletic man
with a military bearing and handsome, even features. Labrecque wears
conservative suits and speaks slowly and deliberately. He is thoughtful,
sober, and thorough, without a speck of flash. At times he comes across
stiffly. Even so, Labrecque's competence and knowledgeability shone
throughout his banking career. His discipline extends to personal matters such as where he puts his ego. This is Thomas Labrecque's extraordinary strength: his uncommon willingness to be number two to give his
company a shot at number one.

TAKING THE REINS

Labrecque was born in New Jersey, the second of his family's eight children. His father was a lawyer, but Labrecque purposely decided to
break his own trail. He joined the Navy in the early 1960s and, as he tells
it, was by happenstance the head of merchant marine intelligence during the Cuban Missile Crisis. "I was in a job I should not have been in,"
he says modestly, "and once the crisis started I was never taken out."
When his tour ended, Labrecque tucked his MBA under his arm and
joined Chase in 1964. CEO David Rockefeller, scion of the legendary
New York Rockefeller family, liked what he saw in young Labrecque
and took him under his wing.

Chase Manhattan Bank, number 23 in the Fortune 500, was founded
as the Chase Bank well over a century ago. A merger with Equitable
Trust in the 1930s made it the biggest bank in the world, and the bank

of choice for shareholder John D. Rockefeller Jr. Son David joined the firm in 1937 and eventually would run the place. Early and midcentury, Chase was known for international banking and as a lender to major corporations. A second merger in 1955 with Bank of Manhattan gave birth to Chase Manhattan and added to the company a strong retail banking presence in New York.

The entire banking industry, Chase included, took a battering in the 1980s and 1990s. Chase was holding hundreds of millions in bonds when New York City went broke. Then developing countries defaulted on billions in loans in the early 1980s. Finally, in the late 1980s and early 1990s, it was undone by the real estate industry. By 1990 Chase was fighting for its life. Rumors circulated that it was too weak to stay upright on its own legs. Instead of turning to CEO Willard Butcher, the board of directors called in Labrecque. "I knew damn well we had to take a fresh look and that's what they wanted to hear," he recalls. Butcher was eased into retirement and Labrecque took the reins. Rethinking the company was a matter of survival. "We sat down," Labrecque says of himself and the board, "and we went at it. We needed to do two things: clean up our asset problems and reset our strategy. We were asking, what is it we want to be?"

STRATEGY SWITCH, CULTURE CHANGE

Chase at that time had "pockets of retail all over the world," Labrecque notes, but "none of them large enough to be a major factor." Labrecque switched strategies. Instead of striving to offer services all over the map, Chase began to concentrate where it had the competencies and resources to dominate. The bank focused on building its wholesale business locally and its retail business nationally. What was Labrecque's contribution to this thinking? "All of it," he says, in a rare display of ego. "That was my recommendation, and it had been my view long before I was chairman."

The company culture also needed a good shake. Chase was highly balkanized when Labrecque took charge, and operations had been weakened by internal politics. Exiting the silos took three years, Labrecque says, and required hundreds meetings that cascaded down to the ground floor. "You can't inculcate change without taking it down to grass roots," he says. Labrecque was after a "team-based, values-based" culture. Chase published new values formulated with plenty of employee participation. They included a customer focus, teamwork, respect for each other, and a dedication to quality.

With his industry in financial upheaval and his own bank facing a crunch, Labrecque had to steady the faith of his workforce. He talks about going to the bank's 42nd Street branch in Manhattan to speak directly to employees, cutting through about twelve layers of management. This is not a jaw-dropping move in some industries, but in banking it is practically unheard of. "If you really want to change people, you have to convince them this is for real, and not just the flavor of the month," Labrecque says, "—that you're not just going to write a nice memo and put it in the annual report and everybody forgets about it by June."

Most employees understood that the bank was aiming for a better culture, Labrecque says. "They saw that it was necessary and that the end result would be very positive for them. That helped people keep their heads screwed on." Labrecque was implementing his own strategy, and one he believed in. Even so, he pegs this period as his career low point.

MERGING FOR MARKET SHARE

Labrecque by 1994 had cleaned up his balance sheet and cleared away credit problems. Chase was fortifying its global businesses and making strides in regional banking and national consumer services. Earnings were up. But Chase still didn't dominate any niche, a must in the new banking environment. Revenues were still a problem. The bank was profitable again, but Chase's performance on Wall Street continued to underwhelm investors.

Chase had become a healthy company with an undervalued stock. Takeover rumors surfaced and intensified when activist investor Michael F. Price acquired a 6.1 percent stake, making him Chase's largest shareholder. Price pressured Labrecque to liquidate. Instead, in mid-1995, Chase announced a merger with Chemical Bank. Labrecque denies any cause and effect, or that Chase sought and found a white knight. "All of this strategy was in motion long before Michael Price bought the stock," he says. "He didn't know anything about a merger, or how fast we were going to get there. He didn't want a merger, he wanted the reverse. He saw value, we did too. He wanted to liquidate, we wanted to build."

The merger came about, Labrecque says, because at the end of 1994 he had gone to the board and issued a warning. "I said that despite all this progress, it will take seven years to achieve our goals, and if this industry starts consolidating faster we may not get there." Chase had the correct strategy, Labrecque says. "But we needed to accelerate it. And the answer to this was Chemical." As Labrecque tells it, Chase and Chemical separately but simultaneously reached the same conclusion: They needed a merger partner to become an industry leader. "Their first choice was us; our first choice was them," he continues. Neither Chase nor Chemical will say who made the first phone call. Team player Labrecque sticks to the game plan. "We got together," he glosses over. "In six weeks we had the merger."

The 1995 Chase Chemical merger created the biggest banking company in the United States and came at a time of hastening industry consolidation. At both banks the merger goal was better market position, which was a necessity for growth, which was a necessity for survival. The new bank had $300 billion in assets, and branches in 51 countries and 39 states. The plan was to cut $1.7 billion a year in expenses by eliminating 12,000 of its combined 75,000 employees and closing scores of overlapping branches. The combined bank kept the Chase name, but Chemical, the bigger partner, was expected to dominate.

"WE TOOK OUR EGOS AND PARKED THEM SOMEWHERE ELSE"

The megamerger was attention-getting but not extraordinary in its time. More exceptional was the relationship that sprang up between the two former CEOs, Labrecque and Walter Shipley. "The two of us were unusual," Labrecque says. "We had come from institutions that went through tough times; we saw a chance to build a world-class institution. We took our egos and parked them somewhere else."

Shipley was no amateur. By the time of the Chase-Chemical merger he had almost 40 years of banking under his belt, most of it at Chemical. Most important, he had already led his company through a megamerger in 1991 with Manufacturers Hanover. In the course of that merger, Shipley had ceded his chairman and CEO title to Manufacturers Hanover's John F. McGillicuddy. A few years later, all according to plan, McGillicuddy had turned the company over to Shipley.

The new Chase went a different route. Shipley, older and the head of the larger bank, remained chairman and CEO. Labrecque accepted a step-down position, the presidency. No one announced a future job swap or put a retirement date on the calendar. Instead, Shipley and Labrecque were announced as "totally coequal partners," ordinarily a fragile, barely credible arrangement. For the first two years they worked out of adjoining offices with connecting doors. "Walter and I were a team, physically together every day unless traveling," Labrecque says. "We walked into each other's office any time day or night, but we also attended scheduled meetings every Monday morning." Labrecque says Shipley never claimed 51 percent of the vote, and there were no hot fights. "We never surprised each other," he explains. The two men talked everything over before a decision, usually more than once, and Labrecque says they never had a buttoned-down meeting where they sprang things on each other. "It took a lot of hard work to make the relationship work," Labrecque says. He pauses, then adds, "It doesn't come naturally."

PLAYING SECOND FIDDLE

Labrecque's role was extremely unusual. Onlookers were sure he would fold his tent. When he didn't, they expected him to be killed off in post-merger infighting.

Labrecque survived and stayed on through a string of prosaic assignments without complaint. Off on the margins, he built Chase's securities processing business into a top performer. In time he outlasted several other senior executives and inherited oversight of the ongoing merger. Shipley understood Labrecque's position. In 1991, he, too, had engineered a merger and then accepted a second-stringer role. Shipley could have forced Labrecque out. Instead these two modest, conservative men formed a comfortable power-sharing relationship that over time became a real partnership.

Bank mergers don't usually play this way. The former boss rarely can handle playing second fiddle. Labrecque was different. He took the number-two position, he says, because he believed it substantially improved the merger's prospects. "It was not the easiest thing personally, but that was not the most significant criterion," he says. "You can argue that I gave up a lot doing that. I'll argue that that may be true, but I'll also argue with you that the results are absolutely worth getting."

GETTING RESULTS

The results were not instantaneous. The merger period was characterized by anxiety and confusion, and Chase suffered through a period of demoralizing layoffs, branch closings, and some bad press. Shipley and Labrecque made several foresighted decisions early on, however. Instead of stretching personnel decisions out, they were announced swiftly. "Walter and I decided it was better to make a mistake and do it quickly and then try to fix it than to string people out," Labrecque says. Were there concerns about merging cultures? "If you don't think you can handle that, you shouldn't do a merger," Labrecque says.

Soon the merger proved a large financial success. Chase earnings were up 50 percent in 1997, to $3.7 billion, and prosperity continued into 1998 and 1999. Labrecque says these earnings were driven by improved market position. Falling interest rates and a strong economy also helped. In addition, Chase has shown great skill at risk management. International events in 1997 and 1998 rocked financial markets around the world. Many powerhouse banks reported large trading losses. Not Chase. While other banks and Wall Street firms licked their wounds in 1999, Chase enjoyed record earnings.

The merger did not solve all of Chase's problems; in fact it exacerbated one. In 1997 the Securities and Exchange Commission changed its regulations in a way that prompted every major Chase competitor to join forces with an investment bank. Chase was still executing its merger and couldn't yet handle another partner, even though the bank very much wanted a piece of the action. By the time Chase was ready there were no willing partners, although the company did a brief tango with Merrill Lynch. Determined to upgrade its equity research and stock underwriting capabilities and erase a serious shortcoming, Chase in 1999 finally cut a deal with San Francisco–based Hambrecht & Quist, which had underwritten the initial stock sales of both Apple Computer Inc. and Amazon.com Inc.

SUCCESS, AND SUCCESSION

Labrecque for a long while was considered a possible—if long-shot—successor to Shipley. He was certainly qualified. Shipley and the board more than trusted him. In 1999, however, Chase named William B.

Harrison as Shipley's heir. Labrecque says he was a contributor to the succession planning. "The decision was made with the board that Walter and I would go out together and put in the new team," he says. "We decided that two successions over two years was not desirable. If Walter left, the speculation would begin about who would come in after me." Chase had cultivated a talented senior team, Labrecque says, and there was no guarantee they would wait around a few more years. "We decided the best, cleanest way was to make the ultimate move." Labrecque says he never put his personal needs first at Chase. "I didn't in this case, either."

Labrecque retired from Chase, the nation's third-biggest bank, in June 1999. He hopes he will be remembered for developing strategy after the Chase-Chemical merger. "Also for my willingness to put the ego aside and be the kind of partner who could make this a success," he says. "Yes, it requires burying one's ego, but for a great outcome. Lots of people said it couldn't be done, that I couldn't have an impact in that position. They were wrong."

Labrecque describes his management style as inclusive. "My office in the old Chase didn't have a desk; it had a round conference table," he says. "I am a team-based player and I wanted my office to have that ambiance. I didn't want supplicants."

Some have misjudged him, Labrecque states. "I'm a very collegial team player, there's no question about it, but you can be a very good team player and be very strong," he says. "People never fully see that. The diplomacy comes across and they equate that with not being strong. But personal strength is not letting it come apart, keeping people's eye on the ball, not personalizing it. That's what made a difference." Labrecque considers, then adds something interesting and a little more complex. "I think people here at Chase would honestly tell you, if you gave them sodium pentathol, that the role of being able to be perceived as number two is very important."

LEADERSHIP ON THE QUIET

Now a newly retired banker, Labrecque has followed his personal interests into foundation work. He also has time for less cerebral pursuits like tennis, cycling, and swimming. He picked up golf recently, and does a little bit of rappelling. He likes to tinker. "I'm mechanically inclined," Labrecque says. "If something breaks I can usually figure out how to fix it."

Labrecque is a good example of leadership on the quiet. His ability to set personal ambition aside in the interest of building the new Chase makes him a peacemaker. This is the approach he urged on all Chase employees to make the merger a success. Like a true peacemaker, he led by example. Chase Manhattan Bank, now one of several leaders in the financial services business, is the better for it.

>—◆—◄

CHAPTER 3

Brilliant Brutes
Respected and Feared

Brilliant Brutes:

⇨ Live in a world of raw power and punishment
⇨ Believe in going nose-to-nose
⇨ Laugh off the nicey-nicey human relations stuff
⇨ Know precisely what they want and are hell-bent on gaining it
⇨ Are extremely quick studies and relish detail
⇨ Survive on a kind of glorious self-confidence until the results arrive

---

Brilliant brutes are a combination of brains, guts, and power with a shot of attitude. They are surefooted and tenacious. They make the opposition wilt and subordinates snap to it. This rugged approach requires uncommon skill, but it can also be enormously successful. Sometimes it is the only way to get results.

Brutes laugh off the nicey-nicey human relations stuff fostered by touchy-feely consultants. Instead they are forceful with competitors, suppliers, employees, or anyone else foolish enough to stand in the way. They believe the most effective way of resolving differences is to go nose-to-nose. These managers live in a world of raw power and punishment. They know precisely what they want and are hell-bent on gaining it, no matter who they have to flatten. This can be deeply offensive, particularly to adversaries who expect to hammer out mutually tolerable solutions or at least engage in some free-flowing give-and-take.

Onlookers often harbor a deep if covert respect for this type of manager. Brutes are direct. What you see is what you get, and sub-rosa agendas are rare. Brutes don't waffle on decisions or second-guess themselves. They don't kiss up to anyone. They are gracious in public and can turn on the charm with the media, but only if they believe it will further their campaign. Most executives don't have the nerve to operate like this, in part because it directly contradicts common wisdom. That doesn't mean they don't envy the audacious approach, or its results.

These managers are typically workaholic loners who don't give a hoot about companionship or collegial relations. Brilliant brutes are one-man shows. Even so, they aren't lonely. A constant stream of fine ideas and hard-won progress against long odds keep them busy and happy. They are a creative breed—some because of their superior mental dexterity, others because their disciplined minds run all hours of the day. They are also quick studies. One brief exposure to the facts and they usually can imagine the rest.

These domineering executives do their best work in fast-paced, trouble-prone industries or sclerotic companies begging for a shake-up. Like military commanders, brutes issue the orders necessary for survival. Their skills suit cash-strapped industries or investment enterprises that must move swiftly and strike hard to capitalize on opportunities.

When a brute arrives at a new company he instantly raises its heart rate. These demanding executives promise big things. They believe in action. They don't dillydally on cost cuts or layoffs or any other needed change. Investors, lenders, customers, suppliers, and so forth are enthusiastic about brute leaders but keep them on a very short leash that lengthens only when they deliver results. The media loves brutes because they charge in and polarize people. Headhunters swarm when the new boss is a brute. They know that top people who don't make the team will bail out.

This high-handed management style looks far more simple in concept than it is in practice. It's easy to shout orders, but misguided brute-types who get carried away or misjudge their circumstances land hard. A brute can destroy a fragile business in need of patient nurturing. They also risk sending dangerous signals to subordinates who may conclude that all's fair in the pursuit of success, including immoral or even criminal behavior. Brilliant brutes must define moral and legal standards for their organizations or watch their companies and their careers self-destruct.

Brilliant brute-type bosses aren't running many world-class companies these prosperous days. Most boards fear them because they demand so much control and are often so disruptive, even when it's for a good cause. There are also few business leaders who pair such sheer brainpower with this kind of undeflectable drive. The ones we do have are legends. Former American Airlines chairman and CEO Robert Crandall reinvented an industry and an airline. CFO Jerome B. York helped restore financial vigor at Chrysler and IBM, then teamed up with billionaire Kerk Kerkorian and grabbed for control at Chrysler. Sam Zell is leading a revolution in the world of real estate investing. These executives have the stomach to muscle their way into position, ditch the rules, ignore the naysayers, and survive on a kind of glorious self-confidence until the results are in. Call it hardened competence.

Robert L. Crandall

Robert L. Crandall
at American Airlines

"I'm feared? I don't know what's to fear, although the notion of fear has always followed me around."

Former American Airlines chief Robert Crandall is deeply and deservedly respected. His brilliance and drive catapulted his company to the top of a relentlessly competitive industry.

Through a string of foresighted innovations, Crandall shaped modern air travel more than other airline chief. His long career was distinguished by master strokes, and he is also remembered for making a goodly number of enemies. His obsessive attention to detail is legendary. Crandall once cut $100,000 from American's annual operating budget by removing the olives from in-flight salads. He shaved $12,000 more on Bloody Marys by yanking out the celery sticks.

Crandall has a cleft chin, slicked-back hair, and a voice made gravelly by thousands of cigarettes. His forehead is deeply creased after 18 years of squinting at tiny columns of numbers and glaring at labor leaders. Even when relaxed he crackles with energy. Crandall is gracious and good-natured, but cross him and he quickly and forcefully sets you straight. He was known at American as a bullying workaholic capable of calling a 5 A.M. meeting. "I did that for a while," Crandall admits calmly. "I wanted to get people's attention."

His intensity and competitive drive are legendary. Crandall's mental jaws are constantly chewing on something. He craves order, and orderly solutions. If Crandall ran the world it would be a place of precise efficiency. Forty identical dark blue suits hang in a closet in his Fort Worth, Texas, home. His wife, Jan, has sewn the same number into each jacket and its corresponding pair of trousers. "They all look the same," Crandall says. "Blue. But I get a match every time."

HARNESSING AN EDGE

Crandall joined American Airlines in 1973, a Wharton grad with six years in the finance department at TWA and brief stints at both Eastman Kodak and Hallmark Cards. When he became CFO, he was appalled by American's halfhearted cost controls. Crandall dissected the budget and spent long hours grinding away at spending practices. Employees and colleagues were not charmed. Behind his back they called him Darth Vader, or Fang. Higher-ups were more impressed and made him president in 1980. Five years later Crandall added the titles chairman and CEO.

Crandall fought deregulation, but when it was a done deal he moved aggressively to make American a competitor. He grasped before other airline chiefs how to harness information technology to competitive advantage and dreamed up innovation after innovation. The Sabre reservations system put computer terminals right on the desks of travel agents and prioritized American Airlines bookings. When regulators nixed the system as biased, Crandall figured out an end run. "We said, OK, no bias, but can we charge a service fee? They said sure. So American wrote its own software to make it happen that way." The software, of course, restored top billing to American bookings.

Crandall also created the first frequent flyer program and devised a powerful yield management system that allowed American to anticipate ticket demand and set fares accordingly. "People think of an airline seat as a commodity," Crandall states, "but by attaching different conditions to it, you can decommodify it." Under Crandall, American also implemented a powerful hub-and-spoke airport system.

Crandall considers himself an uninhibited thinker. "If I have to solve a problem and the common approach won't work, I'll go off and think about alternative ways to attack," he says. The supersaver fare concept, another Crandall innovation, came to him this way.

"We were sitting around a boardroom one day in 1977, all very depressed because a charter had been authorized between New York and Los Angeles that would charge the public half as much as our cost per seat," he says. "We sat there, we sat there. We scratched our heads, we scratched our heads. Suddenly I realized we were thinking about the equation all wrong! If we were flying between New York and Los Angeles and our seats were half-full, I realized the cost of our empty seats was much less than the cost of seats on that charter. If we could fill up our empty seats without losing people in previously purchased seats, we could undercut the charter guy."

GETTING TO NUMBER ONE

These innovations over time would become very important, but back in the early 1980s Crandall's airline was still unprepared to compete in the newly deregulated skies. "We had the wrong fleet, we were transcontinental, we had no hubs, we were the highest-cost operator in the business, and new airlines were coming along every day," Crandall rattles off. In addition, labor costs were eating the company alive.

Crandall was determined to slash those costs. In 1983 he hit on the idea of creating an "airline within an airline" that would pay lower wages and sell lower-priced tickets. Crandall bore down on his pilots to accept the plan. "I spent a lot of time persuading," he says, "and arguing." Sign on, he pressed, and I can expand this company much more rapidly, create more jobs, and accelerate promotional opportunities. When Crandall finally wore them down and they signed, he was jubilant. He had cut labor costs sharply without a strike. Crandall calls this "the most important thing at American in the last 75 years." It would allow him, for a time, to make American the world's number-one airline.

Crandall deployed an aggressive growth plan. He poured billions into new planes and expanded operations. As other airlines merged madly in the mid-1980s, Crandall stayed largely on the sidelines. He fattened his workforce instead. By the decade's end, American was the biggest domestic airline in the country and had earned more consistent profits than any rival since deregulation. As other carriers staggered through the skies carrying heavy debts, Crandall could afford to pounce on foreign routes. Growth and prosperity provided a fast-paced, promotion-rich environment that kept labor relatively subdued.

CRASH LANDING

The party ended in 1990. Increasingly price-sensitive travelers began beating the bushes for low fares, and no-frills carriers had no trouble picking them off. The Gulf War boosted fuel prices and scared travelers out of the air. Deep discounting proved devastating. Awash in empty seats, many airlines figured they'd rather sell a raft of cheap tickets than a scattering at full price.

Every large U.S. carrier faced these straitened circumstances, but Crandall had additional aggravations. After he had expanded aggressively in confident anticipation of a growing market, the market was contracting. It also particularly galled Crandall that bankruptcy protection laws were saving weaker competitors from going belly-up and allowing them to restructure at lower cost. Crandall felt that American had proven itself a better competitor and now was being penalized for it. To his horror, American began posting record quarterly losses.

Labor relations at American were also coming unglued. American's second-tier pilots were now in the majority—and resentful. They told Crandall they would no longer work for second-class salaries. Crandall had long viewed employees as competitors for resources rather than as team members. He considered labor a greedy sponge, an inside force with too much power, that threatened American's future. The labor unions, in turn, viewed Crandall as a stingy tyrant who treated them with contempt. Each side bore grievances that had deepened over time, and distrusted the other.

Early in 1991 AMR, American's parent company, reported its worst quarterly loss ever, about $215 million. Crandall shook his fist at discounters and upstart regional carriers for tearing up the market. He was furious at foreign governments for restricting access to their markets, and spitting mad at the U.S. government for protecting bankrupt airlines. Those airlines were in turn angry at Crandall for lobbying for their extermination.

Crandall turned on his unions. He ran newspaper ads asking customers to be patient while his "hardheaded" pilots conducted an alleged illegal sick-out. American pilots retaliated by toppling the two-tier wage scale, and soon they were taking home some of the fattest paychecks in the industry. "The union snatched defeat from the jaws of victory," Crandall says. All these years later, with deep feeling, he still describes the union's decision as "a tragic mistake."

THE TURBULENCE WORSENS

In the spring of 1992 the airline industry was still in a dour mood. Air travelers, by contrast, were all smiles. Most of them were flying on cheap tickets. Crandall had been gritting his teeth and matching discounted fares, but he detested his backseat role in an industry he was accustomed to leading.

In an effort to turn the tide, Crandall announced a bold new pricing structure that cut ticket prices, some by as much as half. The catch: no more special fares of any kind, period. No corporate rates, no group discounts, nothing. Crandall's plan spread to nearly every major U.S. carrier, but quickly deflated. Crandall hadn't built a coalition around his plan in advance, and after years of expansion most airlines were struggling with so much excess capacity that the choice was to fill seats or die. An all-out fare war exploded. Prices were so ridiculously low that they triggered a disastrous run on tickets. Industry stocks plummeted. Weaker airlines accused Crandall of engineering the whole shebang to drive them into Chapter 7, and two of them, Northwest and Continental, hauled Crandall into court. His company was exonerated after Crandall's convincing testimony, but Crandall left the courtroom expressing utter outrage.

The weakened and weary airline industry began to retrench. This was a terrible time for Crandall, who had to admit that his grand plan at American had failed. Consumers did not want to pay for a high-cost, full-service airline. Instead they wanted transportation without frills. Maybe American had a great product, but it was all wrong for the market.

Crandall scaled back aggressively and spoke out bitterly. Industry problems might be insurmountable, he said. Maybe it was time for AMR to get out of the airline business entirely. But by this time Crandall had built up such a reservoir of distrust inside and outside American that few accepted this beaten statement at face value. Critics called it pure theater. Crandall, they said, was a foxy strategist. First he'll knock labor off balance, they predicted, then he'll go gunning after concessions.

TO WAR WITH LABOR

Crandall has long argued that labor costs make or break an airline. He has loudly derided the "unnatural work restrictions" and "inefficiencies" created by labor agreements. In 1993 there were many economic, political, and legal forces buffeting American Airlines that Crandall couldn't finesse or muscle his way through. Crandall decided his workforce would have to be more flexible. "There's only one really controllable cost in the airline business," Crandall says. "It's labor."

In 1993, just days before Thanksgiving, American's 21,000 flight attendants hit the bricks. It was the biggest U.S. airline strike in nearly five years and exquisitely timed to inflict maximum punishment on the company. Crandall wasn't surprised by the strike, but he wasn't prepared, either. He had reassured ticket-holding passengers for weeks that a strike would not affect service. Crandall had to eat crow. Many flights flew empty because American couldn't scrape up enough attendants to transport passengers but needed to move equipment from one hub to the next. The airline canceled flight after flight over a five-day period. Thousands of travelers were stranded, and many swore never to buy an American Airlines ticket again.

As Crandall saw it, labor was slitting American's wrists. TWA and Continental had recently emerged from bankruptcy as low-cost carriers, and Northwest had won hefty labor concessions. Never big on conciliatory statements, Crandall trashed his pilot's suggestions for improving profitability to a crowd of Wall Street analysts. "If the pilots were in charge, Columbus would still be in port," he was widely reported as saying. "They believe assertions that the world is flat."

It took White House intervention to end the Thanksgiving standoff. President Bill Clinton placed personal telephone calls to both Crandall and the head of the flight attendants' union. When the strike was over, Crandall saw how much ground he had lost. He was left at the mercy of an adversarial workforce in a service industry, where employee interactions with the public mean everything. Crandall could no longer ask employees to be courteous or go the extra mile for customers: They would or they wouldn't, but not based upon his wishes. He had also lost control of labor costs, which moved on to arbitration.

PROSPERITY RETURNS, LABOR BURNS

Crandall's relationship with labor stayed sour, but the economy sweetened. By the fall of 1994 the airline industry showed new signs of life.

Industrywide downsizing began to pay off, and a dip in discounting practices and lower fuel prices helped, too. Crandall's mistakes with labor weren't enough to keep American down, and in fact his brilliance in other management areas began to shine through again. In late 1994, American released its best third-quarter results in five years.

Prosperity over the next two years kept the machinery at American well-oiled. Crandall made several strategic adjustments. For a decade he had held all three top jobs at AMR, savoring concentration of power and the commanding view, but in 1995 Crandall named Donald J. Carty president and made plans to use him as a buffer in coming contract negotiations. The following year American announced a huge marketing alliance with once-rival British Airways. AMR's profits in 1996 exceeded $1 billion. It was the company's best year ever.

While enjoying the good numbers, Crandall cranked up for one more contest with labor. He seemed determined to get this one right. Crandall told his pilots upfront that he wouldn't take a strike but would try to be more accommodating; then he turned the heavy lifting over to Carty. Long, difficult negotiations resulted in a tentative accord. American's 9,300 pilots, already the best paid in the business, were offered a small raise and stock options as part of a four-year contract that tightly capped wage increases. Crandall very quickly announced a $6.5 billion plane order, the biggest in years—but contingent upon ratification. The rank and file told Crandall to take a hike. Many called the plane order a bribe. American was earning record profits, and labor wanted a bigger piece of the pie.

Once more the dispute escalated into a hardened standoff. Labor distrusted Crandall so intensely that his very presence, in the background or foreground, good deal or bad, made any transaction suspect. For all Crandall's genius he had failed to build a workable relationship with labor. American began to shut down in anticipation of another crippling labor action, but just one minute into the strike the White House intervened again. It is a testament to American Airlines' critical role in the U.S. transportation network, and its obviously disastrous labor relations, that the government intervened from its highest level so swiftly.

CLIMBING OUT OF THE COCKPIT

In 1998, following four years of record profits, Crandall turned over the company controls. "I had done it long enough," he says. "The company was in very good shape, with a strong succession team in place, and it felt like the right time. I certainly wasn't bored, but if you've been around the track three or four times it gets repetitious."

He left American healthy. The air carrier's alliance with British Air promised a leadership position in the expanding world of global alliances. New planes were on order, and a labor contract was in place. AMR shares had taken off and then some in anticipation of another quarter of record profits. Excess capacity no longer haunted the industry, and the fare wars had faded. A brief period of relative calm began. Other carriers were also enjoying good times and several had imported leaders from other industries. Crandall's departure seemed to end an era.

SWEATING THE DETAILS

Crandall continues to speak about American Airlines as if he were still in charge. After 18 years of living and breathing the job, retirement is probably a tough switch.

Describing his management style, he says, "I want to have a very detailed understanding of how a business runs and how it interfaces with customers." Business models are important, Crandall states, but a hands-on understanding of "real life" operations is critical. "I try to build effective communication links both up and down. You have to do all you can to understand what the front-line people think needs to be done. They have a feel for the customer." It's important, Crandall continues, that management be accessible. "But it's very, very, very hard. Peter Drucker says the last guy who knows what needs to be done is the boss. I think that's often right."

His obsession with detail, he says, is just common sense. "A good boss has to be obsessed with how his company runs. You can be sure that if you don't care, others won't." What if someone claims to be a leader but shrugs when it comes to the small stuff? "Walk away," Crandall says. "If he doesn't know the details, he doesn't know which way to go, and he ain't going to be able to measure the progress of the army." Crandall's scrupulousness is joined to a restless, almost relentless drive to root out inefficiencies. His mind organizes the world into two parts: problems outstanding and problems solved. "If I see a hole in the wall or a deficiency in the plumbing, my mind massages the problem until I come up with a solution," he says. "A lot of people's minds don't work that way."

SATISFIED WITH THE JOB

Crandall acknowledges his detractors. "If you went around American Airlines and asked people about my leadership skills, you would get different answers. If you went around in the '80s, people would have said 'great leader, terrific, genius kind of guy.' In the '90s a lot of people—including a lot of union people—would say various expletives I won't say."

Even so, he claims not to understand his bogeyman reputation. "I'm feared? I don't know what's to fear, although the notion of fear has always followed me around." He compares himself favorably to General Electric CEO Jack Welch. "You know, if you look at Neutron Jack, he's just not going to tolerate an inferior performance. I'm the same way. I had to do lots that was not much fun. But I did it. It's called facing reality. And that's nothing to fear."

Crandall says his bad-guy image is one thing that he can't fix. "The media is populated by very young people with short institutional memories. If I have to go out and reduce the number of my employees, there's no way to avoid being called callous and hardhearted," he says, still in the present tense. "But I have to choose between the welfare of the few and of the many."

Did Crandall the perfectionist finish all he set out to accomplish at American? Of course not. "I'd like to see American even more successful and an even larger company. But I do feel quite satisfied."

He is candid about his failure with labor. "I fell short. I couldn't ever find the common ground. They didn't share my conviction that it was in everyone's best interest, including theirs, to. . . ." Here Crandall runs down a list of concessions he asked of his unions, and the thinking behind those requests. His voice starts out patient and explanatory, gains an edge, and then snaps shut on five frustrated words: ". . . because unions have uninhibited power." In the long run, Crandall says, U.S. labor laws will have to change if the major air carriers are to remain viable. "We need mandatory arbitration. The cost of a strike is so enormous, no management can realistically sustain it. Arbitration would make clear to unions that they're not going to be permitted to exercise economic power."

The AMR-British Air alliance remains in regulatory limbo. A so-called "open skies" treaty is mired in politics. "These two airlines have forged partnerships and are working together in many ways," Crandall says. "One part of the partnership is intended to be a joint venture to operate across the Atlantic. It hasn't come to pass. But I think, in due course, it will. We'll have to wait until politicians get themselves arranged."

IMPERFECT BUT BRILLIANT

Crandall says he is enjoying retirement. His current office is a near-exact duplicate of his former space at AMR. He is a fanatically organized, everything-in-its-place type. Crandall's desk stays orderly, no matter what. Ironically, the man who used computer power to remake his airline has just learned how to use a PC himself. "I know the plumbing but I don't know how to apply it," he explains. He recently went out "for the first time in 20 years" to see a movie with his wife. For many years, Crandall says, he just didn't have the time.

Now, in his free time, he sits on a handful of corporate boards. He has also taken to the sea in a custom-built English sailboat, which he navigated across the Atlantic with his wife and a crew of one. He still smokes. Crandall also jogs. "I jog so I can smoke," he states. This is classic Crandall: Ornery. Determined to prevail. Set on outsmarting the status quo, and even his own mortality.

Crandall ran American Airlines imperfectly but brilliantly. He made it a stunning competitor and the industry pacesetter. Nobody else in the business has ever matched his innovative genius—no one even comes close. Crandall more than once has compared the airline industry to a battleground, and that's precisely how he approached it: as a place to fight and win, even if that meant getting bloody. It's an understatement to say Crandall never got labor relations right. His successor, Carty, has inherited a raft of labor problems. Crandall alienated other airline executives, too. Even so, Bob Crandall's fingerprints are all over the modern airline industry, and it is a far smarter place for his having been there.

Jerome B. York

Jerome B. York at Chrysler, IBM, and Tracinda

"We had a very narrow road to walk."

Jerry York is as invisible as he is good. He is the unsung person behind the financial recoveries at both IBM and Chrysler, and he played a pivotal role in unlocking Chrysler's stock price before the DaimlerChrysler merger.

York has silvery hair, fair skin, and pale piercing eyes behind spectacles. One-on-one, he can be disarmingly soft-spoken. York favors starched white shirts and dark suits, but beneath this restraint lies a risk-taker who knows what he wants, enjoys a calculated danger, and will rip up the rules to get things precisely right. He has been married four times, twice to his current wife. He used to ride motorcycles; now he drives big pickup trucks and hunts deer in Mexico for pleasure. He's notorious for speaking his mind in streams of four-letter words.

York earned his taskmaster reputation early on. Once, after a Chrysler all-nighter, he fainted. "I'd been working around the clock," York chuckles. "It finally caught up with me one Monday morning." All these years and workaholic hours later York seems amused that "it" could catch up at all.

"GET TOUGH, GET IT DONE, GET IT DONE QUICK"

York is the son of an army officer, but an injury while a cadet at West Point prevented him from following in his father's footsteps. Instead he studied engineering at MIT and joined General Motors. "After a year I figured out the way up the ladder, and the odds of getting there through engineering were not great," he says. York had also discovered broader interests. He took his MBA at the University of Michigan and then worked up through management positions at, among other places, Ford, RCA, and Hertz. Chrysler hired him in 1979.

He started out as a "third-level person in finance," he says, but his versatility soon gained attention. "I got a reputation as "Mr. Fix-It," York explains. He was sent south in the early 1980s to rescue Chrysler de Mexico. "We were bleeding profusely down there. Gerry Greenwald told me, 'You've got to fix it quickly and we don't have any cash to send you, you have to do it on your own.' " York chopped his Mexican work-force in half, down to 4,000. His management style the first six months was, he says, "get tough, get it done, get it done quickly, make the hard decisions, let the chips fall where they may." Then he rebuilt. It's a point of pride for York that he is good at both tearing down and building back up, but it was the "get tough, get it done" York that would become well-known, and who was welcomed back to the States in 1985.

Chrysler was in clover when York returned. "Money was pouring in, Lee Iacocca was a celebrity, Greenwald a very capable number two," he recalls. "But '85 to '89 was a huge food fight for resources. It was the worst intramural warfare I've ever seen in my life. By '88, margins had deteriorated severely to the point where we were only keeping a penny of every dollar we brought in." Management had to squelch the warfare and arrive at a consensus on how to improve efficiency. York was made controller. He rose to CFO in 1990. "My fearsome reputation as a cost-cutter came during that '89, '90, '91 period," York says. By 1993 he had wrung some $4 billion out of costs and sold off another $3 billion in non-core assets. At the same time, Chrysler had spent a chunk of change developing new products like minivans, Jeeps, and the Neon subcom-pact to lure back lost customers. Chrysler posted record profits in 1993 and 1994. York had spent 14 years with the automaker and performed exceptionally well in jobs across the company.

Readying for retirement, Iacocca plugged York as his successor. The board ignored Iacocca's wishes and picked General Motors executive Robert J. Eaton instead.

THE BIG NUMBER FLOPS OUT

Shortly afterward, IBM announced a search for a new CFO. "That got my attention," he recalls. "I thought, I hope I hear from those guys. Sure enough, I did."

York left Chrysler for IBM. He saw the job as "the last really big chal-lenge of my career." After 30 years of rip-roaring success, Big Blue's senior management had failed to respond to a market shift away from big computers to PCs. The company was in a severely aggravated state. Its margins and stock price were way down. Costs had ballooned, and revenues had tumbled. York and new IBM CEO Louis V. Gerstner Jr.

were hired to perform the rescue. "Lou focused on what it would take to turn negative revenue growth to positive," York summarizes. "I focused on what it would take to pull several billion out."

York remembers his first days at IBM. "I walked in and met a bunch of people who came across as extremely capable, but it was quickly clear to me that there was no game plan. The company was highly decentralized and there wasn't anything approaching consensus on what should be done." York remembers being astounded by the company's precipitous decline. "In 1990, IBM had its second most profitable year ever, with a $10 billion pretax profit. In 1993, it was just breaking even, and that was in a hugely improving economy."

York spent his first month immersed in numbers. He set his staff to work benchmarking feverishly. "Then the big number flopped out," he says. "We had to take $7 billion out." York closed plants and unloaded real estate. He traveled the country from facility to facility and forced plant managers to explain, then justify, every small operational step. He cut the workforce and scrutinized supply orders. He slashed $1 billion from the R&D budget, consolidated in-company services, and cut every tuft of budget fluff. A large parcel of his time was spent fishing for redundancies between feuding divisions and then forcing them to work cooperatively. "The good news was that because IBM was highly decentralized, there were substantial redundancies that did not require a rocket scientist," York says self-deprecatingly. York is no corner-cutter. He didn't skip a detail.

By the time York was done with IBM, he was respected and appreciated for his efforts. He also admits he was aware of "considerable grousing" and was feared by some. By the time he left in 1995, he had taken $6.5 billion out of IBM's cost structure and sold off over $2 billion of noncore assets. Revenues were growing again after three years of decline, and IBM was posting record profits. The company stock price had more than doubled.

NOT FOR SALE

While York was chopping budgets at IBM, Chrysler was enjoying its best run ever. Minivans were hot, Jeeps like the Grand Cherokee were popular, and the company's improved sedan line was selling well. Compared to Ford or GM, Chrysler was making more than twice the profit on each car it sold. It was enjoying a record string of quarterly profits and gains in market share. The company's weak spot was quality. Chrysler was working to address this shortcoming. Meanwhile, the money was rolling in. CEO Eaton, cash-rich, had salted away $7.5 billion to ease his company through the next economic downturn.

Billionaire investor Kerk Kerkorian had more than a passing interest in Eaton's rainy day money. Kerkorian, the son of poor Armenian immigrant fruit farmers, had made his fortune as a gambling impresario. Now the septuagenarian dealmaker was wrapped up in building the gargantuan MGM Grand Hotel & Theme Park in Las Vegas—but not too wrapped up to think about his Chrysler stock.

Kerkorian in 1994 owned 9.8 percent of Chrysler, most of it purchased at fire sale prices in 1990 when the automaker was in dire financial straits. Kerkorian knew and respected Iacocca and he believed the company would come back strongly, if not swiftly. "Kerkorian was willing to sit there and be very patient," York says.

In 1994, when his patience paid off, Kerkorian pressed Chrysler to divvy up more of its profits. Kerkorian was the company's largest stockholder. He was peeved at Eaton's cash hoard, and at Eaton personally for ignoring his suggestions over the years to improve Chrysler's stock price. A recent slide had added to his irritation. Kerkorian demanded a stock split or a dividend increase. He also asked Chrysler to eliminate a poison-pill restriction. Then, late in 1994, Kerkorian joined a takeover attempt on Chrysler led by Northwest Airlines cochairman Gary L. Wilson. Chrysler was rattled. It increased its dividend and launched a $1 billion stock buyback. Chrysler's board also changed its rules so that Kerkorian could buy more shares.

Kerkorian was not pacified. The following spring, after extensive private talks between Chrysler and Tracinda, Kerkorian's holding company, Eaton and Kerkorian exploded at each other in public. Tracinda issued a press release announcing a management-led buyout. Eaton called the press release a mistake. Kerkorian said Chrysler had encouraged the buyout for months. Eaton fired back that Chrysler was not for sale.

In truth, both sides were in shock. Top Chrysler people had been negotiating behind the scenes for months with Tracinda and also thought the deal was a go. Kerkorian said he had been double-crossed. The media chalked it up to a series of unfortunate miscues, but it's clear from this distance what happened. There was no misunderstanding.

Chrysler's board had given the numbers and the players a long, last look. Something it saw gave it cold feet.

HIRED BY TRACINDA

Now, in addition to his investment interests at Chrysler, Kerkorian had a huge ax to grind. In April 1995 he made public that he had enlisted former Chrysler CEO Iacocca to attempt a hostile takeover. Iacocca could analyze the company for Kerkorian and bring star power. Besides, Iacocca had his own ax to grind with Chrysler for declining his offer to stay on past retirement age. Eaton discouraged Chrysler's top dozen banks and several Wall Street firms from backing Kerkorian's $22.8 billion deal. Kerkorian got the cold shoulder. The takeover stalled.

Iacocca had twice saved Chrysler. Now, as the public saw it, he had hitched his star to a would-be raider. Iacocca was supposed to bring credibility to the takeover bid, but his name hadn't excited investors. His disavowal of any desire to actively manage his old company again had deeply amused Chrysler's senior managers. Kerkorian, short on cash and out on the dance floor with the wrong partner, ditched his takeover attempt. Instead he went to war with the Chrysler board. In the summer of 1995 Chrysler's largest shareholder raised his stake higher, to 13.6 percent. Then he hired Jerry York.

York's job at Big Blue was done. He had chopped $6.5 billion in expenses, and IBM was prospering again. When Big Blue announced York's departure, the company dropped more than a billion dollars in market value. Chrysler's market value rose a billion. York became the vice chairman of Tracinda. "I wanted to move my career in the direction of private investments," he states. "Kekorian sought me out." Then bought him out, richly. Some speculated that York was after bigger game: a chance to run his old company.

POINT MAN

In a single move, by hiring York, Kerkorian became a contender. York's conservative, cost-cutting reputation and his intimate knowledge of Chrysler erased doubts on Wall Street about Kerkorian's credibility. Greenmail rumors dried up. Chrysler's stock price by this time was too high for them to attempt another takeover, but Kerkorian and York announced they would try for board representation through a proxy fight.

York quickly became Tracinda's point man. He had to convince investors that Kerkorian's approach to Chrysler's finances was superior—even though York himself had personally mixed and poured Chrysler's financial foundation just years before. York jumped in without hesitation. He says he hoped it wouldn't get personal, and says he told higher-ups at Chrysler as much. When it did he jumped in with two feet.

"Things deteriorated between Chrysler and Tracinda," York states. "The press sees a small fight and turns it into a large fight, it sees a large fight and turns it into a war." York blames the media, then, but he also blames Chrysler. "Eaton gave a speech that was quite inflammatory. The decision whether to respond in kind was the most difficult decision we had to make about the goings-on." This is York's scenario, and Eaton would surely tell it differently. Still, York says, Tracinda decided to match fire with fire. When Eaton called Kerkorian a troublemaker, York retorted that Chrysler was afraid to have real shareholders sit on its board.

WALKING A NARROW ROAD

York hit the road. For six straight weeks he met with Chrysler's largest institutional shareholders. On Tracinda's behalf, York played the heavy. He criticized the Chrysler team as financially ultraconservative. He hammered on the company's $7.5 billion stash. His former employer was complacent, he said, where it should be aggressive, timid where it should be decisive. He needled the automaker on quality. "We had a very narrow road to walk," York says, reflecting back. "We didn't want to trash the company, but we needed to have legitimate issues with shareholders." Eaton, behind the wheel during Chrysler's most successful run ever, was deeply upset. He said that instead of building shareholder value, Kerkorian was destroying it. Eaton accused York of actually trying to drive a wedge between himself and his number two, Bob Lutz.

York told Chrysler in late 1995 that Tracinda would back off when it got three board seats, a study of how much cash the automaker actually needed in reserve, and the right to buy another five percent of the company without penalty. A board seat, he said, was nonnegotiable. Chrysler took the demands under review.

In the meantime a board seat opened up. Early in 1996, in a rebuff to Kerkorian, Chrysler filled that seat with prominent mutual fund manager John B. Neff, who was well-known for calling for Iacocca's eviction after he refused to name a successor. The appointment was a slap at Kerkorian, at York, at Tracinda, and at Iacocca. And in the end, Tracinda did not have the votes to win a proxy battle. Proxy fights at healthy companies are rare to begin with, and Chrysler shareholders were far too pleased with their company's performance to revolt.

CEASE-FIRE

Chrysler and Tracinda quite abruptly called a truce. Tracinda executive James D. Alijian got a seat on the board, and Kerkorian entered into a five-year standstill agreement with Chrysler in which he promised not to buy more stock or attempt a takeover. Chrysler agreed to double its stock buyback plan for 1996 and make an additional $1 billion buyback in 1997. It also agreed to return excess cash to shareholders. Kerkorian reportedly signed the final paperwork on the deal via fax, from his yacht off the coast of Florida. He had turned down his own chance to sit on the board. York says it wasn't Kerkorian's style. York himself never got an offer. "Chrysler didn't want me," York says.

The agreement also spelled out a $53 million payment to Iacocca, to be absorbed by both sides, ending Iacocca's tangle with Chrysler over $42 million in stock options. Chrysler accused Iacocca of leaking confidential documents to Kerkorian. Certainly he had broken unwritten rules about badmouthing a former employer and former colleagues. "None of us will really ever know what was on Lee's mind," York states, but he says it like he does know and won't say.

In the end, then, Tracinda got its board seat. Kerkorian's long efforts combined with York's strategic know-how paid off in stock appreciation. Chrysler's shares had more than doubled in value. Eaton had saved his own skin and preserved Chrysler's independence. In May 1996, just a few months after inking the agreement, Chrysler surprised its investors with a two-for-one stock split and an increase in its quarterly dividend. During the same month the automaker sold more cars and trucks than during any other month in its 71-year history. "Chrysler got what it wanted," York says. "We got what we wanted." Did both sides win? "You can make the case."

RUNNING THE ARMY

York's management approach is to find the best people, increase their responsibilities as quickly as possible, and clear out underperformers. York is as brutal about financial tasks as they come. He says his "tough guy" characterization is accurate. "My general view on American business is that there just aren't enough companies striving every day of every week of every quarter of every year to do all they possibly can to make their business better. In many companies there just isn't that push. If they get 80 percent of the way there, that's considered just fine."

York says he varies his management style to fit the circumstances. He uses a peacetime army–wartime army analogy. "When at war you have to move quickly and decisively. I think of General Patton during the invasion of Sicily, when he's on the front line and the company commander isn't getting the job done. Patton relieves him on the spot and promotes someone right in the moment. In a peacetime army it wouldn't happen that way, but in a warlike situation, speed is essential. You don't have time to build consensus." In a crisis, York is saying, his "get tough, get it done, get it done quickly" approach works best.

York doesn't relish his gun-for-hire image. As previously noted, he believes he's equally good at building a weakened company back up to full strength. If he could change one thing, he says, it would be his one-dimensional image. "If you need to fix a company and part of that fix is very substantial cost reductions, that's what I'm associated with," he says. "But at IBM it wasn't just about fixing the cost structure, but figuring out what to grow. I was very involved in that strategy."

STILL STRATEGIZING

At Tracinda these days, York is deep into Hollywood dealmaking at MGM, another Kerkorian investment. He's mixing with a different crowd than the one at Chrysler, or IBM for that matter. "Sure, there are prima donnas in Hollywood," York says, "I've found a few of those in other companies I've worked for, too." In mid-2000, when his Tracinda contract runs out, York plans a move into the private investment sector. He says he has no use for retirement.

Jerry York is a brilliant brute. He savors a high-stakes challenge, demands excellence from everyone around him, and throws every ounce of himself into a fight. York left IBM in far better shape. He fought for team Chrysler and then turned right around and fought against it. Ask anyone who has worked with York, or against him: This is one fellow you want on your side.

Sam Zell

Sam Zell and his REITs

*"I don't care what people think of me riding motorcycles
and wearing jeans to work. The world can do what it wants.
I do what I want."*

Sam Zell is plotting a real estate industry revolution. He's hip-deep in
the process of building a nationwide empire out of publicly traded properties. No one owns as much publicly traded real estate as Zell. Down
the road, Zell predicts, three or four public companies will define the
real estate industry. If Zell is right, he will be calling a lot of the shots.

Billionaire Zell is the Antichrist of the buttoned-up business world.
He speaks his iconoclastic mind vigorously in a rapid, raspy voice. If Zell
has a suit it doesn't see much daylight. Instead, he favors blue jeans and
white banded-collar shirts. Bald and bearded, he roars around his
Chicago hometown on a Ducati motorcycle. Zell's charismatic dash is
tempered by a ragged edge. His irreverence sometimes refreshes, other
times distracts from his superior management skills. "I don't know what
the media's expectations are of me," Zell says, annoyed. "Am I the kind
of guy to sit down, cross my legs in a three-button suit and answer questions slowly and carefully? Not likely." Management skills are what
count, Zell says. So he jumps around. So he swears. So what?

"NO ONE HAS EVER OWNED THIS MUCH"

Zell was born just after his Polish parents immigrated to Chicago. He
earned his J.D. at the University of Michigan, but his legal career was
over in a blink. "I practiced law for a week," he says. "It wasn't a good
use of my time. I was much more productive making deals than paper-
ing them." He cemented his "grave dancer" reputation in the 1970s and
1980s by buying dying companies at bargain prices and restoring them
to health. Zell's investments have ranged from radio stations to mattresses, from mobile homes to drugstores. At present he owns a dozen
or so public companies, including a cruise ship firm, a seafood restaurant chain, and a fertilizer concern.

But Zell's most ambitious undertaking is in the real estate industry, where he has bundled enormous amounts of property into real estate investment trusts (REITs). Zell's office, apartment, and prebuilt-home REITs are the nation's biggest, and Zell is their chairman and largest individual shareholder. In mid-1999, U.S. Equity Office Properties (EOP)—the king of REITs in terms of market capitalization—owned 80 million square feet of office space, more than any other public company. "No one has ever owned this much office space," Zell states. Equity Residential manages 200,000 apartments, also more than any other public company. His manufactured home (mobile-home) REIT is also an industry leader. What Americans are witnessing, Zell asserts, is "the oligopolization of the real estate market."

Congress created REITs in 1960, but the first ones collapsed in the early 1970s when interest rates skyrocketed. Congress eliminated most property-related tax shelters in 1986, prompting another real estate slump. The industry began a recovery in the early 1990s, but the market was overbuilt and drowning in debt. Commercial banks weren't feeling generous. Zell and other industry operators, scrambling for capital, rediscovered REITs and their special tax status. REITs pay no corporate tax as long as they distribute at least 95 percent of their income as dividends. Property owners also realized in the early 1990s that they could convert their holdings into REIT shares without immediately paying capital gains taxes. So Zell turned three of the private real estate funds he comanaged with Merrill Lynch into REITs and hit the public equity markets. REIT operators could also use their own stock as currency to snap up other properties. Which Zell did in quantity.

FEEDING A REVOLUTION

Zell is not a developer. Like most current REIT operators he consolidates and manages existing buildings. Unlike other REIT operators, or any other property owner ever, Zell is attempting this on a grand scale. Real estate has always been a local endeavor, but Zell is assembling a sprawling national network of properties to leverage deals with suppliers. According to Zell, the strategy is working. "We've never looked at these integrated networks before, and they benefit from economies of scale," he states. "When I owned 3,000 apartments in Seattle it used to cost me $150 to paint each one. Now I own 12,000 apartments, and it costs just $50." There's more. Zell says that because of his size and track record, and because lenders have confidence in his scheme, Equity Office Properties can raise a billion dollars in unsecured debt in the capital market. Zell says he can just walk into the bank, sign his name, and waltz out with the money. "Compare that to some schlub at the corner of X street and Y street who goes out looking for a mortgage," Zell says, satisfied.

The real estate revolution has begun, Zell says. The bad old days of boom and bust are dead, and soon the industry will behave just like every other publicly traded part of the economy. Real estate has always been an unruly industry, distinguished by overdevelopment and hefty borrowing. Soon, Zell predicts, the Street will discipline the industry. REITs as publicly traded companies are subject to full financial disclosure, must meet reporting requirements, and bear up under the scrutiny of the media and investment analysts. Management will have to focus on building efficient operations that generate steadily improving earnings.

Zell's properties have generally received good marks for management. Unlike rival operators, Zell has years of experience running public companies. He knows his way around the equity market, and in 1997 it showed. Shares of Zell's Office Properties and Residential Properties companies were trading at lofty multiples of their cash flow, while the average REIT was trading below that level. 1997 was in fact a stellar year for Zell. His office properties REIT purchased its leading rival, Beacon Properties, for $4 billion in stock and assumed debt.

FORECASTING THE FUTURE

The trip hasn't been all champagne and roses. Since 1991, more than 150 REITs have gone public. The industry's market capitalization has risen from $13 billion to $131 billion, with Zell's companies alone accounting for $25 billion. But in early 1998, while everyone else in the stock market was celebrating, REIT holdings fell from favor. A credit crunch and overbuilding fears dashed Zell's predictions about real estate market stability—for the moment, anyway. In 1998 the total return on REITs was minus 17 percent. REITs got off to a rocky start in 1999, too, even though interest rates were low and office space was renting. Zell's REITs alone remained durable.

But Zell is fully convinced that REITs are the future. He predicts a huge wave of companies going public, then a surge of consolidation. His conviction that the historic real estate market boom-and-bust cycle is dead seems almost defiant, given the likelihood of tax law changes, interest rate adjustments, and economic dips and rises. But Zell says the securitization of real estate will spread worldwide.

RUNNING AN ECLECTIC SPREAD

Zell is no one-trick pony. In addition to his REITs he owns and dominates a flock of other companies. They include a cruise ship enterprise, a cable products company, a seafood restaurant chain, a fertilizer and animal feed concern, an independent supermarket chain in Washington state, and an oil and gas exploration company in Scotland. This is an eclectic spread, and Zell admits as much. "I view myself as an investor," he says simply. "As an investor I respond to opportunity."

A short time back he sold Jacor Communications, a radio station group that he describes as a particularly enjoyable investment. "I was dealing with a bunch of really talented, quirky people. It was awesome." Zell now relishes managing American Classic Voyages, his cruise ship company. Chart House Enterprises, his restaurant chain, is a more personal venture. He is backing a restaurateur friend. "We put up the money," he says. "I don't know if it will work, but I think it will." What does Zell enjoy most? "Putting together both the strategy and properties for companies, then watching them get better and better," he says. "It's real exciting stuff."

Not all Zell touches turns to gold. From 1991 to 1993, the Zell/Chilmark fund invested in Broadway (previously known as Carter Hawley Hale), the aging California department store chain that had taken a header. Zell couldn't revive this one. It was sold in 1995 to Federated Department Stores at a sizable loss. "We bought control of the Broadway, we brought it out of bankruptcy, but we underestimated how long it would take to recover. We were hurt to some extent by earthquakes, fire, flood. Owning that deal was like the ten plagues, but I would say the biggest mistake was hiring the wrong guys to run the business."

Zell's track record, however, is largely enviable. Each of his companies is run by a handpicked CEO with full line responsibilities. Zell does the strategic thinking and serves as a top-level combination field general and motivator. "I've done a pretty good job of reducing my administrative and bureaucratic functions to almost zero," he brags. He is good at picking talent and keeping people motivated. At Equity Residential, for example, employees can participate in a profit-sharing plan. Top executives get stock options, but so do regional managers. A training program serves to fast-track promising talent. This corporate approach is a real estate industry rarity.

"AM I BEING TOO SUBTLE?"

Asked to describe his management style, Zell shoots back, "I've always believed the definition of power is never having to take a vote." He considers, then adds, "I encourage people, I steer them. I may have no line responsibility, but I do have strategic responsibility, judgment responsibilities, and people coming in to see me all day long. Usually their consensus is the correct one and I encourage them. Sometimes I make a slight correction." A typical Sam Zell workday is devoured by appointments. "I spend the whole day making judgments," he states. His office is cluttered. His calendar is busy, but most meetings are ad hoc. "Fortunately I'm blessed with an extraordinary ability to compartmentalize," Zell says. "It's common for someone to talk to me, disappear for two weeks, then come back and I can continue the conversation exactly where we left off."

Zell's style is a far cry from collegial. When he gets cranked up on a subject his raspy voice turns the air blue and his opinion is the only one that counts. Any consensus-building effort dies. Zell's overbearing style is tempered by bright flashes of superior thinking. Anyone who can't keep up should wait in the hall. People don't generally walk away from one of these meetings trying to decipher the finely turned nuances of the exchange. If Zell is anything, he's blunt. "One of my favorite lines, and I use it two or three times a day, is 'Am I being too subtle?' " Zell says. This is a joke, and not at Zell's expense. "I want to make sure everybody comes away from meeting me understanding what I said. I don't talk in circles. Why would I want to create misunderstandings?"

TESTING LIMITS

Zell knows that he is extraordinarily unlike most of his business world peers, and he thrives on that difference. "If you're comfortable being different, you don't spend a lot of time thinking about it," he says. "Am I concerned that people think I'm honest? Yes. Am I concerned that people think my word is my bond? Yes. But I have learned that even if I'm consistent on those, sometimes I'm a hero, sometimes I'm a bum, even if I don't change my actions." It's very important that the world thinks he's straight, Zell says. "It's not so important that the world thinks I'm smart. I don't care what people think of me riding motorcycles and wearing jeans to work. The world can do what it wants. I do what I want."

Zell says his high public profile is unintentional. Since 1985, when *The Wall Street Journal* published a long article about him that set his net worth at $300 million, Zell has tried to draw a curtain around his private life. There are a few standard morsels he tosses to hungry reporters, he says, such as his motorcycling. "I've basically created a personage that serves a public purpose," he says. "As long as I run a public company, I have no right to hide." But Zell says he detests being well-known. "You go to a restaurant and people come up and talk to you about some deal," he says. "I can't go anywhere. I was riding my motor-cycle recently and guy comes up alongside me on his Harley. He says, 'What's your name?' I say, 'Sam.' He says, 'Sam Zell?' I say, 'Yeah.' He says, 'I know you.' This is in rural Georgia! So I've gone to great lengths to protect who I am."

Motorcycles do play a large and pleasurable role in Zell's life. His "Zell's Angels" group schedules an annual tour. "It's spectacular, real therapy," he says. "We go all over the world looking for twisty, turny roads." Past destinations have included Nepal, Thailand, Greece, Chile, Argentina, Slovenia, and Serbia. He reads "escapist stuff," genre not specified. "It's a way of turning off, of getting lost for a while." Zell also describes himself as a "reasonable art collector." He goes for the surre-alists: Dali, Magritte. It's no great surprise that he gravitates toward such vivid, over-the-top art. Zell explains the attraction: "This stuff tests your limits."

Testing the limits is what turns Sam Zell on. His real estate endeavor is another attempt to do just that. This would-be revolution is well worth watching. Zell is, too, for his brash, break-down-the-walls style.

CHAPTER 4

Healers
Restoring Health

> *Healers:*
>
> ⇨ Parachute in from the outside
> ⇨ Exude confidence
> ⇨ Resist surrendering to adrenaline
> ⇨ Build up, instead of beating up, an already demoralized workforce
> ⇨ Are scrupulous about their credibility
> ⇨ See the job through, then clear out

Healers are like doctors. They make housecalls on very sick companies, and matters invariably improve after they arrive. Healers know just how to examine a suffering company, how to read the symptoms, and when to pull out the medicine. Then they offer expert hands-on care until the organization is healthy again.

Healers understand how quickly a downed company can be dismembered, but they resist surrendering to adrenaline. Instead they cultivate a healthy but controlled sense of urgency. Healers are an overwrought company's best friend: They listen well, focus on the positive, plot a course through the trouble, and then lead the company out.

Restoring hope is part of the remedy, so healers exude confidence with a purpose. They take charge, express optimism, and get out front to shake hands instead of wringing their own in the back room. When they do it right, employees stop mass-mailing their resumes and buckle back down to work. Doubters and the distraught get a grip. Shareholders stop agitating, and spooked customers trickle back. Healers are not the command-and-control type, but they operate with a restoring authority.

Executives seldom lead with the soft stuff because most of them believe a muscular approach works best, and often it does. But healers are different—they're nice guys. They know their workforce is staring unemployment or worse in the eye. By the time most healers show up, demoralized employees are starved for leadership. There is usually plenty of buried strength remaining, something healers verify through due diligence before they accept the job.

This is no place for an amateur. Healers trade on their credibility, and a respectable track record is priceless. Chances are the party across the table is a lender, customer, competitor, or employee who feels abused and won't put up with any garbage. So healers are scrupulous about saying what they mean, telling their company story straight and following through on promises, with no exceptions.

Healers work best at companies operating on the brink, when all the hope has boiled away and morale is shot. Firms near bankruptcy are a good fit, as are companies that have exhausted the public's good will, are out of cash, or whose products have failed or pose a public threat. Companies that have broken the law in some unforgivable manner are also a good match. The more crippled the firm, the more welcome the healer. In fact, a little despair helps. Anything less makes it difficult to rally the troops and bring off the cure.

Only a handful of top-notch healers exist. At any one time, in any single industry, there may be only one or two. Consultants like to fill this breach and they may offer good advice, but they can't take charge as needed or build the same confidence that a real healer can. And there are no second acts here. Either the healer produces or the next one through the door is the undertaker.

But healers don't just stabilize a teetering firm; they send it off in a more productive direction. Healers not only cure the ailment but advise the patient how to live a better life. Then they move on. These folks are a mobile lot. They'll take on a mammoth, complex project, but they don't accept custodial positions. Waste Management chairman Robert S. "Steve" Miller parachutes in and out of troubled companies. Kmart CEO Floyd Hall and Advantica CEO Jim Adamson also will depart when the job is done.

The practice of medicine is an art. It is science-based, but its effectiveness depends upon the skill and judgment of the practitioner. Healing a company is like this, too. Healers have the experience and the know-how. They can't guarantee recovery, but they are dedicated to it, and they are a sick company's best hope.

Steve Miller

Robert S. "Steve" Miller
at Morrison Knudsen and
Waste Management

*"Saving a great enterprise on the brink of extinction
is far more satisfying than tweaking a company
already in pretty good shape."*

Steve Miller has spent his entire career preparing for and then practicing business medicine. No one is better qualified or credentialed. Miller's greatest professional satisfaction these days is helping a desperate company back up onto its feet and restoring its vitality.

CHOOSING THE EXTRAORDINARY

Miller is over six feet tall, almost totally bald, and wears rimless eyeglasses. He has prominent ears and good teeth that show. When he laughs he roars. He always wears a suit but never seems caught up in the rat race. Even after a string of top-level positions managing anxious or angry people, Miller is amazingly accessible. He might be mistaken for an avuncular professor of English literature, harmless and smart, not a bit concerned about measuring swords with anyone. His low sonorous voice and level-headed, thoughtful style inspire tremendous confidence—it feels as though nothing could throw this guy. In fact, he is as solid on business insights as they come.

Miller was born into a prominent timber-owning family in Portland, Oregon. His father was a top-flight corporate lawyer and so Miller trooped off to Harvard Law School (which he hated). He took an MBA at Stanford and spent his early career at Ford as a finance executive in international operations. The job took him to Mexico, Australia, and Venezuela. "Others said to me, 'Out of sight, out of mind,' " he recalls, "but I had vastly better business training than if I had stayed in the bowels of Ford's headquarters building." Miller migrated to Chrysler and in 1982 became the automaker's prime negotiator in its bailout and loan crisis. For a time Miller was in the running to succeed Lee Iacocca.

Then he badmouthed Iacocca to the board. Bad blood followed, and he quit. After a year with the investment banking firm of James D. Wolfensohn Inc., advising the Reichmann family's real estate empire Olympia & York during its $20 billion real estate crash, and then some time working on the Canary Wharf project in England, Miller settled back home in Sun River. He turned down a string of job offers that he deemed "too ordinary." Then some extraordinary ones came along.

WANTED: MORE OOMPH

The first was at Morrison Knudsen, the giant Boise-based engineering and construction firm famous for mammoth projects like the Hoover Dam and the Trans-Alaska pipeline. Tunnels, bridges, airports, superhighways, and power plants around the globe bear MK's stamp. But in 1995, MK was a company courting disaster.

The seeds of trouble were planted in the 1970s, when MK moved beyond its core business into land development and shipbuilding. The company coasted along nicely for more than a dozen consecutive years on earnings gains, only to wobble in the mid-1980s, when a recession kicked the chair out from under many engineering and construction projects. Real estate investments failed; shipbuilding sputtered as oil prices rose; and rail-car manufacturing operations ran into production glitches. MK's losses grew, and share prices rolled downhill.

MK's board decided it needed a CEO with more oomph. The directors unanimously voted in outside director, visionary, and hometown boy Bill Agee. Agee was a financial whiz who had survived (but not unscathed) several legendary falls. He'd had a hand in building Boise Cascade into one of the first big conglomerates of the late 1960s, then left before the company took the second of two writedowns that ranked at the time among the biggest in U.S. corporate history. Next, at Bendix, Agee boosted earnings magnificently through clever financial maneuverings, only to blunder famously. First he briskly promoted a young, inexperienced assistant, Mary Cunningham, to a top-level position and fudged the truth about their romance. Cunningham was forced to leave the company, and Agee married her soon afterward. Then Agee made a hostile bid for missile and technology company Martin Marietta, only to watch his own company get eaten alive in a so-called "Pac-Man" defense. Agee was out of work. He temporarily retired to Cape Cod with Cunningham and a $9.5 million severance package.

BETTING THE COMPANY

At MK Agee pursued what seemed like a textbook turnaround. He sold off losing real estate and shipbuilding operations, cut the payroll, and strengthened MK internationally. But instead of restoring MK's construction core, Agee repositioned MK as a leading transit equipment maker. The United States was on the brink of a new railway era, Agee predicted, and public and private investors would soon pump huge amounts of money into domestic rail transportation. In anticipation of Agee's vision, MK bid on a $6 billion high-speed train linking five Texas cities; a new commuter line project in Honolulu; and new transit cars for California, New York, and Chicago. The company nailed contract after contract by lowballing its proposal prices. MK had little experience with new rail cars and was no locomotive expert, but soon it was juggling a bulging order book for just these items on a double-quick timetable.

It was viewed by some as a bet-the-company strategy, and it was doomed. By 1990 Agee was selling off assets. He reassured his board regularly that prosperity was just around the bend, but by 1992 there were signs of the coming train wreck. MK faced a staggering backlog of rail car orders. Huge rail projects had been delayed, and government projects had fallen through. Morale at MK was terrible. Agee had fired a raft of senior executives. Many more had jumped ship, and their replacements were largely less experienced or knowledgeable. MK's board of directors was forced to rely upon Agee for information on the state of the company. "They only heard what Bill wanted to tell them," Miller says. Even so, it grew painfully obvious that MK had grossly underbid contracts and promised too much from its engineering talent. MK spiraled downward. Salaries were frozen. Animosity toward the boss exploded.

"SHOOT FOR THE HEAD"

Agee was under excruciating pressure during this period "He was very security conscious," Miller says. "He worked behind locked doors." Even so, bodyguards failed to halt the delivery of an innocuous-looking package in October 1992. It contained a black rose. Agee interpreted it as a death threat and moved his office from Boise to his seaside estate in Pebble Beach, California. For two years he ran the company by phone and fax while employees jetted back and forth from Boise. "When he did come to town he wore a bulletproof vest," Miller says, not joking. "The graffiti in the men's room counseled, 'Shoot for the head.' " Perhaps this is a joke, or perhaps not.

Agee was already deeply disdained for lavish spending on personal perks. More than once he had been warned about using the company jet as a private taxi. His wife was reported to have once busied MK's graphics department making birthday party decorations. "Agee was a local hero when he first became CEO, but he soon alienated the company and the town with his high pay and regal lifestyle at corporate expense," Miller says. "That sort of thing might have gone unnoticed in New York or Beverly Hills, but he happened to do it in Boise."

In early 1995, after massive losses, the board stripped Agee of all his titles: chairman, CEO, president, and director. Agee had appointed two former White House officials to his board, Zbigniew Brzezinski and William P. Clark, who discovered aggressive and misleading accounting practices. Familiar with high-level intrigue from his White House days, Clark blew the whistle and resigned. Agee's appallingly cozy relationship with MK's board was promptly exposed. He had handpicked most board members, many of whom knew next to nothing about construction. A sizable number were also Agee's personal friends and also sat on the board of a small private charity promoting alternatives to abortion, his wife's pet project. Also on the board: stockpicker Peter Lynch and former baseball commissioner Peter Ueberroth. As late as 1993 this board had voted Agee a very generous $2.4 million in compensation, a company record.

A COMPANY ON ITS KNEES

Wall Street cheered Agee's departure, then attacked the company's questionable accounting practices designed to obscure its dreadful financial performance. MK announced a $310 million loss in 1994, almost twice the company's original estimate.

While MK struggled to scrape itself off the floor, Miller was at home working on his model trains. "I got a phone call," he remembers. "Agee had been fired and the acting chair [Clark] had just quit in despair. Cash was so low MK would miss a payroll in two weeks; they were drowning in a complex web of shareholder litigation; and how would I like to be chairman?"

It took Miller just a few days in Boise to confirm that MK was "a real basket case." "The company had contracted to build hundreds of railcars at a loss of about a million per car," he states. "Agee was an eternal optimist—the original we'll-make-it-up-on-volume guy. I think he thought things would turn out OK if we just had enough time, and in his style of management, he wouldn't tolerate any dissent." In fact there were thousands of dissenters, many of whom believed Agee had destroyed a good company. "My one-liner for Agee: great vision, lousy execution," Miller says. "I don't think Agee was an evil guy, in fact I admired his vision, salesmanship, financial acumen, but he pushed the organization too hard into a field that was not a good match. That business brought MK to its knees."

RESTORING THE TRUST OF THE TROOPS

MK was down but not yet dead. At the operating level, Miller says, there remained substantial experience, know-how, and a still-hardy pride in MK's history. "But at the corporate level it was in disarray," Miller says. "The board was falling apart, our shareholders were litigious, we had a life-threatening cash crisis, and then there was a whole bunch of hostility largely aimed at Agee." Employees were incensed. "Besides ordinary anger at the destruction of a proud company, Agee had converted employee pension plans into MK stock, which had tanked. They'd seen their life savings go. The only good news was that this anger was all aimed at Agee and Cunningham, and that made it easier for me to come in."

During his first days at MK, Miller tried to phone Agee, just to get his perspective. "I couldn't get anyone to tell me his phone number," Miller says. "No one wanted to be associated with him. After a few days I decided I was better off if I could say I'd never talked to him." Agee's wife, Miller says, was resented by employees who believed that she had long played unofficial second-in-command. "Executives said they might meet in the morning to choose between path A and path B," Miller recalls. "Agee would agree with path A, then come to an afternoon meeting and say path B. Everyone was sure he had talked with Mary and she had a different view." Miller's office at MK was not the CEO's room, but "another room, nicely decorated, spacious, somewhat feminine, and referred to as 'Not Mary's office,' " he says. "People would say 'Hey, where's Miller?' The answer was, 'In Not Mary's office.' " Employees, warned not to call it the real thing, had turned the non-name on its head.

One of Miller's first tasks as a healer was to restore the trust of his troops. MK would never recover from its swoon unless employees felt confident about its future. Healing a company means being decisive, but also being a good listener. "You have to be very open, understand and appreciate people's problems," Miller says. "Their lives were threatened with destruction over this, their pension was dependent on MK stock, their savings were gone, and they didn't know if their jobs were going to be saved." Miller knew many employees were looking for new jobs. He began holding town meetings and invited everyone—secretaries, engineers, janitors. Miller spoke; he listened; he was accessible to people starved for leadership. "My style was a combination of humor and candor and it made a big difference," he says. "I had to be visible, approachable. I took a lot of hard and angry questions in those town meetings. I also had lunch in the cafeteria every day. Agee never did that; he had his secretary bring a tray up to his office."

"THEY HAD US BY THE THROAT"

Simultaneously, Miller faced a mind-boggling financial task. His fragile company was in delicate negotiations with lenders in a frantic attempt to avoid bankruptcy. MK was in technical default on hundreds of millions in bank loans. Company stock was down 80 percent from the previous year, and debt was mounting as MK struggled to honor contracts and cover shortfalls. Miller needed to secure credit, lots of it, just when lenders were least likely to feel even moderately inclined in MK's direction. But largely on the basis of his personal credibility, Miller arranged a bridge loan and then $30 million in new borrowing power, and access to as much as $200 million more in proceeds from asset sales. The plan left MK's balance sheet heavily leveraged.

"The banks had us by the throat," Miller says. "They wanted to auction off pieces of the company, sell engineering to Raytheon, sell construction to Pactel, sell mining to someone else, and break it up before the thing went down." Miller was sure that under the banks' proposed plan, MK would "die on the operating table."

MK stayed in critical condition right through early 1996. Miller overhauled the board, shed unprofitable transit businesses, and sold noncore assets in an effort to recapitalize. But viability remained a real question, even in Miller's mind. "In truth, there were times I worried that MK would simply disappear," he says. "Our new bookings had come to a standstill. When GM is investing a billion dollars for a plant slated to start job one on Sept 5th next year, they want to know you're going to be around to finish the job." MK's customers knew the company was technically competent, Miller says, but the financial chaos scared them off. "Fear took away our ability to get any work, and our inability to get any work was what justified the fear." There was no end to MK's bad press.

SAVING A MELTING ICE CUBE

Fortunately for MK, Miller says, many banks gave up on the company in disgust and sold off their positions at 50 cents on the dollar. Miller is a master at exploiting the best side of bad financial circumstances, and here was his opening. Vulture bankers who bought up that debt "wanted management to make something good out of their 50 cent crapshoot," Miller says. "So all of a sudden we were dealing with people with an entrepreneurial approach, rather than workout guys trying to squeeze blood from a turnip."

Miller and MK President Robert A. Tinstman used a "melting ice cube" analogy with these lenders, Miller says. "The flow of new work was coming to a standstill," he explains. "We made it clear that we needed bold action or we would have a dead company not worth two cents to anyone. It would've just melted away." The new set of lenders were persuaded that it was in their best interests to agree. When Dennis Washington, a Montana tycoon, showed up with an interest in acquiring MK, Miller had talked the banks into just the right frame of mind. "The banks started jumping through hoops to keep him on board and not let him spook and go away."

After what Miller describes as a "nailbiting drama," MK won the unanimous approval of all its creditors and litigants. In mid-1996 it was acquired by the much smaller Washington Construction Group, a Highland, California, company largely owned by Washington. The equity/

debt swap was part of a prepackaged reorganization plan and just about wiped out existing shareholders. The combined companies kept the MK name, and MK emerged from Chapter 11 with a net worth of about $300 million, mostly debt-free. Miller turned MK's reins over to new CEO Tinstman, a most able successor. Then Miller moved on to his next patient.

WASTE MANAGEMENT: GARBAGE INTO GOLD

Garbage hauling is hardly glamorous, but on Wall Street in the 1970s and 1980s, garbage turned into gold, and Waste Management was one of the highest flyers. Most people know the Oak Brook, Illinois, company's burgundy garbage trucks.

Waste Management was built in the late 1960s by former insurance salesman Dean L. Buntrock and former south Florida garbage hauler H. Wayne Huizenga. Buntrock took it public and acquired hundreds of mom-and-pop waste haulers to create an enormous firm and a great growth stock. Profits piled up high. Huizenga left in 1984, but Buntrock kept the stock hot. Shares rose from $3.41 in 1984 to $46.63 in 1992. Acquisitions continued. Analysts sang the company's praises.

At the top of the heap, with fewer companies around to acquire, it grew harder to sustain such growth, but Buntrock in the early 1990s hatched a grand plan to do just that. He recast WM as a global environmental services organization. WM branched out into hazardous waste disposal, water treatment, lawn care, and recycling. The company also began to offer waste-to-energy incinerators, air pollution control, toxic dump site cleanups, and engineering and construction services. Buntrock scooped up hundreds of overseas acquisitions and WM sprawled across the globe, a $16 billion company with 73,000 employees.

BREAKDOWN

Then Buntrock's plan went awry. The company, caught up in becoming a global entity, allowed its basic collection and disposal business to deteriorate. Its huge patchwork of acquisitions was scattered and inefficient. Some newer services weren't generating returns. A glut of dump space murdered disposal prices, costs ballooned, and WM's hot streak on Wall Street had generated a throng of competitors. WM had additional financial problems overseas, where it had overpaid for many acquisitions. Buntrock's worst fear came true: WM's stock stalled. But instead of accepting that it was no longer a hot growth company, WM sugar-coated its problems with aggressive accounting. Assets were overvalued and earnings were plumped by cutting capital spending. Employee morale declined precipitously. Wall Street held its nose. The company's burgundy trucks, slighted on service and parts, broke down everywhere.

WM began a conventional restructuring, but frustrated investors demanded more. They pressured Buntrock to bring in strong outside directors, and Miller, among others, was recruited. When Buntrock prepared to retire in 1996, many hoped for a changing of the guard. Instead, Buntrock kept his board seat and installed his handpicked successor and longtime second in command, Phillip B. Rooney. "The investment community, including financier George Soros, was outraged," says Miller. Investors and WM's board had a history of "taking potshots at each other," Miller says, and now cranky investors turned up the heat. They demanded that Rooney unload everything except the company's North American waste business, pronto. Eight months in, Rooney called it quits.

ANOTHER CEO BOLTS

Board member Miller spearheaded the search for a new CEO. The board zeroed in on Sprint president and COO Ronald T. LeMay, who was reluctant to walk away from his huge compensation package. WM countered with one of the richest executive pay packages in U.S. business. LeMay signed.

He stayed less than four months. LeMay broke the news to Miller over the phone, while Miller was out of town preparing to give a lecture on crisis management. "He said, 'I have two pieces of bad news,'" Miller remembers. "He said CFO John Sanford had quit. Then he said, 'I'm out of here, too. Good luck.'" A corporate jet scooped up LeMay a few hours later and flew him to Sprint headquarters. He was back at his old job the next morning. Determined to keep Buntrock from stepping in, and equally determined to have a CEO in place before the sun rose on a new day, WM's board made Miller the new CEO—WM's fourth that year—while he was still out of town, without much discussing it with him.

WM officials wouldn't and couldn't explain LeMay's sudden departure. Shareholders were shaken by his mysterious resignation, assumed the worst, and sent shares plunging. Miller soon discovered what the Sprint executive had unearthed: monster accounting problems. "LeMay went digging and he never found bedrock," Miller says. "If you talked to Buntrock on accounting problems, he'd say, 'What problems?' But WM had gradually gotten into massaging the books to get a better result. You know, you take a dollar out of the kitty, nothing happens, so the next day you take two until you're taking real money. This was the same thing."

LeMay discovered financial quicksand, but Miller believes LeMay's heart was still at Sprint. "He was damn sorry he changed industries," Miller says. "His wife hadn't moved and he was living out of a hotel— LeMay was not a happy camper. The accounting problems became his excuse, not his reason." LeMay would probably also say he was misled about WM's financial picture, Miller says. "But there was no attempt to mislead, we didn't know. Still, if it had been me, I would have said this ain't what I thought it was, shame on me—but I would stick with it and it wouldn't have occurred to me to walk out."

Miller had been instrumental in hiring LeMay in what he admits was a flawed process. "Don't have an outgoing CEO be part of search for new CEO," he says, meaning Buntrock. "They want to protect their own image and the course they've set the company on, so they look for someone to elegantly carry on in same direction. The search committee should have independent directors with no ax to grind. LeMay looked like a damn good choice, but he was also the only choice at the time. And the need to make the change was urgent—there was pressure from Soros and other investors saying get with it, give him what he wants in compensation and get on with it."

ACTIVATING THE RESCUE

Miller knew the first few days as CEO were extremely important. "It was critical not to leave a gap between leaders. I worked around the clock, talking to employees, shareholders, customers, analysts, and competitors." As he moved through those early weeks, Miller tackled a huge array of tasks. Fortunately, before his abrupt departure, LeMay had almost finished a project with a cost-saving reorganization plan. Miller ran it by senior executives at WM; they agreed the steps looked right.

"I said we're going for it," Miller recalls. "Maybe it wasn't 100 percent the right thing to do, but it was important to get people away from the water cooler talking about this leadership thing and back to work." Miller's active approach is one of his assets. "For better or for worse, I'm able to decide things," he says. "I don't stand around studying things forever in a crisis."

Miller kicked off a massive restructuring, the second in a year. He had to restore financial discipline and investor confidence. In an important symbolic move in that direction he eased Buntrock off the board. Determined to reduce overhead by $100 million a year, Miller thinned out a confusing bureaucracy grown dense and inefficient across years of acquisitions. Sales, marketing, and purchasing were centralized. Miller modernized the company's huge, aging truck fleet and installed a new information systems program. In addition he named two old trusted friends to the board, former SEC chairman Roderick M. Hills and former United Airlines President John C. Pope.

"I also began to dig into accounting discrepancies, because unless we could establish credibility on Wall Street, our business might gradually be destroyed," Miller says. He turned to Hills for help. "Four months in, when we finished the investigation, we took a whopping writedown of $3.5 billion, surely a world's record," Miller says. "Eighty percent of our net worth evaporated in one stroke." It was a painful but necessary remedy to restore credibility. After the writedown, 1997 was the worst year in company history. WM would eventually restate earnings back to 1992.

FINDING AN EAGER SUITOR

WM's board understood that Miller was only temping as CEO and they had to hire a permanent leader. Miller, once again, had a big hand in the search and he says it was a very tough recruit. "I'd say, 'Hello, Mr. Wonderful? This is Steve Miller in Chicago, I don't know if you'd be interested in running a giant garbage company in Chicago? And I'm sorry I can't tell you what the earnings are because we don't have a clue. . . . Hello? . . . Hello?' "

Major shareholders urged Miller to approach "Chainsaw" Al Dunlap. He read Dunlap's book, *Mean Business,* on the flight down to Dunlap's Florida home. The two men shared sandwiches and conversation. "I think he's hard of hearing," Miller says, "so he shouts, right across the room at you." What Miller says Dunlap shouted: a collection of business bromides from his book. "I came away thinking he was one-dimensional, a one-trick pony who knew how to slash but might not know what to do next." Even so, Miller thought Dunlap was campaigning for the job and said as much back in Chicago. His comments made it into *The Wall Street Journal.* Dunlap was furious and retaliated with a vicious press release. "He came out slugging," Miller says. "He said I was a terrible guy, and that he would never work for any company that had me on its board."

WM had a more eager suitor, anyway: CEO John E. Drury, of USA Waste. Miller had spoken to Drury about three days into his WM job. "I said, John, I'd love you to consider us," Miller remembers. "But I can't negotiate the terms of a deal until the accounting is sorted out."

Early in 1998, Miller asked Drury whether he was still interested. "We had finally finished straightening out our accounting, and within a week we had our merger." So instead of hiring a new chief, WM combined forces with an up-and-coming competitor. Drury's smaller but much more robust company took over WM in a $13.5 billion deal. Waste Management's name was retained, and WM remained the biggest trash hauler in the industry.

In 1999, in another dramatic twist of events, WM stumbled again. Once more its accounting faltered and share values plunged. President and COO Rodney Proto was ousted. Drury, sidelined for some time by brain cancer, resigned as chairman and chief executive. Miller was briefly activated as CEO until A. Maurice Myers, a trucking industry executive, became WM's sixth CEO in under five years.

What happened? Waste Management had promised too much, Proto says, and fell short of its own overly optimistic forecast. The board had every reason to believe that financial controls were in order—internal auditors and public accountants had stated as much. But Proto's effort to single-handedly carry his firm through Drury's illness was a mistake. Proto was spread far too thinly. Investors, still trying to forget the bad old days at WM, panicked. These events don't invalidate Miller's contribution—in fact, this once-dying company is now quite successful, even if it couldn't hit the high earnings mark.

SAVING HIMSELF FOR BIG GAME

There is "no one great cookbook approach" to corporate turnarounds, Miller says, but they do share several universal steps. They call for great leadership, he says, usually by an outsider. "Former management spends too much time covering old ground or simply following old strategy. A new person may not know as much but can spend 100 percent of their time focusing on the future." New managers, Miller says, "also instill confidence that things will change for the better."

Miller's rules for anyone trying to turn around a fallen company: Be decisive so that you can start your organization moving forward. Listen to customers. Streamline the organizational structure. Come out of your bunker, communicate, and expect that you may have to deliver bad news. Miller has done this many times. "You don't want them to find out from someone else," he says. Tell the truth, Miller says. Do it the first time around and you'll be trusted next time.

Finally, Miller says, cultivate the people who work for you. "Companies falling on hard times are not necessarily populated by a bunch of bozos. Instead they typically have cadres of experienced, hardworking people who know their craft, want to do well, and are frustrated by poor leadership." With good turnaround management in place, Miller says, "Those same troops who couldn't shoot straight turn into an incredible fighting machine."

Miller speaks with well-earned authority. He has nursed several very sick companies back to health. Speaking of healthy companies, he has zero interest in running one. "There are two kinds of people in the world, project-oriented and process-oriented," Miller says. "I can't stand process. I never want to go to another budget meeting in my life." Or run any company full-time. The daily grind is deadly dull, he says. "I'd get bored. I'd be happier as a fireman. Crises are very satisfying. Saving a great enterprise on the brink of extinction is far more satisfying than tweaking a company already in pretty good shape."

When he's not working, Miller is happiest on skis, or poring over a huge scale-model railroad he's building with his wife, Maggie, at their home in Sun River, Oregon. As well as he relates to other people, Miller and his wife are not very social. Nor do they have fancy tastes. Miller drives a 1993 Dodge Caravan, and his favorite food is razor clams, breaded and fried. What's ahead after Waste Management? "Hopefully, nothing exciting," Miller quips. He is certainly not available for any long-term assignment.

That doesn't stop his phone from ringing. Miller considers a few offers, consults with Maggie, and rejects almost everything. His talent will always be in demand, in good times and bad. Miller saves himself for big game, a troubled few organizations that he believes are worthy. They are exceptionally lucky to get him.

Floyd Hall

Floyd Hall at Kmart

"We fully intend to compete with Wal-Mart. They're a big,
very impressive company, but they don't know anything
about this business that we don't know."

Not so long ago, the Kmart Corporation was on nothing short of a deathwatch. Shoppers had given up on the discount retailer's dowdy stores and dull merchandise. The company's retailing strategy was bombing. Wal-Mart was eating Kmart's lunch. As Floyd Hall saw it, "Kmart was like a tree that had died at the top."

Current CEO Hall changed Kmart's course dramatically. Like a true healer he restored hope and steered the company back into the black. As for all those customers who gave up, Hall is making them think again.

Hall has a gentle voice and is remarkably low-key. He exudes a quiet self-confidence. His manner is remarkably open, friendly, frank. Ask him a direct question and he delivers an answer stripped clean of pretense or façade. Merge Kmart with Kroger? "Good idea." Combine with another retailer to form a larger or more strategically positioned company? "Worth considering." Made mistakes? "You bet." Such disarming candor makes Hall easy to like, and is wholly unexpected from the head of a retailing powerhouse.

Hall's round, fair face and unhurried manner separate him from some of his hard-driving, clock-watching competitors—which doesn't mean he's not vigilant. The most dominant thing in his office is a big sign on his desk that reads, "No Surprises." An Oklahoma native who grew up in California, Hall has a nonidentical twin brother. "He's much better looking than I am," Hall says, "but I'm a better businessman."

JOB OPENING

Hall is a business builder. He has moved from one critical situation to the next, always leaving a strengthened organization behind. His first retail job was furniture sales, which he took to, he says, "like a duck to water." Soon he was selling at Montgomery Ward, then Singer, then

Dayton Hudson. As CEO at B. Dalton booksellers, he built the company from 42 to 500 stores. In 1981 he moved over to Target, which he nearly tripled in size in three years. Before his arrival at Kmart, Hall was best known for resuscitating the 400-store Grand Union grocery chain, which he repositioned for Sir James Goldsmith and then sold very profitably.

After Grand Union, Hall says he pretty much retired. He started a few small businesses purely for pleasure. Then Kmart called with a job opening. Did Hall know anyone qualified?

EARLY WARNING SIGNS

Kmart is the third-largest discount retailer in the United States, behind Wal-Mart and Sears, and the 21st company in the Fortune 500. The company, based in Troy, Michigan, employs about a quarter of a million people and operates more than 2,100 stores around the nation. It was founded by Sebastian Kresge and John McCrory, who opened the five-and-dime stores in Memphis and Detroit in 1897. When the partners split in 1899, McCrory got Memphis, Kresge got Detroit. By the 1950s, S.S. Kresge was one of the largest general merchandise retailers in the US. The first Kmart store, one of the first true discount retailers, opened in 1962.

Kmart diversified in the 1980s by buying, among others, Waldenbooks, Builders Square, and PayLess drugstores. In 1987, the year Joseph Antonini became CEO, it ranked second only to Sears in retailing revenue. Antonini had begun his Kmart career as a teenage sales clerk in West Virginia. He was personable and charismatic, and had made a splash in the mid-1980s running the apparel division by helping Kmart ditch its "polyester palace" image.

But by 1990 trouble surfaced. Earnings at Kmart declined, and stock values dipped to an all-time low. A market shift in retailing meant customers were moving away from neighborhood locations to bigger, better-priced stores with wider selections. Even though Kmart had many more stores and in better locations, Wal-Mart's bright, new, fast-paced stores were siphoning off customers. Kmart stores, by contrast, seemed small and outdated. Wal-Mart and other growing discount chains like Target shot past Kmart in terms of revenues, profitability, and reported customer satisfaction. Antonini wasn't entirely taken by surprise. Years earlier, on the job in Texas, he had gotten an eyeful of Wal-Mart. His first thought: "Uh-oh, we are in trouble, Joe."

To combat that trouble, Antonini launched a $3.5 billion plan to remodel, expand, or relocate nearly every Kmart store. Then he went shopping. Antonini bought up big properties like OfficeMax, Borders Bookstores, The Sports Authority, and Price Savers. He considered the problem solved, and so did Wall Street. Kmart posted record sales and profits in 1992, and Kmart shares doubled in price.

ON THE SLIDE

But by 1993 the giant discounter was on the slide again. Customers were still unhappy with what they saw on store shelves. Profits from Kmart's specialty retailing effort hadn't materialized, and updated stores weren't producing needed results. As cash grew tight, shareholders grumbled out loud about Antonini. They called his company makeover too modest and criticized specialty retailing as a dangerous diversion from Kmart's discounting core.

Fear set in, and Kmart's stock price went into full retreat. Antonini realized he had to move aggressively. In January 1994 Kmart took a huge write-off to cover its store upgrade plan and prepare for future layoffs, then sold off several specialty retail holdings to raise quick cash.

But the $34 billion retailer continued to lose ground. Earnings declined further. Outlet malls and category killers like Staples and Home Depot were also gnawing on Kmart's bottom line. Antonini acknowledged that customers were defecting—in 1993, Kmart lost nearly $1 billion—but he insisted his diversification strategy would prove visionary. Shareholders disagreed, and the company's 1994 annual meeting became a showdown. Antonini proposed a new stock structure and partial spin-off of some specialty retail chains. Shareholders wanted Kmart to forget specialty retailing altogether. "We had inklings that it would be a close vote," Antonini says. In fact, shareholders revolted, and the "no" vote killed a stock sale that might have raised up to $900 million, cash Kmart needed. Shareholders had rejected Antonini's plan and his leadership.

Fairly or otherwise, questions about Antonini's leadership began to swirl. Over the years, Antonini had appeared in an appealing advertisement campaign, much like Lee Iacocca did for Chrysler in the 1980s. The public identified Antonini with Kmart's fortunes. Now, as his company floundered, Antonini became a symbol of all that had gone wrong at Kmart. "Part of our quest to get Kmart away from its dowdy image was to do a PR program to tell our story," he says. "But unfortunately I had to tell it, and I shouldn't have done it; I was too high profile. . . . they had me up on a pedestal as high as the Empire State Building, and when things got tough those last two years, that's where they started shooting at me."

TEETERING

Through the close of 1994, Antonini slashed costs, closed stores, and laid off employees. He reluctantly began selling off his specialty retailing empire. Kmart continued to lose money and market share. Eight months after permitting his humiliation at a shareholder's meeting, Kmart's board stripped Antonini of his chairmanship. Antonini was retained as CEO, but it was a degrading display. Three months later they sent him through the door.

Since 1987, when Antonini took over, Kmart's market share of total discount sales had dropped from 34.5 percent to 22.7 percent. By way of contrast, Wal-Mart's market share was up from 20.1 percent to 41.6 percent. Kmart was looking back at 13 consecutive disappointing quarters. Antonini had admitted Kmart's problems and initiated changes. Most important, he had the Big K and Super K concepts, which would become terribly important in years to come.

But Antonini's efforts had been hampered by execution missteps. He had consistently brushed off suggestions as criticism. Poor communications between headquarters and retail stores had done deep damage. As Kmart's directors ushered Antonini through the door they were certainly aware of then-recent CEO oustings at Morrison Knudsen and W.R. Grace. They may have feared a legal and public relations tangle if they didn't act. Kmart was left teetering, with no clear strategy and no successor.

STARVED FOR LEADERSHIP

Kmart needed a leader who could see the road back, command the respect of dispirited employees, and nurse the company back to health. The board approached Hall, who says he started out with "no interest whatsoever" in the job. "But then I warmed up to the challenge," he recalls. "Topping off my career with a major turnaround appealed to me."

When he walked through the door, Hall says, he found an entitlement mentality. "Also a silo management style. There was a lot of backbiting among senior management." Hall also found a ragged split between new hires and longtime personnel. "Tenured people, you could see the fear in their eyes," he says. "They saw their peers leaving left and right. But I also saw an enormous number of people who hoped I would put the company back together. I saw a lot of hope in their eyes."

Hall called in workmen to remove a large set of steel doors separating his offices from the rest of the building. "Those doors said a lot about the old mentality," he says, "which was, 'They're out to get me.' " Onlookers waited for more. Many people expected a huge, clattering shake-up from Hall, perhaps including massive store closings and layoffs.

Instead, Hall disappeared deep into Kmart for nearly six months to solve a very sudden financial crisis. Kmart's credit rating had just been downgraded to junk-bond status, triggering a debt provision that required an immediate $550 million payoff to bondholders, a "put." Hall says he was "semiaware" of Kmart's precarious financial position when he hired on. "But bankruptcy was never mentioned to me, nor was anyone else thinking about it. I thought we had enough working capital and lines to carry us through the storm. And we did, with one small flaw—that little tiny provision." Kmart escaped Chapter 11 when Hall negotiated a new $3.7 billion credit line and prepared a $1 billion preferred stock offering. "But in effect, I lost about a year," he says. "I couldn't focus on our program as I would have liked to. And restructuring our balance sheet was enormously expensive—and added to our problems, which were already bad enough."

In early 1996, with Kmart's ailing finances stabilized, Hall got down to the business of recovery. He had run two previous turnarounds, he says, and he had learned from both of those experiences. Hall saw a company starved for leadership. He needed to rally his workforce and put able new people in place. "We needed a sense of entrepreneurism, a sense of teamwork throughout the organization," he states. He also needed to restore faith.

TAKING AIM

In mid-1996, Hall reported another huge quarterly loss, but there was good news, too. In the previous year Kmart had replaced 7 board members and 19 of its top 33 executives, and many of the replacements had turnaround experience. Costs were down by about $500 million. Hall had tethered compensation to performance for top executives and store managers, and raised the performance bar. In addition, Kmart had closed more than 200 underperforming stores, unloaded hundreds of millions in aged inventory, and sold off $4 billion in noncore assets.

Hall pushed to rid Kmart once and for all of its image of cheap goods and shabby stores. His predecessor had rightly begun building bigger, brighter stores, and Hall carried on. These new stores had wider aisles, snappier displays, and better inventory. Kmart hired popular actresses Rosie O'Donnell and Penny Marshall to do a string of TV commercials reinforcing its new image. Hall also expanded Kmart's private label and name-brand collections, including the Sesame Street line of children's clothing, model Kathy Ireland's women's apparel, and the Martha Stewart line.

"Martha Stewart was already here but she was doing $10 tinwear," Hall says. "She had magnificent products, but we didn't have the customers for her." Hall raised Stewart's profile at Kmart and greatly expanded her line of home products. The Martha Stewart Everyday Home Collection gave Kmart a needed touch of class. Most Kmart shoppers are women over 25 and under 50 years old, with children and annual household incomes between $20,000 and $60,000. These name-brand clothing lines were aimed directly at their pocketbooks.

AT LAST, SOME ZIP

The turnaround came slowly. Sales in 1997 remained unspectacular. Enormous rivals Wal-Mart and Target continued gobbling up suburban customers and earning between $50 and $100 more in sales per square foot of store floor space, which is how retailers measure productivity. Kmart was still behind—some said way behind. Wall Street questioned Hall's comeback strategy. Analysts said Kmart had no choice now but to deliver on sales because it had already milked the benefits of cost reduction. Hall admitted his frustration publicly and pushed on, shedding the last of Kmart's non-U.S. and specialty retail stores and rebuilding his management team.

Hall also continued to aggressively convert stores to the Big Kmart and Super Kmart format. Big K stores are Kmart's answer to Wal-Mart's big bright formula. They offer shoppers the usual discount items but with more apparel and shelves of "pantry" items like disposable diapers and soft drinks. Kmart launched a new Big Kmart format in 1997 with better store layouts and a new logo featuring a very large orange K. These conversions were pricey, but Hall believed they would pay off.

Kmart began to show some zip in the spring of 1998, when Hall announced the best quarterly performance in five years. Stocks had tripled in value since late 1995. Later in 1998, the company opened 45 Big Kmart stores on a single day. Hall noted that it was the first time in five years that Kmart would have more stores open at the year's closing than at its opening. He also extended his contract another three years, to 2001. "I was trying to settle down the Street. They were preoccupied with succession, and I had to put that to rest." All things taken together, Hall calls 1998 "a very encouraging year. We were finally earning enough money so that our cash flow was taking care of all our needs."

Kmart continued its comeback. Fourth-quarter profits in 1998 were the best in six years. Profits were up 89.7 percent to $353 million, from $186 million a year earlier, beating analysts' expectations. Overhead costs fell to a record low, and more than half of Kmart's 2,161 stores had been converted to the Big K format. "At the end of 1999 we won't have to fix anything from the past," Hall says. "We can focus on looking forward and growing the company."

ATTENTION, KMART SHOPPERS

Kmart's future looks brighter these days, though Hall has work ahead. Shoppers are notoriously capricious, and if the economy takes a dive the retailer could find itself scrambling again. Online shopping may also have the potential, in the long run, to knock the wind out of discount retailing. Hall expresses concern here. "We have a major initiative on this," he says. "We'll need to give people a better alternative."

Hall believes in Big K stores, but he also wants to open more Super Kmarts, giant stores that combine general merchandise with a full supermarket. He's on the prowl for the right partner. "To combine with a national food chain, like Kroger, would make enormous sense," he states. Kmart must also prove that it can stay in the ring with the heavy-weights. Hall is straightforward about how Kmart thinks about big, burly Wal-Mart. "It's like standing out in the middle of street with a tank coming at you," he cracks. "There have been major dynasties—GM was one, AT&T was one—but there has been nothing even remotely close to Wal-Mart in retailing. We fully intend to compete with them. They're a big, very impressive company, but they don't know anything about this business that we don't know."

RUNNING THEM AS IF HE OWNED THEM

Hall describes his personal management style as "guided autonomy." He believes strongly in "a high level of specialization in organizations. Let people do their jobs, and let me worry about how to reward them." But the Kmart CEO says he also expects to "be a partner." He gets his key people together annually to let their hair down and freethink the company's strategic direction. "I'm an entrepreneur at heart," Hall says. "I try to run companies like I own them, and that's my criteria for making decisions when there is no black and white."

For years Hall has commuted between Kmart's sprawling orange buildings in Troy, Michigan, and Montclair, New Jersey, his permanent home. He climbs aboard a corporate jet on Friday, flies an hour and fifteen minutes east and spends the weekend with his family. On Monday morning he reverses the trip. Hall has thrown himself into healing Kmart, but he looks forward to making the trip home one-way. To relax these days he reads authors like Larry McMurtry and James Michener. He drives a new Mercedes SL and owns five other cars, including an Aston Martin. Hall still does his own shopping. It's always interesting, he says, to see how another store does it.

Kmart is prospering under Hall's good care. When his employment contract runs out in 2001, he will leave a healthier company behind. Hall will move on, but don't expect him to retire. The retailing industry, arguably the most difficult business around, is not likely to let a gem like Hall spend the rest of his life collecting more cars.

James B. Adamson

James B. Adamson
at Advantica and Denny's

*"We went from being the poster child of racism
to where we are today."*

Denny's restaurants are roadside fixtures in many American towns. The Denny's sign with its sunny yellow background suggests an upbeat, informal atmosphere—a relaxing place to tuck into a plate of pancakes. In the 1990s, however, this six-sided sign became an emblem of racism. Snowballing allegations threatened to wipe Denny's off the map. It took a healer to restore Denny's health.

James B. Adamson is chairman, president, and CEO of Denny's parent company, Advantica Restaurant Group, Inc. He has straight dark hair and a penetrating gaze. Adamson is both intense and markedly friendly. He describes himself as "shy, extremely introverted," but says he has trained himself to be gregarious because communicating effectively is part of doing the job right. As he sees it, that job is to make Denny's a model of business diversity. Adamson is utterly convinced that this is his mission. At times he sounds less like a businessman, and more like a civil rights activist.

The son of a U.S. Army general, Adamson was born in Japan and grew up on military bases around the world. He calls that experience preparation of sorts for his role at Denny's. "I remember playing basketball in Washington D.C., when I was the only white person on the court and all that mattered was how you played," he recalls. His family also lived for a time in Honolulu. "I was the only white, so I got beaten up the first day of school. I do know what it's like to be on the minority end. I've learned how important it is to stand tall on this issue."

He was already the veteran of several business rescues before he arrived at Denny's—first at Revco, and then at Dayton Hudson. Adamson's proudest prior accomplishment was as CEO of Grand Metropolitan PLC's Burger King. In 18 short months, by streamlining the company and sharpening its marketing focus, Adamson had helped boost annual profits by 28 percent.

Denny's would ask much more of him.

CASH SQUEEZE

Advantica (formerly Flagstar) is one of the largest restaurant companies in the United States. Its 19-story office building in Spartanburg, South Carolina, is the tallest in town. Advantica operates over 2,600 moderately-priced restaurants. Denny's is the company's flagship chain, best known for its $1.99 "Grand Slam" breakfast: two eggs, two slices of bacon, two sausages, and two pancakes. Many Denny's customers are travelers pulling off the highway for a reliable meal with no pyrotechnics. Senior citizens are also frequent customers and in many places become regulars. Denny's motto: "Always Open."

Denny's was founded in 1953 as a single donut stand in Lakewood, California. By 1981 the chain had grown to over 1,000 restaurants. Through the 1980s a flurry of expansions, acquisitions, and leveraged buyouts left Denny's parent company, TW Services, $2.4 billion under water. The company continued to lose money for five straight years. This cash squeeze probably lies at the heart of Denny's race problem. Regional managers and district supervisors in the early 1990s felt great pressure to make cash registers ring. Some of them believed that black customers were bad for business and encouraged, perhaps even instructed, their employees in discriminatory practices.

Adamson disagrees with this theory. There was "no relationship whatsoever," he says, between cash flow problems and the bigotry that raised its ugly head. According to Adamson, discrimination at Denny's "was just unenlightened idiotic behavior." Why, then, at Denny's? Why not someplace, anyplace, else? Adamson laughs. "My mother didn't bless me with a rearview mirror. Denny's—I'm not sure it's more typical or atypical—but it got caught with its hands in the cookie jar. It was a company run by all white men. There were no women, no people of color, and the board was all white."

"Denny's got sued, then the company ran to defend itself instead of admitting the problem," Adamson summarizes. "They did a stupid thing."

". . . BUT THEY CAN'T GET SERVED AT DENNY'S"

The racial allegations began in 1991, in San Jose, California. Eighteen well-behaved black teenagers were asked by Denny's waitstaff to pay a cover charge, unlike white teenagers at a nearby table. The teens called a reporter, then hired a lawyer. Soon there was a second accusation, from a California woman who said her daughter had been denied the restaurant's customary free birthday meal because she was black.

TW Services CEO and Denny's boss Jerome J. Richardson had built his food services career from scratch. A southerner and a former wide receiver for the Baltimore Colts, Richardson as a young man had invested his football earnings in a Hardee's hamburger stand in Spartanburg. By 1989 he was running the company. Richardson's initial response to charges of bigotry at Denny's was lighthanded. This company is billions in debt, he countered, and these allegations don't make any sense because we obviously need all the customers we can get. Denny's does not tolerate discrimination, Richardson continued, and to hammer home his point he arranged sensitivity training for his company nationwide. Richardson was known in Spartanburg for relatively progressive views on race relations. He was sure his conciliatory response would finish off the controversy.

It didn't happen that way. A Justice Department probe found that discriminatory practices at Denny's were widespread in California. Richardson's firm in 1993 entered into a consent decree that required no admission of guilt, but the publicity was terribly damaging—and new allegations sprang up almost immediately. Six black secret service agents en route to a speech by President Bill Clinton said they had been treated rudely and forced to wait endlessly for breakfast while their white counterparts received prompt, courteous service. CBS Evening News anchor Dan Rather reported the story this way: "These agents put their lives on the line every day, but they can't get served at Denny's."

Richardson must have been devastated. He apologized to the agents and fired the restaurant manager. Even so, Denny's argued that the poor service had not been racially motivated. The agents sued—and new accusations kept coming. In June, 1993, members of a black gospel choir claimed that because of their skin color they'd been refused service at two separate Denny's restaurants in a single night.

ALLEGATIONS MOUNT

Richardson moved to kill a mounting public relations disaster. Denny's began broadcasting "The Pledge," an extremely unconventional television commercial. "Everyone who comes to our restaurant deserves to be treated with respect," Richardson states to the camera. "With dignity," continues an employee. "I will make mistakes," says another. "Please know they will never be intentional." Richardson also expedited a so-called "Fair Share" agreement with the NAACP that committed TW Services, renamed Flagstar, to spend $1 billion in jobs and contracts for minority employees and suppliers. Both sides called the agreement historic, but later that same day the NAACP publicly backed Richardson's ongoing efforts to win an NFL expansion team. Many said the two sides had cut a deal.

Attorneys leading lawsuits against Denny's sniffed at the agreement. They publicized an 800 number and encouraged people to report racist encounters at Denny's, perhaps to join a class action lawsuit. Thousands called. The allegations list lengthened: black customers ignored, forced to pay a cover charge or prepay, offered back-room seating and disrespectful service, treated like troublemakers, and threatened with police action. The most outrageous reports were of so-called "blackouts," when restaurants allegedly closed to keep out too many black customers.

Mounting evidence seemed to suggest that at some level, racism might be a tolerated or even tacitly encouraged element of Denny's corporate culture. Back in 1990 a consulting firm had warned Denny's parent company that its lack of diversity was a strategic danger. Industry competitors like McDonald's and Burger King had cultivated connections with the minority community for years. Not Flagstar. Although it served many minority customers, Flagstar had only a sprinkling of minority-owned supply firms. There were no black senior managers and no minority officers or directors. Only one out of 163 Denny's franchises was black-owned. At Denny's, diversity was something other companies worried about.

DANGLING, THEN SETTLING

The lawsuits left Denny's dangling, legally and financially. Its parent company was still trying to cope with billions in debt. Kohlberg Kravis and Roberts had shelled out $300 million in 1992 to take a 47 percent equity stake in Flagstar, and according to Adamson, "that had allowed the company to survive." Despite the cash infusion, Denny's parent company was still on the rocks. Sales were off in some places. Share prices were near their lowest point. Competition for customers was tightening for midscale eateries.

Richardson weighed all these factors and decided that Flagstar couldn't afford several more years of such extreme instability. In 1994,

Flagstar paid $54 million to settle the bulk of its race-bias lawsuits in the largest and broadest settlement ever under the Federal public-accommodation laws, laws enacted in the 1960s to end segregation in restaurants and other places that serve the public. Denny's insisted the settlements were not an admission of policy or any practice of discrimination. We serve a million customers a day at Denny's, Richardson stated at the time. We have 40,000 employees. It would be naive on my part to expect that our customers are always satisfied.

Some said Richardson had done his best to contain the damage. Others questioned the company's innocence and characterized Richardson's actions as superficial, too little, too late. Either way there was mounting evidence and public perception that Denny's didn't want its minority customers.

SHAKE-UP

Richardson, worn down and longing to devote himself to his NFL expansion team, the Carolina Panthers, reduced his role at Denny's. KKR looked for a healer. It found Adamson, who speaks as if he took the job instinctively. "I could have done more due diligence," he says, "but I jumped in, and like anything else, you gotta swim."

Adamson swiftly formulated a strategy. He readied to sell off Flagstar's low-margin lodging and food service businesses that operated in places like Yellowstone Park and the Los Angeles Coliseum. He also decided to sell Flagstar's Hardee's restaurants: "Had to go, we didn't own the franchise." Also a chain of restaurants named Quincy's: "A dying steak house, had to go." Adamson set his sights on luring back market share. He also had to revive Denny's.

Right off the bat, Adamson told employees that anyone who discriminated would be fired, and anyone who disagreed with that policy should resign. In just months, all but 4 of the company's top 12 officers left. In the end only 2 stayed, both women. Adamson says Flagstar, renamed Advantica, had begun a dramatic culture change and many senior people didn't belong in the new company. "They could leave with dignity but they had to go," he says. "We needed a different skill set." The new culture was a shock to the system, Adamson admits. He says if he'd been one of the old guard he would have packed up, too. "We totally shook up the company, but it needed to be shaken up. You don't like to do it, but when you have limited time in a company that needs reshaping, you tend to go to people you know can deliver so you can hit the ground running."

"IF YOU DISCRIMINATE, YOU'RE HISTORY"

Adamson and Denny's CEO J. Ronald Petty, also formerly of Burger King, burrowed into the details. They eliminated three layers of management to get closer to restaurant operations. A massive remodeling effort began. Diversity-oriented programs boosted the number of minority store managers, and talented minority employees in management positions were fast-tracked up the corporate ladder and into franchise ownership. Tens of millions in contract dollars went to minority suppliers. In case anyone had missed the message, Adamson put all employees through an additional round of racial sensitivity training. He made diversity a performance criterion. Martin Luther King Jr.'s birthday became an official company holiday.

Adamson understood that he needed to heal Denny's image with the public, too. He wanted consumers to distinguish between the "old Denny's" and the "new Denny's." Big print ads ran at the end of 1995 to mark the distribution of settlement money to nearly 300,000 aggrieved customers and their attorneys. "It's a New Day at Denny's," the ad announced. "If you discriminate, you're history!" Adamson also contacted Jay Leno, who for years had been riding a wave of Denny's jokes. "I sent him a letter and said you have to get off this, your humor is dated," Adamson says. Leno called back in person. "He laughed, he was somewhat uncomfortable," Adamson says. "But he said he would take a new look at the company." Adamson thinks Leno really did. The Denny's jokes tailed off.

INTO THE FUTURE

Advantica had made progress on diversity issues, but its finances remained fragile. The $1.99 "Grand Slam" breakfast special was still bringing in customers, but sales overall were flat. Interest payments were still crippling, and the company's stock price was stuck near an all-time low. KKR would soon sign off, leaving Denny's to the junk bond holders. "That was my worst moment here, when I had to call the guys at KKR and say we struck a deal in court with creditors and you're out,"

Adamson says. "We lost supportive, challenging, smart partners. But at the end of the day we were talking about warrants, and the most important thing was to restructure."

In recent years, however, Denny's outlook has improved. Nationwide sales have reached record levels. Franchise growth has also boomed. Advantica emerged from Chapter 11 with cash and four restaurant chains. For the first time in years, Denny's is growing into the future instead of expending the biggest chunk of its resources trying to repair the past.

Racism charges still haunt Advantica. "Whenever Denny's gets lots of press we have a spike in the number of lawsuits," Adamson says. "But 90 percent of the lawsuits filed against Denny's today are frivolous, and we litigate every one." Adamson believes the media plays a role, too. "Most media stories, fortunately or unfortunately, are written by the white liberal community, so Denny's will continue to have a smoldering image of racism. We're guilty automatically because we're big corporate America." Adamson clarifies that he does not believe in any concerted effort to go after Denny's. The restaurant chain, he implies, brought some of this trouble upon itself. "Denny's did some stupid things," he summarizes.

The liberal left is not Advantica's only adversary. Criticism has also been leveled from the political right. Conservative critics have blamed Denny's for knuckling under when accused of mass discrimination because it was caught in a highly charged political atmosphere. Denny's capitulated, they've accused, to a gigantic shakedown by enterprising plaintiffs' attorneys fronting for civil rights activists. This, Adamson says, is pure hogwash.

CREATING CULTURE FROM THE TOP DOWN

By any reasonable measure, however, Denny's and Advantica have undergone a cultural transformation. "We have a very clear policy today," Adamson says. "You discriminate, you're fired." Before the scandal, Adamson says, "there was no policy. This was a company run by very unenlightened people." Where did that "nonpolicy" start? "I wasn't there, but from my perspective, when there's a problem with a company, the blame starts at the top. The culture starts at the top." Racism at Denny's didn't disappear overnight, Adamson says, just because some higher-up instituted a no-tolerance policy. When he first arrived "it just went underground. But slowly, surely, people realized that if they wanted to operate that way they'd have to go somewhere else."

Adamson protests that he is not a "turnaround" executive. He says he just keeps falling into positions at troubled companies. Fortunately, he's very good at climbing out of trouble, and carrying out a company intact. "The problems at Revco, I was naive to them, and I just got involved with a troubled company at Dayton Hudson. I don't like steady states," he continues. "I like the reward when I feel progress. But I'm not a turnaround type. It's more like remodeling, reshaping. Advantica was the hardest for me because it was more complex. There were times in 1995 and 1996 when I didn't think this company was fixable. I had to reshape a culture on top of running a business."

Adamson says his management style works because he excels at assembling a top-notch team. "I surround myself with people with skills better than mine, then I leave 'em alone to do their jobs. I'm very good at pushing people to do better and recognizing how well they have done. And I kick people on a roll rather than when they're not doing well. They've already kicked themselves 38 times by then, and there's no point in rubbing salt into the wounds."

"BULL'S-EYE"

Denny's is in the final stages of its transformation. Adamson is excited about the progress he sees but says the effort has taken a toll on him. Like most healers, he says he'll move on sometime soon to make room for "some other skill set." On to another troubled company? "I've had my run," he says. "I don't know if I'd have the same mental energy to do this again." His ambition is to teach, preferably business ethics. "I'll probably be lousy at it and do another turnaround," he laughs. "But if there's something you want to do, at least you should try."

Adamson's personal modesty is striking. His enthusiasm for diversity is also striking. They come together when he describes his efforts and those of his team to get it right at Denny's: "We threw the dart and then drew the board and got a bull's-eye. We set about doing the right thing. Then we looked back and said, 'My God, we did it. We went from being the poster child of racism to where we are today.' " Adamson is a first-rate business healer. His experience is coupled with uncommon conviction and compassion.

>—◆—<

Dealmakers
Gutsy Gamblers

Dealmakers:

⇨ Don't approach negotiations expecting perfect solutions

⇨ Are good at deciphering an adversary's hard points

⇨ Are masters at dressing up and selling an idea so that it appears to favor the opponent

⇨ Seldom feel any guilt or anxiety about maneuvering to clinch the best deal

⇨ Are personable on the outside, driven inside

Dealmakers are extraordinarily skilled at achieving agreement. They find paths to peace that elude others, passageways that nobody else can detect. These accomplished thinkers can juggle the merits of opposing arguments without being derailed by the high emotion that often swirls around disagreements.

Dealmakers don't approach negotiations expecting perfect solutions. They don't even strive necessarily for a deep understanding of the problem du jour. Their single objective is, simply put, agreement. Neither side will get everything it wants. Both sides will make sacrifices, and nobody will walk away completely satisfied. In the end, however, when these topflight negotiators are done, each side will be able to claim victory.

A dealmaker is patient, persistent, analytical, and resourceful. He can track two or more competing agendas on his radar at once. That's the easy part. The more difficult job is identifying an adversary's hard points, or dealbreakers. All the tactical maneuvering will revolve around these points—explicit or unstated—until they are addressed.

Dealmakers plan their maneuvers with a cool eye, but they deeply relish the fray. They enjoy the jockeying for position, the eyeball-to-eyeball bargaining, the back and forth under pressure, and finally buttoning down the deal. Every calculating step of the bargaining process is a pleasure. They are masters at dressing up and selling an idea so that it appears to favor an opponent when the benefits are actually reversed. Born dealmakers seldom feel any guilt or anxiety about operating as necessary to clinch the best deal. They sleep well at night.

These executives are personable on the outside, driven inside. They have the astonishing capacity to meet physically demanding, emotionally draining challenges and still bring their very best forward during negotiations. Dealmakers read other people well. They seldom parade their power. The last thing a sensitive, high-stakes negotiation needs is a public display of vanity, competitiveness, or attitude.

Dealmaking executives and their organizations are usually rewarded by the peace and progress that follow a well-managed conflict resolution. The parties, no longer frozen or flailing away at each other, can shake hands and move on. Dealmakers fashion avenues of escape. They build to a settlement, not a fight.

This style does come with risks. Every successful executive privately considers himself a great dealmaker. Few are. Skills in other business arenas—for example, a superb engineering aptitude or stellar marketing talent—do not automatically translate into effective negotiation skills. Even a gifted negotiator can get himself into trouble when an imprudent deal goes through because of rapidly shifting circumstances, or when a bargain made in haste serves short-term goals but sacrifices the future. Driving a weak opponent to his knees can nail a deal, but it also builds resentment. The vast majority of all deals fail to achieve their purpose, and this kind of overpowerment is a common cause. And sometimes no deal is the best option. The best dealmakers enjoy declawing a conflict, but they also know when to leave the table.

Dealmakers do their best work for companies at major turning points, when the firm's future direction is at stake. At Dow Corning, CEOs Keith McKennon and Dick Hazleton brokered a way out of litigation hell when their company faced its breast implant crisis. Al Checchi and his partner Gary Wilson cut deal after remarkable deal at Northwest Airlines, first to purchase the company, then to save it from drowning in red ink. United Auto Workers boss Steve Yokich is also one of the best dealmakers, particularly when he is putting the screws to General Motors.

Not all dealmakers are loved. A hostile-takeover artist out to line his pockets is universally disliked except by shareholders. Most dealmakers are welcome, however, because they join people in conflict-laden circumstances for a larger goal. Dealmakers are agents of change, the good kind. They are in high demand these days because the business environment has grown superdynamic, and globalization is boosting the need for speedy negotiations. Dealmakers are on the leading edge of business development, and the entire market system depends on them.

Keith R. McKennon

Richard A. Hazleton

Keith R. McKennon and
Richard A. Hazleton at Dow Corning

*"How did I know people thought we were evil?
I knew because I did about 150 press interviews in my
first 40 days as CEO. There isn't much that can
bring it home better than that."*

—KEITH MCKENNON

*"It's not pleasant, expecting to pay $3.2 billion for claims
that we believe are without merit, but we don't have any
alternative. And we've made peace with that."*

—DICK HAZLETON

When Keith McKennon was the boss at Dow Corning he sometimes pushed back from his desk to gaze out his office window. Outside was a gently wooded landscape, home to honking flocks of geese and families of tawny deer. It was a peaceful view. Calming. To CEO McKennon, the flat lands of Midland, Michigan, were home, a place of natural beauty and small-town life. To many Americans, however, Midland was the home of the Devil Incarnate. And McKennon's office was ground zero.

Dow Corning was accused in the early 1990s of knowingly selling breast implants that leaked, ruptured, and ruined the health of hundreds of thousands of women. The company fought back but couldn't back up safety claims. When the FDA booted implants out of the marketplace, drooling attorneys swarmed. Dow Corning cashed out of the implant business, then ran for Chapter 11. When the company finally settled the class action chunk of its legal woes last year, it was no champagne victory. Dow Corning has been vindicated by science, but it will fork over a mountain of cash. Women with implants will never receive the compassion they deserve for living through the hysteria. Only the plaintiffs' bar came out ahead.

There is, however, cause for celebration at Dow Corning. Stand-out leadership saved a worthy company. McKennon, a stocky man with a square face and dark hair, led the rescue effort. Good-natured and disinclined to take himself too seriously, McKennon is the opposite of a hotshot. He prefers to connect with people rather than to dazzle them, and his folksy manner makes him a great communicator. McKennon trained as a chemical engineer, but by instinct he is exceptionally good at diplomacy, at defusing confrontation, and at laying the groundwork for deals with adversaries.

McKennon reset Dow Corning's course during the early years of the breast implant crisis; then successor Richard A. Hazleton carried out the long, tricky piloting job that followed. Bespectacled, balding, a little intense, Hazleton is a steady leader with a keen sense of purpose. He, too, trained as a chemical engineer but performed jobs all across Dow Corning before becoming CEO in 1993. Hazleton is a fair-minded man who appreciates the complexity of the implant controversy and doesn't try to falsely pare the subject down to simple terms. His charge now, and that of his successor, Gary Anderson, is to move his company beyond the implant fiasco.

HUMMING ALONG

Midland Michigan is about a two-hour drive north of Detroit. There are no high-rises in Midland and no need for any. Before the implant crisis, Dow Corning's remote location was a reflection of its conservative corporate culture. The company hummed along, its top officials making decisions in a decidedly insulated atmosphere. Company products were in every home, at use on construction sites, in cars and on airplanes, but Dow Corning wasn't very visible, and direct communications with the public were rare. The company's pioneering corporate ethics program was better known, at least in business circles, and was considered the gold standard.

Dow Corning is often confused with its two sole shareholder companies, chemical maker Dow Chemical and glassmaker Corning, Inc. It was founded in 1943 as a fifty-fifty joint venture between the two to produce silicone, a polymer used in thousands of products ranging from nipples for baby bottles to sealants on the Space Shuttle. Dow Corning today is a $20 billion multinational business with 9,000 employees worldwide. Breast implants never contributed more than one percent of its total revenue, but revenues aside, Dow Corning invented the silicone-gel-filled implant technology. Dow Corning was for years the leading U.S. manufacturer of silicone-gel implants. And Dow Corning was hit hardest when the implants became suspect.

FLAT-OUT DENIAL

Silicone breast implants are supple, gel-filled, and entirely uncomplicated looking. They arrived on the United States market unregulated in the early 1960s, and when Congress granted the Food and Drug Administration (FDA) jurisdiction over medical devices in 1976, implants were simply "grandfathered in." The FDA for 12 years didn't seek out safety data, and even then the agency didn't enforce its mandate until 1992. By then it was too late.

Quality-related complaints trickled into Dow Corning in the 1970s, mostly concerning leaks and ruptures, mostly reported by surgeons and implant recipients. A few uneasy Dow Corning employees also expressed safety concerns. One accused his employer of conducting "experimental surgery on humans" and quit in flagrant protest. *Ms.* magazine also printed a finger-pointing article and called on women to protect themselves. Dow Corning flat-out denied safety problems, real or perceived. Silicone implants are safe, the company asserted. And for sale.

Early in the 1980s a clutch of unhappy women sued Dow Corning and other implant makers. Silicone from their implants had migrated within their bodies, they alleged, causing chronic pain, fatigue, and intense allergic reactions. A number took Dow Corning to court, alleging a causal connection between breast implants, cancer, and autoimmune disorders including lupus and scleroderma. In 1984, the first big court award rolled in when a California jury ordered Dow Corning to pay $1.5 million for fraudulently marketing silicone breast implants as safe. The company snoozed through what should have been a wake-up call. Instead Dow Corning blamed its lawyers for blowing the case and was indignant in public about being soaked by a frivolous lawsuit built upon unsubstantiated claims.

The implant controversy picked up steam. Ominous reports about implants crawled across newspapers and television screens, including a famous Connie Chung segment showing the disfigured chest of a woman whose implants had been removed. Implant recipients formed advocacy groups and demanded answers. Prodded into action, federal regulators gave Dow Corning three years to pony up sufficient and credible safety data—data that Dow Corning didn't have and couldn't have for years. Dow Corning stonewalled. Its public image began to slide. The company's inability to produce rigorous supportive research appeared downright sloppy, and its indifference to anxious women seemed coldhearted (and blockheaded). Dow Corning played into a nasty stereotype: Here was another greedy company cutting corners on safety to boost profits, or so it seemed.

ALARMS SOUND

Implants in 1991 yielded only a tiny sliver of Dow Corning's total revenues. Other product lines were healthy; earnings elsewhere in the company were robust; and cash was flowing. "Dow Corning's board wasn't much concerned during these early days," McKennon says. "Implants were not the biggest topic of the week at meetings." CEO Lawrence Reed handed off the implant matter to Health Care Division chair Robert Rylee. When aggressive new FDA commissioner David Kessler convened a panel on silicone breast implants—including public hearings—Rylee played hardball. He released documents slowly or not at all. The implant debate hurt women, Rylee asserted, by scaring them and threatening to eliminate a legitimate option. Dow Corning insisted on its innocence. The company set up a hotline to counteract "half-truths" about implants, but investigators caught staffers reassuring callers by describing implants as 100 percent safe, even though the research was incomplete. The hotline was suspended.

Dow Corning's bad year grew worse when the company lost a second, extremely important lawsuit. A woman named Mary Ann Hopkins sued the company for allegedly concealing evidence linking implants with autoimmune disorders. Hopkins did have a serious connective tissue disease, Dow Corning countered, but it had been documented well before her implant surgery. The jury disagreed and ordered Dow Corning to pay Hopkins $7.3 million.

The Hopkins verdict was a turning point. "Believe me, that got the board's attention," McKennon says. "We thought we would win, or at most it would be a $100,000 judgment." The board could no longer treat implant litigation as a distraction, McKennon continues. "Before that, management was telling us this is not a big deal, we are not seeing any increase in these things, we've got all of these doctors writing to tell us how wonderful these things are, we've got all these happy patient letters."

The court award wasn't the company's only problem. Dow Corning had lavished millions of dollars on out-of-court settlements to keep potentially incriminating documents sealed. Now thousands of documents from the Hopkins case went public. Page after page suggested that safety concerns had been ignored for years. Consumers smelled a cover-up. Contingency fee attorneys smelled blood in the water. Dow Corning took the first of several hefty charges to cover implant liabilities, and its debt rating slipped. Then the FDA slapped on a temporary but consumer-confidence-shattering sales moratorium.

What had Dow Corning learned? Nothing, it seemed. The company blustered on that silicone implants were safe—not risk-free, but safe. The risks were known and understood, and women were free to make an informed choice. This mixture of legal positioning and evasive public relations infuriated implant recipients. Dow Corning's renowned ethics program was roundly ridiculed, and to management's horror the breast implant controversy was now routinely compared in the press to some of the worst business disasters ever, including the Exxon Corporation's Valdez oil spill, the Johns Manville Corporation's asbestos mess, and A.H. Robin's Dalkon Shield fiasco.

Dow Corning's two shareholder companies sat on their hands as long as they could stand it. But in early 1992, their Dow Corning connections began giving off dangerous sparks. Dow Chemical and Corning saw their own well-tended public images scorching and blistering. Both companies were also afraid Dow Corning would burn down the bank. After intense top-level talks, Dow Chemical Corporation executive Keith McKennon was dispatched to douse the fire.

UNCIRCLING THE WAGONS

McKennon arrived on his first day feeling uneasy. "It was no strange situation," he says. "But to take the assignment it was necessary to retire in 24 hours from a company I'd been with for 36 years. I was asked to take the job by people I respected, in a way I couldn't refuse. I was feeling surprised that first day, maybe even sorrowful."

McKennon had been metaphorically strong-armed because he was a seasoned crisis manager with a reputation for diplomacy. Born, bred, and schooled in Oregon, he had become president of Dow Chemical U.S.A. in 1987, then vice president of the corporation in 1990. McKennon had been Dow Chemical's point man on Agent Orange, the controversial defoliant used in Vietnam, and had managed the controversy over the morning sickness drug Bendectin. He arrived on the job with a vastly different hand of cards than any of his predecessors.

McKennon discovered an organization in a state of shock. "That company had never really tasted adversity," he says. "It had increased sales and earnings every year. Now there was this immense controversy, and 99 percent of the people working at Dow Corning had never seen an implant. All of a sudden they pick up a newspaper and read that they work for a terrible company that's done awful things." McKennon moved quickly to restore morale and productivity. He fired off a memo to employees. "I said, 'Gang, this company has developed a magnificent reputation in 50 years and we're not going to lose it.' " The biggest risk, he told them, was "that you all sit around and worry about this implant controversy and you don't set about making this a bigger, better outfit around the world." McKennon's pep talk sent employees back to their regular work, except for the team handling the implant controversy.

Next he moved to "uncircle the wagons," as he describes it. McKennon dropped the company's confrontational tactics in favor of a more open, conciliatory posture. "I believe that in any significant public controversy of this kind, the first thing to do is decide where your fundamental responsibility lies," he says. "I said our responsibility as far as I was concerned is to women with implants, not to shareholders, tomorrow's earnings, etc. Once you say that, once everyone knows you mean it, and you start to demonstrate that, decisions start to get a whole lot easier."

THROWING IN THE TOWEL

These days companies are expected to bend over backwards for consumers who feel victimized, and McKennon understood this. He assembled an advisory committee composed of implant recipients and met with company adversaries face-to-face. Dow Corning funded new research at a cost of over $10 million. McKennon released piles of documents and offered to pay medical bills for women electing to have their implants removed. "You have to accept as real that the people on the other side are not a bunch of idiots or out to get rich or out to do you in," he explains. "Some of them may be each of those, but in this case, we had a lot of concerned women with implants."

McKennon also stopped feuding with the FDA and the media. "I went to see Kessler right away. He said, 'Who are you?' " McKennon laughs. "I said, 'Good question.' " McKennon hoped to cultivate a rapport. "It became a suitable relationship," he says. "I didn't say warm and fuzzy." Mediawise, he says that he "quit ducking and being adversarial. I did about 150 interviews in the first 40 days on my job. We answered every question." McKennon isn't a blame-the-messenger type. Now years away from the controversy, he has nothing to gain by saying the media treated Dow Corning fairly, but he says it anyway. His decision to appear on the Larry King Show, McKennon says, was "the one thing I'm absolutely certain I did right. It was a high-pulse-rate thing to do. It was a dice roll. You have seven million people not liking you already, and if it doesn't go well, you will add fuel to the fire." The appearance went well, and he calls it "the single event that put a face on Dow Corning."

McKennon defused some of the fury directed at Dow Corning, but he never shook company lawyers and he couldn't derail the FDA. In the spring of 1992, the FDA banned silicone breast implants except for use in clinical trials or reconstructive surgery. Kessler ordered them off the market, not because they were explicitly dangerous but because there wasn't enough evidence to prove their safety. McKennon threw in the towel and abandoned the market. For good. The shutdown was strictly a business decision, Dow Corning said, and not in response to safety concerns. "The decision to never again reopen was mine," McKennon says. "There was no commercial opportunity. I thought Dow Corning should get as far away as possible."

A COMPANY ON ITS KNEES

Dow Corning's retreat did nothing to resolve the controversy. After 30 years on the market, gel-filled implants were in the chests of more than a million American women, and personal injury lawyers had signed up great numbers of them as plaintiffs in class-action suits. Dow Corning said some $250 million in company insurance policies would cover their legal fees and judgments in pending lawsuits. Contingency fee attorneys snickered and said the grand total would sneak closer to a couple of billion dollars. Stockholders at Dow Chemical and Corning accused their companies of failing to disclose implant risks and sued for hundreds of millions in damages. Dow Corning's insurance companies balked at paying claims for the same reason.

McKennon in late 1992 retired unexpectedly. A non-Hodgkin's lymphoma survivor, McKennon's experience with cancer had probably allowed him to manage the implant controversy with more compassion than his predecessors. Unfortunately, during his difficult year in charge at Dow Corning, McKennon suffered a relapse. Dick Hazleton stepped in to fill McKennon's shoes.

Hazleton, a Chicago native, had joined Dow Corning in 1965 and held positions from engineering to finance. He'd been tapped in 1983 to run Dow Corning's big Midland factory, then sent on to Europe to streamline operations. His new assignment was to carry the breast implant crisis to a conclusion and bring the company out alive.

"Things were quiet when I took over," Hazleton says. "I felt my job was not to pull people out of a trough, but to make sure we wouldn't go back in, and to get this thing resolved. I couldn't predict that it would stay quiet and calm and I didn't rule out the possibility that things would heat up again. And of course they did. Considerably."

Hazleton believed one unanswered question stood at the center of the implant controversy: Did silicone breast implants sicken recipients with systemic diseases? But as Hazleton saw it, mass tort litigation and class-action suits had made the answer to this question irrelevant. Contingency fee attorneys had already rounded up vast numbers of plaintiffs. No court could cope with the logistics or finances of such an onslaught. The sheer volume of litigation was forcing Dow Corning into a brokered solution, but a settlement would have little to do with what Hazleton thought should come foremost: the science of implants. So-called expert witness testimony and "junk science" had figured largely in Dow Corning's courtroom battles and kicked the company to its knees. As Hazleton saw it, Dow Corning was the victim of a legal system run amok. Early, influential verdicts against the company had arrived before the completion of definitive research trials. A body of epidemiological evidence was only beginning to form that would confirm or debunk a connection between implants and the autoimmune diseases alleged in many lawsuits. When the facts finally arrived, Hazleton realized, they wouldn't much matter.

BITING THE BULLET

A string of class-action settlement proposals straggled in. The first one bit the dust when a whopping 440,000 women registered for a piece of the $4.2 billion pie and another 6,000 women opted out to sue on their own. The blizzard of claims left Dow Corning aghast. In 1991, the company had faced 137 pending lawsuits. By 1992 there were 3,500. Three years later the number was up to 19,000. Hazleton thinks this "great wave of litigation" was an organized attack, part of the business of practicing tort law. "We literally would see the same documents filed all over the country with identical typos," he charges.

Dow Corning had by this point already spent about a billion dollars on legal fees. Now there was a new worry: a judge stripped shareholder company Dow Chemical of legal protection.

The most difficult period personally for Hazleton was in early 1995, the four months leading up a Chapter 11 filing. "I absolutely believe in hindsight that it was the right decision, but Chapter 11 is a drastic solution," he says. "It wasn't a hard decision because we didn't have many options, but the question was whether we would be destroying the rest of the business by doing it." Hazleton bit the bullet in May and blamed the bankruptcy on "Litigation, Inc." Some others said Dow Corning had dug its own grave. Finger-pointing aside, the filing killed off the global settlement proposal.

Hazleton was under great pressure. He somehow had to satisfy a bankruptcy judge, creditors, fractious insurers, jittery employees, and furious implant recipients backed by a knife-sharpening army of litigators. "There were almost no times I lay awake at night or had chest pains," he says. "But maybe that's who I am. I'm the kind of person who understands that when there's a situation you can't control, you don't get all bent out of shape. I like to think I spent my energy thinking about how to manage, rather than wringing my hands." By the end of 1995, breast implant manufacturers Baxter International, Bristol-Myers Squibb, and Minnesota Mining and Manufacturing had agreed to huge payouts to put away their class-action legal woes. Hazleton knew a settlement of the same sort remained his company's best hope.

Dow Corning filed a new reorganization plan offering to pay claims, but with a catch: No one could collect unless a "science trial" determined that silicone leaking from implants caused the systemic diseases listed in pending lawsuits. The plan was rejected. A series of other amended plans also fell short. Finally, in July 1998, a $4.4 billion plan—including a $3.2 billion payout for implant recipients—got the thumbs-up. Implant safety questions were not addressed.

GROWING VINDICATION

Beyond the range of settlement talks, however, scientific evidence has mounted in Dow Corning's favor. More than a dozen studies at eminent research institutions seem to vindicate implant makers. In late 1998 an expert panel appointed by the judge coordinating federal breast implant litigation accepted these findings. In 1999 an independent panel of 13 scientists convened by the Institute of Medicine at the request of Congress also concluded that silicone breast implants do not cause any major diseases. This research does not diminish concerns about other implant complications: Breast implants can cause localized problems. They can and do rupture. They can and do leak and cause pain, chronic inflammation, and breast deformities. These possible complications are well-documented, and implant makers do not dispute them. Even so, real science has largely ruled out any link to life-threatening diseases. The fact remains that expert witnesses practicing junk science for years perpetuated the breast implant controversy, distorted the legal process, and squeezed Dow Corning into bankruptcy.

Hazleton has been outspoken on this subject. McKennon's management approach was largely defensive and focused on cooperation and resolution, but Hazleton is more righteous, more concerned with justice for his company. McKennon suited Dow Corning's needs in the early 1990s; Hazleton is the right man now as Dow Corning emerges from bankruptcy and enters its next life. These differences in style speak volumes about how far Dow Corning has come. Hazleton admits that Dow Corning made naive mistakes, and he wishes his company had undertaken epidemiological research much earlier to rule out the risk of disease. Was Dow Corning morally corrupt? "Absolutely not."

Corrupt, no. Poorly managed in crisis, yes, for a time. Dow Corning denied its incipient troubles for years, then stonewalled like crazy. It showed a paucity of sympathy for frightened women with implants and hunkered down behind its lawyers. The company squandered its credibility and forfeited the public trust. Certainly Dow Corning might have stopped production sooner, although McKennon has said that physicians wanted implants, and the company back then believed that pulling them off the market would send the wrong message. Dow Corning might have conducted human tests on implants back in the 1970s, although had they done so it would have been precedent-setting.

Hazleton disagrees that had Dow Corning taken these options its crisis might not have spun so wildly out of hand. "Changing public perception in a situation as inflamed and emotional and out of control as this—I don't believe there's much we could have done differently even if we'd been as skillful as possible," he says. "It might not have gotten quite as out of control, but the difference would be at the margin rather than fundamental."

"One of the biggest challenges has been how to strike the right balance between forcefully defending what you think needs to be defended and at the same time trying to show compassion, concern for, and respect for women with implants. It's been very, very difficult to balance, and difficult to keep from getting defensive."

"UNFAIR, UNTRUE, AND INACCURATE"

McKennon says he made tough decisions at Dow Corning by following what he calls a "set of first principles." In so many enterprises, McKennon says, a company's direction is "fuzzy, figured out in the moment. Here there was very little room for experimentation." McKennon says he developed the command-and-control style he used at Dow Corning by dealing with the Agent Orange and Bendectin controversies. "My ordinary style is much less hands-on. I usually like to hire the best, give them the tools, and encourage them to take the initiative in an overall game plan." The implant crisis, he says, called for something different.

McKennon is now back home in Oregon. He has gone on to serve as chairman and CEO at PacifiCorp, an electric utility company in Portland. His cancer is again in remission. He plays tennis and travels around the world to fish for bonefish and steelhead. After his stint at PacifiCorp, he says, he will "retire from the field of battle for all time."

Hazleton still heads Dow Corning as chairman. "This company has a very bright future," he says. "We've been through a very painful exercise, and no question that it has caused some damage, but it has not fundamentally destroyed our vitality." What about the lessons of the breast implant controversy, specifically regarding junk science and mass tort litigation? "I don't believe Dow Corning has changed the world," Hazleton says. "It's my personal view that under the circumstances, the conventional wisdom had us as a big bad corporation led by evil people that couldn't be trusted to say anything that's not self-serving. That's grossly exaggerated, unfair, untrue, and inaccurate. I don't quarrel with the view that people should take what we say with a grain of salt, that self-interest is involved, but I would hope that when people understand the facts they will modify their view." Hazleton is still deeply rankled by the skepticism he encountered, particularly because the same skeptical questions were never aimed at plaintiffs' attorneys, the media, and many so-called medical experts—what Hazleton, when polite, refers to as "the other side."

NEARING THE ENDGAME

Hazleton describes his own management style as consensus building. "I'm a good listener," he says. "I can draw out other points of view and create a shared sense of commitment." He prides himself on bringing a sharpened sense of purpose to Dow Corning and in helping his organization preserve a measure of self-respect even when it was being pelted from all sides. Hazleton is also a team player. "I am the CEO and the buck stops here, but a team pulled this thing out of the fire." Other team members included Dow Corning president and now CEO Gary Anderson, vice president Barbara J. "Bari" Carmichael, corporate counselor Jim Jenkins, and CFO John Churchfield.

Dow Corning's position in industrial products has "not at all been negatively affected," Hazleton says. But why would a company convinced that its product was absolutely safe lay out so much money to settle claims? Why cut this deal? Hazleton has several answers: It costs Dow Corning about a million dollars to defend a case, win or lose. With tens of thousands of cases pending, the math made sense. Settling also ends litigation against Dow Corning's two corporate shareholders, the Dow Chemical Company and Corning Inc. And finally, Hazleton says, the controversy has been a long, painful experience for almost everyone involved, and the company wants to move on. "I believe we are nearing the endgame," he says. "It's not pleasant, expecting to pay $3.2 billion for claims that we believe are without merit, but we don't have any alternative. And we've made peace with that."

What about Dow Corning's highly-touted ethics program? Some say it failed spectacularly, either by not detecting potential product problems or failing to fully register the public perception crisis. Hazleton is emphatic here. "The ethics process is as robust as it's ever been." It's natural when a company enters a crisis to conclude that its ethics program is flawed, Hazleton says. "But I don't believe the evidence supports this." Dow Corning can look at the loyalty of its customers, its employees, and others that know the company well, McKennon says, and see that the company is sound. "I say the ethics process is robust," he repeats. "Maybe we ought to look a little more critically at the allegations."

Dick Hazleton intends to retire some day, he can't say when. A self-proclaimed introvert, he plans to read and get out on the golf course. At the moment, however, he is still very much a factor in Midland, Michigan. Thousands of women have settled their cases with the company in private, and the $3.2 billion settlement proposal is progressing. "Dow Corning continues to perform remarkably well," former CEO McKennon says. "That's no mean feat, with the eyes and ears of the world pressing down on you and everything you do."

Keith McKennon was a breath of fresh air at Dow Corning. He put the company on the road to recovery, steered it out of the implant business, and his decision to file for Chapter 11 was the right call. Hazleton navigated the treacherous waters of bankruptcy and litigation. He negotiated the final settlement deal, and is carrying his company beyond its crisis. Dow Corning must still regain its balance and finally exit Chapter 11, but it has more than survived the phalanx of attorneys who got rich on the company's troubles. The legal onslaught was unrelenting and, science now indicates, unjustified. Only superior dealmakers could end the nightmare. Dow Corning was fortunate enough to have them.

Stephen P. Yokich

United Auto Workers President Stephen P. Yokich and General Motors

"Nobody wins a strike. Absolutely nobody. Workers don't win, corporations don't win, neither does the community win. Everybody suffers. We don't take strikes lightly. I don't."

Stephen P. Yokich works at the apex of a vast, vibrating pyramid of deal-makers. Layers and layers of people beneath him are charged with brokering agreements for their locals, plants, and regions. Yokich negotiated his way up through these ranks. He became the United Auto Workers' top strategist by making deals exceptionally well, time after time, and by having the political know-how to capitalize on them.

Yokich is an interesting wrinkle in a book full of heavyweight business executives. In many ways, he's a businessman, too, managing a workforce of thousands that requires the same watering and feeding as any other business organization. Yokich must think like an executive on many scores, with a difference: His organization's only product is peace. Yokich must produce enough of it to stay in the good graces of those who elect him.

Yokich was in charge during the 1998 Flint strike, a local dispute that shut down GM's North American operations and threw 190,000 workers out of work for 54 days. It was the longest, costliest battle between the UAW and GM in 30 years. Both sides were caught off-guard when the stakes blew sky-high. It took top talent to bargain a way out.

BORN TO IT

Yokich is slim and jug-eared, with a receding hairline. Behind his outsized eyeglasses he looks mild-mannered. He is, in fact, a pussycat until the subject of GM comes up. Then Yokich's voice hardens. He makes sweeping, accusatory statements. Running beneath the rant is an irreverent sense of humor and streetsmarts that don't come from books or business school. Yokich is also a stand-out politician. He knows how to work over a subject, how to answer a question, how not to answer. He can purr or be pugnacious, and it is this last quality that wins him the loyalty of the rank and file.

He was born in Detroit in 1935, the same year the United Auto Workers union was formed. As the story goes, his mother pushed his stroller along a GM picket line when he was 22 months old. "My mother worked at GM for 43 years, my dad bounced around the union, and so did all my uncles, aunts, and grandparents," Yokich says. "When we had family dinners it was like a UAW meeting." After a stint in the Air Force, Yokich trained as tool and die maker and then began climbing the UAW ranks. He was elected president in 1995. "

Now I do my work in the same office that Walter, Leonard, Doug, and Owen did," Yokich says. That's Reuther, Woodcock, Fraser, and Bieber. Union leaders have come and gone, Yokich says. The office looks "pretty much the same as it always has." It's the world outside that's changed.

"THE DUMBEST THING I'VE SEEN A CORPORATION DO"

The 1998 strike began at an aging Flint, Michigan, stamping plant. GM was in the midst of investing hundreds of millions in the plant and tooling up to make parts for a very important and fussed-over new pickup truck, the GMT800. But as Flint local members celebrated their new job security, GM retreated. The automaker was curtailing its investment, GM said, because labor had reneged on promised work rule changes. Workers were incensed. Grievances skyrocketed. GM sensed an impending strike. Anxious to preserve its pickup truck production schedule, the automaker quietly pulled crucial dies out of the building over Memorial Day weekend and shipped them to another plant. Some 3,400 angry workers trooped out.

"I was at home, doing my honey-do list, when they pulled those dies," Yokich recalls. "Was I surprised? Absolutely. In all my years as an officer, this was the dumbest thing I've seen a corporation do." Yokich says GM's "stupid mistake" rallied UAW members across the nation. "We do focus groups on ourselves, and when we asked, do you know what the strike was about in Flint, people answered, 'Yeah—about pulling them dies out of the GM plant.' People remember that and not the real issue: a promise to invest in the plant."

GM doesn't commonly comment on labor disputes in progress, but this time it went on the offensive. Noncompetitive work practices are killing this company, Vice President Donald Hackworth stated, and the Flint plant was one of GM's least efficient operations because workers had forever resisted work rule changes. GM officials said they were particularly fed up with so-called "pegged rates" that permitted engine cradle welders to lay down their tools when they finished a pre-set number of parts, no matter how many hours remained in their shift.

Yokich called it differently. "It was part of a local agreement to bring in new presses to raise productivity in that plant, and then the company decided they weren't going to make that investment," he says. "The company also came in with unreasonable production standards. They said people were leaving early. Certainly they were, and they were working through their breaks and through lunch for all I know." Yokich declines to state a position on pegged rates. "Every plant, every situation is different. It depends on what you're building." He does, however, object to GM's opinion and the way the company chose to express it. "When they pulled out," he says, "it was unbearable."

SHRINKING

Yokich since 1989 had threatened or authorized dozens of strikes at GM factories. Now he authorized another one. "Sometimes a corporation will put you in a situation where even if it isn't worth doing you have to do it," he explains. "If you both put your names on a piece of paper you have to do it, to preserve what little trust there is. We had no choice."

The Flint strike was about local issues, Yokich says. Perhaps it started there, but it sure didn't stay there. The dispute quickly escalated to include national issues, specifically, jobs. In the 1980s and early 1990s an auto industry downdraft had dashed car sales and forced massive lay-offs at Chrysler and Ford. GM had furloughed workers, too, but in smaller numbers. Over time GM had become the least efficient automaker in North America. A surge of nonunion transplants like Toyota and Honda had further weakened GM's position. Analysts said GM needed to shed another 30,000 to 50,000 jobs to stay competitive, and GM had pressed the UAW for workforce reductions and improved efficiencies for years on the grounds that the company was losing its footing.

The UAW begged to differ. Yokich and other labor leaders pointed to GM's record profits, its growing overseas operations, and its overtime needs. GM needed more employees, the UAW said, not fewer. Still, membership spiraled dramatically downward. The reasons were many and included auto industry downsizing, changes on the factory floor, new technology, NAFTA, outsourcing, and the UAW's failure to organize transplants. By the mid-1990s, jobs were the UAW's top priority. When GM halted its Flint investment, then pulled the dies, the union local fought back with job security on its mind.

THE STAKES RISE

The union soon gave GM a second strike to think about. Six days after the stamping plant walkout, 5,800 workers at GM's Delphi components plant, also in Flint, hit the sidewalk. Delphi made parts for almost every GM vehicle and supplied assembly plants across the country. GM felt the squeeze quickly. By the end of June the double strike strategy had closed 24 of 29 assembly plants, idled 122,400 workers, and was costing GM an estimated $80 million a day. New car production was stalled, and the new pickup launch was in jeopardy.

Even so, GM Chairman Jack Smith and his board decided that GM could no longer afford labor peace at any price. GM stood its ground. The UAW was paying a price, too. Most of its membership was out of work. The conflict had escalated in an eyeblink to a nationwide shutdown with no end in sight.

At the end of June, top UAW officials left for their annual convention in Las Vegas amid a smattering of criticism. "I had no choice, it was our constitutional convention," Yokich defends. "It isn't like I wanted to go. If I could have been anointed for the next four years I would have taken it, but it doesn't work that way." Yokich rode his popularity to a second term. He said little in public about the strike, deferring instead to Vice President Richard Shoemaker, head of the union's GM department.

Two weeks of regularly scheduled vacation followed at all GM plants. Negotiations continued, with Yokich working the strike behind the scenes. "I don't get involved with direct negotiation when it's the locals," he says. "It's not a hand-holding situation. We're part of a team, we're all one team, and that's how we think about it."

Yokich did go to Flint during this time, though he denies that extraordinary circumstances motivated the trip. He minimizes his role, perhaps in deference to Shoemaker, perhaps as part of a strategy to keep GM guessing. "I didn't go to the local strike," he says. "I stayed on the outskirts of town." At the end of two weeks, GM's top negotiator, Gerald Knechtel, broke off face-to-face talks with Shoemaker. He snapped his briefcase shut and left town. Neither side had budged.

"I THINK IT'S UN-AMERICAN"

The UAW's resolve surprised GM. The automaker didn't expect labor to fight back over a local issue so hard or so long, or to elevate the dispute to a national level, or to shut down the company. Union leaders had also miscalculated. They were used to holding the upper hand with GM, but this time GM wasn't blinking, despite its suffering. GM hadn't planned for an extended strike and did not have the inventory or cash on hand to carry it much further. Now only 3 out of 29 assembly plants were running. Each week of the strike was costing the automaker $500 million and the production of 105,000 new cars and trucks. Impatient customers were opening their wallets to the competition. The pickup launch looked sunk. In mid-July, GM announced that second-quarter profits had plunged 81 percent, mostly due to the strikes.

Then GM made a second, startling announcement: It was hauling the UAW into court. The union had fabricated disputes over legal issues, GM said, so that it could strike over GM's investment decisions. This was expressly forbidden by the national contract. GM called for an arbitrator to rule on the legality of the strikes.

This was unprecedented. Disputes in other industries might go to arbitration, but the auto industry had always settled labor conflicts with its bare fists, in its own backyard. GM's legal tactics may have been born of frustration, or fear, or courage, or even a desire for revenge. Yokich found them despicable. "Trying to put pressure on the UAW like that is wrong," he states. "I think its un-American. Bringing in outside parties doesn't help."

Yokich was upset about the judge, too. U.S. district judge Paul V. Gadola Jr. was a Reagan appointee. He was also the son of a judge who almost 60 years before had declared the UAW's 1937 sit-down strikes illegal. "The courts are supposed to be neutral," Yokich says contemptuously. "They got that judge, they got him, and he steps in and plays hero."

SAVING FACE

Arbitration hearings sent labor and management running for the bargaining table. Neither side wanted to risk a damaging ruling. The UAW was broadly expected to lose, or perhaps that's just the way it played in the papers. "The media, God bless the media," Yokich says. "Who owns the media? The largest corporations in this country. Who advertises? GM, Ford, Chrysler. Who writes for the media? The shills." Labor can't win against corporate giants, Yokich says. "Who're the biggest giants in this country?" he asks. "The media. You don't get a fair break."

GM and the UAW needed to craft a deal that allowed both sides to save face and claim victory. All the heavy lifting was carried out by GM's top negotiators and the UAW's Shoemaker, but the overall strategy and the final deal were made at the very top of both organizations. This is Yokich's amazingly understated description of his role in those talks: "On the 44th day of the strike I went to Flint. I went back and forth, working with Shoemaker. I talked to Dick, we're good friends, we came on staff together in 1969, and the others with us were all part of Walter Reuther's youth group in 1959. I said, 'Dick, I want to talk, just you and I.' I thought I should go up there and see if there was anything I could do to help. So I went up, I spent some time with Dick."

Four days of marathon talks ensued. Soon 18 flatbed trucks carrying the disputed dies rolled up to the Flint plant and unloaded. Finally, after 47 days, the strike was declared dead. The final negotiations were personally monitored by Yokich and senior GM executives.

The deal was remarkably narrow. Most important, GM agreed to complete its $300 million investment at the stamping plant. The dies were already back in place. UAW Local 659 preserved its "pegged rate" policy for engine cradle operations but promised to improve productivity. A limited set of no-strike and no-sale clauses at three GM assembly plants were signed all around to create a period of stability until contract talks in 1999.

Of course both sides claimed victory. The two UAW locals said they had prevented a pivotal loss and forced GM to make good on its investment pledge. The union also pointed out that it had shut the world's largest industrial corporation down cold. GM said it had preserved its pickup launch and gained a period of stability. The automaker also had a new weapon: the courts.

These were very small gains at huge cost. GM had lost $2 billion in after-tax profits and 50-odd days of production. Some 190,000 UAW members were out about $1 billion in paychecks. The strike had few implications beyond Flint. Outstanding national issues raised during the dispute remained as raw as ever. It's hard to say that important principles were established, and in fact some unworthy practices were reinforced. As GM factories all over North America clattered back to life, each side continued to regard the other as the enemy.

Shortly after the 1998 strike, GM announced plans to spin off its gigantic Delphi parts-making unit in what might well be the largest IPO ever. The strategy shift was long expected, but the announcement came on the heels of the Flint strike. The UAW interpreted it as a slap in the face. Yokich promised that when 1999 contract talks rolled around he would come out swinging.

DANGER DOUSED

What mattered most in 1998, then, was that a dangerous, out-of-control strike was doused. It took the tremendous dealmaking skills of Yokich, Shoemaker, and top GM brass to put away this ugly, overgrown, overheated local dispute before it had mammoth and unintended national ramifications.

Yokich says he hates walkouts. "Nobody wins a strike," he states. "Absolutely nobody. Workers don't win, corporations don't win, neither does the community win. Everybody suffers. We don't take strikes lightly. I don't." That said, Yokich is willing to march his people out the door when necessary to protect their jobs, their pay, and their dignity. "People say autoworkers are overpaid and underworked," he says. "Every time I hear that I say, does anybody want to volunteer and go work on an assembly line? I'd be more than happy to let you have one day on an assembly line. We'd have to give you three days' training so you can assemble something, but I want you to spend one day there, and *then* you tell me about the underworked and overpaid auto worker."

OUT WITH A BANG

Yokich at this writing is still the UAW's chief strategist. He describes his management style with simplicity. "To be the president here, you have to be strong on your convictions," he says. "When you have to make a decision, you make it, even if people don't agree." Does Yokich encourage dissent? "No, I encourage discussion. I have strong opinions, but I don't think my opinion is always right." What does he consider himself particularly good at? "Fishing," Yokich snaps, and then laughs at himself. "I wish. Actually politics and negotiations. My biggest strength is at the bargaining table."

Yokich describes himself as a clean-desk type. He wades through a foot of mail a day. He doesn't wear a beeper and doesn't want one. The job is demanding enough, and sometimes he just wants to get away. For Yokich that means fishing or hitting the links. What does the president of the United Auto Workers union drive? "An SS Impala," he says. "The last Impala made, built in '96, a four-door, the last big iron [automobile] built in this country."

Yokich has plans for when his UAW term expires. "I'll be 66," he says. "I'm going to do everything I didn't get to do the first 66 years. I'll fish, I'll golf. I'd like to get a bigger boat. I'd like to relax—I hope I can do it."

With or without Yokich, the UAW will continue to contest GM's efficiency drive and local disagreements will continue to escalate into full-fledged national showdowns. The Flint strikes set a new standard for brinkmanship. They ended with a cease-fire and not a solution. GM is determined to return to respectability. New products are ready, and management is poised.

Yokich, meanwhile, has negotiated the final Big Three contract of his career. In the fall of 1999 he led the UAW through a final round of deal-making, masterminding the most lucrative set of agreements for UAW members in all of that organizations's history. He will be remembered by the outcome.

Alfred A. Checchi

Alfred A. Checchi
at Northwest Airlines

"Why did Mozart write music? Why did Van Gogh
paint? I can't look at something or someone
without seeing how to fix it."

When Al Checchi and his business partner Gary Wilson bought into Northwest Airlines in 1989, they cut a heck of a deal. The airline industry was flying high and Northwest was very profitable. Checchi and Wilson were experts at using other people's money for enormous daredevilish deals, and they nailed Northwest using just such a scheme.

Checchi had grand plans for Northwest even though he had zero airline experience. Some respected such raw confidence, others waited for Checchi to hang himself. These countering views were tested when Northwest flew straight into some of the worst years in aviation history. Only masterful dealmaking and solid operational talent steered Northwest out of a nosedive and restored it, against all odds, as a profitable competitor.

SEEKING A CHALLENGE

Checchi, the son of a Washington financial consultant, was raised in Wheaton, Maryland. He earned a Harvard MBA, then sharpened his own financial skills from 1975 to 1982 at Marriott Corporation. After four years of brokering deals for the Bass brothers and a brief stint helping Michael Eisner restructure at Disney, Checchi was ready for a big, brainbusting challenge. It had to be big game, offering outsized rewards, personal and professional. This was the Al Checchi who arrived at Northwest Airlines.

Checchi is personable and articulate. He just barely contains a restless, almost impatient intelligence that is both his great asset and a sometimes liability. Dark-haired and athletic-looking, he is handsome enough to play a businessman on television. Checchi has a basketful of skills, some of them extraordinary. He likes to talk about the big picture. He craves big, complex, adrenaline-popping challenges, which means he doesn't fit well into the day-to-day world of business. "I am not a CEO," he states. "I don't preside over things. I leave when the job is done."

OPPORTUNITY SPOTTED

Airline industry deregulation in the late 1970s created a hot new marketplace. Even so, most big trunk carriers tried to carry on with their pricey tickets and bloated cost structures. Northwest was among the foot-draggers. Longtime chief Donald Nyrop ran a conservative organization and controlled every decision, right down to choosing fabric for airline seats. Labor relations were frigid. Northwest employees toiled in a windowless building and Nyrop didn't much care how they felt about it. Nyrop's successor, Joseph Lapensky, defrosted the atmosphere but hardly led a revolution.

That's not to imply that Northwest wasn't successful. By the time Stephen G. Rothmeier took over, the airline could brag about 36 consecutive profitable years and enviably low costs. Rothmeier wanted more for his company, and in 1986 he engineered an ineptly executed merger with Republic Airlines that he hoped would make Northwest a major player. The merger blew up in Northwest's face. Machinists staged a slowdown, travelers were enraged by delays, and suitcases bound for Memphis sometimes deplaned in Minneapolis. Passengers nicknamed the company "Northworst," a sobriquet it has never entirely shaken. In 1987, at the end of a long hot summer, a Northwest flight crew in Detroit failed to properly set the wing slats on an MD-80. It crashed on takeoff, killing 156 people.

Rothmeier pulled his organization back to its feet. He opened new company headquarters in Eagan, Minnesota, and belatedly began integrating Republic. Labor relations remained messy, but the airline rebounded with a very strong capital structure and a lagging stock price. Northwest board member Gary L. Wilson spotted a sweet takeover target. Wilson, a Checchi pal, was a behind-the-scenes operator with an extraordinary command of detail. He didn't know the airline industry well but he had no trouble appreciating Northwest's unleveraged balance sheet. Checchi and Wilson conferred, and in 1988 they began scooping up NWA stock.

CLOSING THE DEAL

Checchi and Wilson went way back. Wilson had hired Checchi at Marriott, where the two devised a novel financial strategy that tripled the hotel chain's earnings—for a while. Later the real estate market collapsed and quintupled Marriott's debt, but by that time Checchi was helping billionaire investor Sid Bass engineer a stake in Disney. After Checchi made the introduction, Eisner made Wilson his CFO. Wilson went on to structure funding for the $2.6 billion Euro Disney project, then left before the troubled, debt-laden park could open. Checchi by this time had also moved on. When Northwest appeared on the Checchi-Wilson radar screen, they were both ready and available

There were thorny problems at Northwest, but instead of scaring Checchi off, they sucked him in. "It was a company in trouble, he says. "It had a broken culture. It lacked a strategy. The airline had very good properties and the franchise was unreplicable, but it had one of the worst managements I've ever seen, and it had some of the worst labor relations in the industry." Other draws: "There was organized labor, I hadn't run into that before. And government relations. I wanted to deal with that, too."

Northwest had more than one suitor, and the ensuing bidding war more than tripled Northwest's stock price, from $40 to $121 a share. Wanna-be owners included billionaire ex-oilman Marvin Davis, Pan Am, and New York leveraged buyout firms Kohlberg Kravis Roberts and Forstmann Little & Co. Northwest's machinists' union, miffed over failed contract talks, also made an offer. When the shouting was over, Checchi and Wilson owned an airline. The giant $3.65 billion LBO was financed by $700 million in equity from sources including Australian brewing executive John D. Elliot and San Francisco money manager Richard C. Blum. KLM-Royal Dutch Airlines came forward with $400 million for a 20 percent stake and made plans to pool resources with Northwest in a transatlantic alliance. A consortium of lenders assembled by Banker's Trust Company supplied the debt portion of the deal, some $2.9 billion, heavy leverage that would come back to haunt its owners. In many ways, however, the deal was remarkable. Checchi and Wilson, relative unknowns in the world of leveraged buyouts, suddenly owned 44 percent of an airline on the basis of a puny $40 million personal investment, and they'd done it without a single junk bond. Before the closing, Checchi asked for labor's endorsement. "We have work to do, but we can't do it in a hostile environment," he told them. All three unions signed on.

LABOR FIRST

The Northwest LBO was a gutsy move, even for Checchi. His highly leveraged formula was a huge gamble—some thought a death wish—in such a capital-thirsty, labor-intensive, competitive industry. Checchi and

Wilson, both airline novices, had planned to piggyback onto Rothmeier's know-how but Rothmeier quit immediately and several top managers followed him out the door. Now Checchi and his team had to figure out how to run an airline.

Checchi made labor relations his first priority. "When we got there the place was like a gulag," he says. "These were the most angry employees you've ever seen in your life." Checchi traveled the company for three months, talking, talking, talking, something he is good at. Sometimes he spoke to a sea of faces, sometimes it was a clutch of people around a table. "Every time I got on a plane I would end up with all these envelopes from employees, loaded with suggestions," he says. "My pockets were bulging. These people craved leadership." To boost morale, Checchi abolished a slate of rules that, for example, prohibited relatives of Northwest employees from working there, too. "I said this is the stupidest thing I've ever seen in my whole life," he recalls. "You had to say to yourself, what kind of lunkheads would produce these rules?" Checchi replaced 200 of Northwest's top 300 managers and retrained the rest, angling for a culture change. By treating labor well, Checchi wagered, labor would reciprocate. It was a farsighted bet.

NOSEDIVE

Checchi and Wilson called in former Marriott colleague John H. Dasburg to handle operations. Freed up, the two men tackled Northwest's finances. By early 1991, through a series of savvy financial moves, Northwest had repaid more than half of its massive buyout debt. It was still waist-deep in debt, however, and extremely vulnerable to bad luck, poor planning, or an industry downturn.

Northwest got all three in the early 1990s. The Persian Gulf war sent the entire U.S. airline industry into a tailspin. Jet fuel prices soared, price wars exploded, and fears of terrorism kept travelers home. Northwest was damaged further when a company pilot was arrested for drinking just hours before a flight. In a separate incident, a Northwest 727 crashed into one of the airline's DC-9s, killing eight people. By midyear, Northwest's cash flow barely covered interest payments and aircraft rentals.

Checchi's plan when he purchased Northwest had been to snap up assets as other carriers failed and eventually to play in the big leagues with American, United, and Delta. Now he was strapped for cash. Checchi went shopping anyway. He bought some routes and gates. He talked deals with Eastern, Trump Shuttle, America West, Midway, and Continental. Checchi also snagged an improbable $740 million loan from Northwest's home state of Minnesota and squeezed Airbus Industries and General Electric for more huge low-interest loans.

But imaginative financing could carry Northwest only so far. It was still billions of buyout dollars in debt. Bankruptcy rumors swirled. KLM Airlines chairman Pieter Bouw wrote off his company's entire $400 million investment in disgust, and a mutual resentment began to fester. KLM and Northwest had won unique U.S. dispensation to act as one airline, free of antitrust scrutiny, but the alliance became a poisonous power struggle.

Northwest in 1993 was by no means the only airline in trouble. Three other steeply leveraged airlines—Midway, Eastern, and Pan Am—were already out of business. Others were operating in bankruptcy. Even United, American, and Delta had announced layoffs. That said, Northwest's reversal of fortune was still stark. Once known for its strong capital structure and sterling balance sheet, Northwest had become a company built on risk and begging for funds. It had lost nearly $1.7 billion, used up most of a $600 million revolving credit line, canceled billions in aircraft deliveries, and laid off thousands. In the spring of 1993, Northwest would miss a billion-dollar debt payment. KLM refused to help.

Checchi's reputation looked finished. "I was in New York City walking down Park Avenue with Wilson," he says. "We knew that if we didn't pull off a miracle, all the work we'd done would be overwhelmed by events." Suddenly, Checchi says, he had a moment of clarity. "I said this is the finest work I've ever done in my life. I'm not going down. I actually thought of that scene in *Rocky,* where the fighter has taken a tremendous beating in the ring but decides he's not going to get knocked down again. I just decided at that moment that there were no circumstances beyond my control—that I would make it happen."

CLOSING THE DEAL, PART TWO

Operating on what Checchi calls "sheer will," he and Wilson for the umpteenth time asked labor for concessions. Labor was willing but only after lenders made concessions, too. Lenders were willing to stretch out their terms, but only after labor agreed to make serious sacrifices. With negotiations deadlocked and working against the clock, Checchi and Wilson lashed together an intricate restructuring package larded with conditions. Every single party—unions, lenders, suppliers—had to sign on the dotted line or the deal would die. On July 6, 1993, Northwest's attorneys went to bed expecting to be in bankruptcy court at 8 A.M. the next morning. Late that night, at the very last possible moment, the pilots okayed a concession package worth $838 million in exchange for a 30–odd percent stake in the airline. Lenders agreed to defer principal repayments. Improbably, the deal fell into place.

"The unions had to come to it," Checchi summarizes. "It was a struggle, and I got vilified." Teamster leader Ron Carey flew into town, Checchi says, strode out onto the tarmac, and announced to the assembled rank and file that he had arrived to save Northwest from a "rapacious capitalist." At dinner, Checchi says, Carey turned to him. "He said, 'Al, I've never met an owner or manager as well liked by his employees.' I said, 'Ron, then why did you say those things?' 'Every deal needs an escapegoat,' [sic] he said to me. 'In this deal, Al, you are the escapegoat.' "

The restructuring reduced costs by more than $1.2 billion over three years and established a new repayment schedule for another $1.5 billion in outstanding debt. Everyone associated with Northwest relaxed a little, but Checchi says he felt no great pleasure when the dealmaking was done. "This was a titanic effort," he says. "I was assaulted on many sides. The press was very, very hostile, and I had to take a public beating while I worked behind the scenes. Frankly I felt only relief, not exhilaration."

RIGHTING THE AIRCRAFT

As Northwest pulled out of its fiscal emergency, the aviation industry outlook began to brighten. Fuel prices fell, business travel picked up, fare wars died back, and the Gulf War retreated. Over the next year profits surged back. Cash began to flow again, and net margins became the best among the larger airlines. Northwest was back. It still owed big bucks, but its debt level was no longer life-threatening. Dasburg, a financial (and as it turned out, an operations) expert, had carefully selected markets where Northwest would face less competition and could charge premium fares. His strategy was working. Checchi and Wilson, supported by Dasburg's know-how and a strong economy, had turned a leveraged buyout disaster into a most amazing recovery story.

AWE-INSPIRING, AND IMPERFECT

Northwest's turnaround was inspiring. And imperfect. Relations with KLM remained rocky. Employee wages were slated to snap back in 1996. Debt payments to the tune of $2 billion were creeping up. During its restructuring Northwest had postponed plans to modernize its fleet or take delivery on new planes, which meant that it would shortly be piloting an extremely creaky fleet. None of these chickens was inconsequential, and each came home to roost.

In the end, KLM's alliance with Northwest did come very close to detonating. Just as the two companies finally began to very profitably exploit their transatlantic relationship, hostilities exploded into accusations and lawsuits. The bitter power struggle was finally resolved in 1997 when KLM Chairman Pieter Bouw resigned and KLM agreed to sell its 20 percent stake back to Northwest. Each side dropped its lawsuit and signed what promised to be a profitable new 10-year pact of cooperation.

Labor relations were another matter. Northwest was posting record profits in 1996 and paying down its remaining debt when wages for 45,000 employees snapped back. Contract talks went poorly. Two years later, Northwest's pilots were still holding out for an "industry-leading" contract. Labor concessions had saved Northwest when it mattered most, the unions argued, and they wanted their due. The strike that followed cost Northwest $630 million and bloodied its reputation.

There are other issues at Northwest. On-time performance has been spotty. The Asian recession hammered Northwest's Pacific routes. The company continues to operate the oldest fleet in the commercial airline industry, planes that will gradually become more costly to operate. Low-cost airlines are a source of continuing pressure. Finally, a serious Department of Transportation examination of predatory airline pricing practices is underway. Northwest is a primary target.

"WHY DID MOZART WRITE MUSIC?"

Wilson and Dasburg still run Northwest, as chairman and chief executive, respectively. Checchi left in 1997, after he and Wilson split about a billion dollars on their combined original $40 million investment. "I put a team together and it became the best airline in the world," Checchi says. "Then I moved on." His job was finished, Checchi says. There was no reason to stick around when he could be doing the next thing.

Checchi and Wilson once lived across the street from each other in Beverly Hills. They still live only a mile or so apart. Wilson is the detail man, Checchi is the dreamer. "I tend to come up with grand ideas," Checchi says. "I tend to be an inspirer. I bring good people together and I'm a very effective recruiter." Checchi also calls himself a motivator. "I've often gotten institutions and people to do what they've never done before. Most people are afraid of change. They think that if they keep doing things the same way they won't do anything wrong. My view is that if you keep doing things as you've always done them, you are by definition doing something wrong. We live in a changing environment. You have to adapt."

At this writing Checchi is weighing his next move. In 1998 he ran as a probusiness Democrat for governor in the state of California. Checchi pumped about $40 million of his own money into the campaign, but with no political resume in a state bristling with Democratic power he did not survive the primary. "A lot of what elected politics is about has nothing to do with skills or positions on issues or vision," Checchi says disappointedly. Running for office is about opinion surfing, he adds distastefully. "You lie in the water, you pick up a little ripple from the public, and you ride it home. I'm not into that."

It's a surprise when he says he doesn't want to do a Marriott, or a Bass Brothers, or a Disney, or a Northwest again. "I don't think I got pleasure out of those," he explains. Why do them, then? "For the complexity, for the challenge. Why did Mozart write music? Why did Van Gogh paint? I can't look at something or someone without seeing how to fix it. It's almost a compulsion." Still, Checchi says, he doesn't always take pleasure in it. "An artist can paint, a writer can write, but the things I undertake require you to blast through the inertia of individual and large institutions," he explains. "The unfortunate byproduct is a lot of conflict. It's like being a warrior."

Checchi has no grand life plan. He makes it up as he goes. At this writing he is learning to play classical piano. He devours biographies, he golfs, runs, and lifts weights. And he thinks a lot about what to do next. His specialty is marrying complex financing with carefully selected talent. Northwest has encountered some rough air lately, but Checchi checked out long ago. He is no manager. He's not even an executive. He's a dealmaker, and we haven't heard the last from him.

Sizzle Sellers
Winning the Heart of the Market

Sizzle Sellers:

⇨ Add meaning to products far beyond any practical utility
⇨ Make buyers feel cool
⇨ Create demand
⇨ Possess incredible antennae
⇨ Attend to the numbers, but trust intuition

The best sales approaches convince people that no matter what they may already own, there still is something far better out there to buy. Sizzle selling is a variation on this approach: It makes products meaningful far beyond any practical utility. Sizzle selling tells people that buying a certain product will make them part of a discriminating group. The shopper goes to the store and gets the widget she wants, but she also gets much more. She gets to belong. It's like buying a kind of cool.

Sizzle sellers convince customers and the marketplace that their product deserves respect far beyond its precise ability to function. Pushed to its extreme, this kind of thinking quickly grows ridiculous—who would buy a $70,000 car for the nameplate, or just to join an elite group of drivers? Yet thousands of BMW owners have done exactly that. BMWs are great cars, but they don't sell just because they handle well. Bavarian Motor Works sells snobbiness. It sells a cultivated superiority. The sizzle is what sells BMW's automotive steak.

Sizzle sellers know how to build a good product into something that, completely aside from its outright usefulness, feels fantastic to buy, and then to own. (This is commonly considered a part of brand management, but that term is too broad and bland to apply here.) Sizzle sellers understand that what people buy represents a fantasy image of who they think they are or want to be. Once sizzle sellers have figured out how to appeal to this desire for social status, escape, pride, or a cutting edge of some sort, they cut through the marketing mumbo jumbo with the right emotional and symbolic stuff.

Sizzle sellers have an incredibly accurate set of antennae. They are able to read, articulate, and translate into precise marketing terms what their customers want and need, and to do so not just once, but on an ongoing basis. Sizzle sellers attend to market research and study the numbers, but they also very much trust in intuition. They are pursuing something subtle—often something that cannot be named or articulated. Call it a vibration. When they tune in properly, watch out. The buyers will flock, followed closely by competitors eager for a piece of the action.

Sizzle sellers reap the rewards created by their legions of enthusiastic customers. The product moves itself. In stand-out cases a hot product sells out before it even hits the store, and wanna-be owners end up on a waiting list. Get this: They don't mind. Red-hot products like these produce enormous profits because price is not a purchasing issue. A premium price may even add cachet and improve sales volume. This kind of reverse curve drives economists bonkers.

Sizzle selling only works when the product or service is first-rate to begin with. A gizmo sold on sizzle will go nowhere unless it's near-perfect, no matter how beautifully it's peddled. Quality must come first—*then* a company can afford to shout about its product. That same company must be ready to stand behind its product or service, anytime, anywhere, and spend whatever it takes to make a correction or replacement if something goes awry.

Few companies today are doing this extremely well. Most companies are so volume-hungry that they settle for mediocrity. The cost guy says watch the bottom line; the production guy says make it easy to manufacture. The marketers say keep the retailers happy with a good price, and bottom-liners hate low volume and high margins. There is tremendous pressure in every industry just to be plain good enough, never mind special.

Some industries play the sizzle selling angle, however. Think fine perfume, upscale jewelry, and luxury hotels. The entire fashion industry is built on sizzle. Harley-Davidson and Intel have both gone the sizzle selling route, with spectacular results. One sells quality heavyweight motorcycles; the other sells state-of-the-art microprocessors. Although they come from vastly different corporate cultures, Vaughn L. Beals and Richard F. Teerlink, both formerly of Harley-Davidson, and Andy Grove and Dennis Carter, at Intel, would understand each other. Stranded together on a desert island, they would have plenty to talk about. Fortunately for the rest of us, they're not. Their motorcycles and microprocessors are everywhere. And because those products are of such good quality, and because they're sold on sizzle, the rest of us are doing the talking.

Vaughn L. Beals

Richard F. Teerlinck

Vaughn L. Beals and Richard F. Teerlink at Harley-Davidson

"I believe in what Harley-Davidson is: an emotional attachment. People think I'm weird talking about family, love, and emotion but that's what it is."
— FORMER CEO RICHARD F. TEERLINK

"I've never seen anyone tattoo 'Chevrolet' on their body."
— FORMER CEO VAUGHN L. BEALS

It's hard to describe the sensation of standing in a sea of Harley-Davidson motorcycles revving their engines. It's the sound of raw power, a deep rapturous roar that thrums through every bit of your being until you tingle. It makes you want to ride. And own. It explains why, when Harley riders look at blow-dried, clock-punching, minivan-driving America, they see a land of drones stuck in the system.

Harley buyers get more than transportation. They get an ownership experience. A typical Harley is customized to the gills with lots of sparkly pipes and custom paint. Depreciation? Harley's don't depreciate, they just gain value. Some riders wear black leather and belly-length beards. Others pack American Express cards and cell phones. Buttoned-down or blue collar, Harley owners share a passion for their motorcycles and a desire for freedom, for camaraderie, for an escape from everything serious, boring, middle-aged, and middle class.

Former Harley-Davidson CEO Richard F. Teerlink owns five Harleys. Teerlink, who ran the company from 1989 to 1997, sports enormous brown-rimmed eyeglasses. He steeples his ham-sized hands when he listens and paces with them in his pockets. Long brown hair covers the tops of his ears. Teerlink is an old-shoe type of executive, friendly and unpretentious. He hates regimentation, but at Harley-Davidson he was hands-on and deeply disciplined. Teerlink still rides about four or five thousand miles a year. The last time his motorcycle broke down was

110 miles outside of Alberta. A dealer hauled him in, made repairs, and sent him back into the wind.

Teerlink was hired by Vaughn L. Beals Jr., CEO and chairman from 1981 to 1989, and chairman seven years beyond that. Beals owns a 1986 Liberty Edition Electra Glide. A patrician-looking man with bushy eyebrows and a Roman nose, Beals speaks plainly and persuasively. There isn't a phony bone in his body. Beals has a take-charge personality but is no dictator and can laugh at his mistakes. He still can recall every tiny facet of Harley-Davidson's business—odd parts prices, even loops of decades-old conversation. Mention the name and manufacturing date of any Harley model and Beals could probably tell you the carbon deposit on the cylinder walls at 30,000 miles. Beals has a pair of engineering degrees from M.I.T. His most memorable riding experience was crashing his bike on the Autobahn while finishing up a European vacation. "The hospital released me after three days," he says. "The Harley was totaled."

Harleys are so hot these days that there is a two-year waiting list to buy a new one. They're also pricey—about half-again what other motorcycles cost. Harley riders don't much care. Nine out of ten say that when they finish roaring around on their current bike they'll go out and buy another. Employees tattoo the company name right on. Annual sales at Harley-Davidson during the last decade shot up from $350 million to $1.6 billion, and stock values soared from $5 to $50.

It's astonishing to remember that in the early 1980s many people wrote the company off. Japanese manufacturers were siphoning off the last of its American market. Manufacturing was such a mess that half of all Harleys coming off the assembly line were missing parts. The 1982 recession nearly cooked what was left of Harley's goose. Beals and Teerlink snatched Harley-Davidson back from the grave and built it into a phenomenal performer. First they solved crippling manufacturing and management problems; then they reinvented Harley-Davidson's marketing. If there is a company on this planet doing a better job of selling the sizzle, we aren't aware of it.

EARLY RUMBLINGS

The motorcycle maker was founded in 1903 when William Harley and Arthur Davidson, soon to be joined by Walter and William Davidson, set up shop in a shed in the Davidson family's Milwaukee backyard. The first year the company hand-built three motorcycles. In 1907 it cranked out 150. In 1909 the brothers built in a 45-degree V-Twin engine, still the company standard, which could power a rider down a dirt road at a shocking 60 miles an hour.

Motorcycles were fast, noisy, frightening. They caught on. By 1911, 150 motorcycle companies were competing for road time. Police departments ordered Harleys. The military used them in border skirmishes with Pancho Villa, and the United States ordered them into service during World War I. In 1953 Harley-Davidson produced just over 14,000 motorcycles, and Indian, its only surviving U.S. competitor, closed its factories. Harley-Davidson became the entire American motorcycle industry, a card the company would learn to play deftly. Motorcycle riding exploded in the 1960s. The big bikes acquired glamour and spawned a black leather jacket culture that attracted bikers, wanna-bes, and the just plain fashion-conscious who borrowed the look. Motorcycling acquired a sexy, safely dangerous image. By the mid-1960s the heavy Harley owned a niche that nobody else could touch.

GROWING INTO TROUBLE

Harley-Davidson ended family ownership in 1965 with a public stock offering. Four years later, at the height of the conglomeration era, the company was acquired by the American Machine and Foundry Company (AMF), a big recreational goods concern. AMF had financial resources and chairman Rodney Gott loved Harleys. Labor relations decayed but production exploded. AMF pumped $40 million into Harley-Davidson, an investment Beals characterizes as "more than generous." Harley expanded, modernized its manufacturing, streamlined old models, and introduced new ones, including the Super Glide and the Low Rider. These heavy Harleys, or "hogs," were designed by William G. Davidson, known as Willie G., the designer grandson of a company founder. Buyers reached for their wallets.

SEIZING

But beneath its gleaming surface, Harley-Davidson was slipping. A swarm of smaller, sporty, less costly Japanese imports was attracting

Americans, particularly first-time buyers. By the early 1970s Harley-Davidson's share of the entire motorcycle market was down to 3.6 percent from a high of 50 percent in the 1950s. The motorcycle maker experimented with smaller bikes, then washed its hands of the whole effort to concentrate on motorcycles 1,000cc and larger. Lucky for Harley, demand swung sharply toward the heavyweights. The company capitalized on the trend but not by pitching performance details. While foreign manufacturers had year by year upgraded their products, Harley-Davidson had fallen farther behind on mechanics and design. Engine vibration made long trips uncomfortable. You could tell where a Harley had been parked, the joke went, by the puddle it left in the parking lot. When Japanese manufacturers came after the lucrative heavyweight market with their own big, reliable, more comfortable bikes, Harley-Davidson's dominance began to slide.

Competition aside, Harley-Davidson was already seizing. Quality problems were killing sales. Harley was shipping motorcycles that leaked oil, broke down, betrayed their owners. Dealers fumed because they had to thoroughly service new bikes before they would even run. Loyal customers were disgusted. Beals, an AMF vice president back then, recalls a personal moment of reckoning. "The guy that ran our service shop knocked on my door," he says. "This guy received all the returned parts. He took me down and showed me what was coming back. We were making junk."

Then, in a stunning display of either vanity or ignorance, AMF plastered its name on Harley-Davidson motorcycles. Perhaps Harley's parent company misunderstood the brand concept, or simply was willing to toy with an important asset. Maybe senior management was spending too much time hunched over balance sheets, where intangible assets like brand names don't appear attached to dollar signs. Consumers treated the AMF logo as a warning label.

Thinking back, Beals is surprisingly exculpatory about AMF's role. "I can criticize AMF for expanding production as they did, but I might have done the same thing," he concedes. "They bought Harley-Davidson and the market started to take off like a rocket. All these years, Harley-Davidson had been this static, family-owned company, and all the major departments were run by somebody in that family." Ratcheting up production probably made sense, Beals concludes. He sighs. "But that's where the place blew up."

With its rank and reputation hurting, Harley asked AMF for more help. Beals appealed to AMF for $80 million to help build a new kind of power train that he believed could make a difference. AMF balked. "They were starving us," Beals says. "We were going to end up with a dead Harley-Davidson."

BUYOUT

So in 1981, 13 Harley-Davidson managers banded together and bought the company. Beals led the $65 million leveraged buyout. The new owners celebrated on their bikes, with a ride to company hometown Milwaukee. They were exuberant. "We were sure we were going in the right direction," Beals says. But Harley-Davidson was a weak player in a fiercely competitive industry, heavily in debt and hemorrhaging cash. No parent company with deep pockets would throw money at it anymore, and there was no capital. Many of the motorcycles rolling off the assembly line were incomplete. Honda had blown by Harley in the superheavyweight market. By year's end the new Harley-Davidson had lost $25 million, and its mystique was scraping bottom.

The 1982 recession delivered a near-deathblow. Across the Midwest, Milwaukee included, the Rust Bowl was born. Motorcycle sales died as first-time buyers faded away. High unemployment levels, interest rates, and insurance costs kept everyone else at home. Japanese manufacturers Honda, Yamaha, Suzuki, and Kawasaki were stricken, but Harley-Davidson was devastated. CEO Beals switched his company into survival mode, but nevertheless that year the motorcycle maker lost $32 million. "If I had known what the recession would do to us, and what would happen to our market share, I wouldn't have touched the Harley-Davidson buyout with a ten-foot pole," he says. To stay out of bankruptcy, the motorcycle maker needed to get smart and tough, and perhaps get lucky.

Beals patched together a rescue plan. His strategy included stringent cost cuts and employee sacrifices. Beals also had to figure out quickly how to capitalize on Harley-Davidson's two remaining assets. The first was the company's brand name, worth more than the motorcycle maker ten times over. To millions, Harley-Davidson meant escape, adventure, freedom, and life on the road with the wind in your hair. The branding concept was just dawning on Harley executives in 1983. In coming years the Harley name would grow into the company's most powerful tool.

The second asset was the fierce loyalty of its customers. Thousands of diehards had built a lifestyle around Harley ownership and were waiting out the company's hard times, ready to resume a relationship when Harley-Davidson righted itself. Beals, Teerlink, and other Harley executives were slow to understand this attachment, or how to exploit it. Teerlink remembers his top engineer coming in one day and admonishing him. "He said, 'You folks are nuts!' " Teerlink remembers. "He said, 'You have a group of people who want to love you and you're not letting them!' "

WINNING TARIFF PROTECTION

Beals focused in public on an outside adversary: the Japanese. Honda and Yamaha were flooding the U.S. market with motorcycles, and Harley-Davidson saw killer price cuts coming. Its plants were already operating at only 50 percent of capacity, and layoffs were at 40 percent. Beals begged Washington for protection. We're fragile, Beals warned. We're surviving, but that's all. Harley joined a chorus of motor vehicle manufacturers complaining about so-called offshore predators. In 1983, President Ronald Reagan slapped a stunning tariff increase as high as 49 percent on imported heavyweight motorcycles. "Without that tariff, the industry of Harley-Davidson would have been out of business," Teerlink says. *The New York Times* was less hopeful. "It's not hard to imagine that eventually Harley will, even with the protection, fall or be merged into oblivion," an editorial predicted. Winning the tariff was a neat trick—and a piece of the much-needed luck Harley needed. It won the company sympathy. And time. It set the stage for a comeback.

CONFRONTING THE DEMONS AT HOME

Now Beals was charged with the real work of saving Harley-Davidson. Time was short. "The company needed a foundation to make it grow," Teerlink says. More bluntly, Harley-Davidson needed a revolution. Management's first task was to solve a tangle of connected problems—inefficient production methods, poor quality, and out-of-date designs.

Beals had criticized the Japanese, but one of the first things he did was copy some of their manufacturing practices. Harley-Davidson adopted just-in-time (JIT) inventory control, where parts move through a plant on the basis of actual orders rather than on the basis of projected need. This change cut the company's work-in-process inventory by a staggering two-thirds, freeing up cash. Harley adopted statistical process control (called statistical operator control at Harley), which helps employees catch production errors early. SOC cut the percentage of new motorcycles with defects from as high as 50 percent to about 2 percent. Beals also enrolled his whole workforce in a program that rewarded problem-solving suggestions with wage incentives and cash bonuses.

Harley-Davidson also confronted its management deficiencies. Loudly, publicly, and probably too often, the motorcycle maker had blamed cost and quality problems on overseas competitors. Beals finally conceded that Harley-Davidson's demons were at home. He reshaped weak divisions and hired better managers. One of the least effective departments at the time was engineering. "We had good, enthusiastic people with little technical training," he remembers. Beals is superb at spotting leadership. Just as he had identified Teerlink and brought him in as CFO, now Beals placed another future CEO, Jeffrey Bleustein, in charge of engineering.

"THE BRIGHTEST THING WE EVER DID"

These improvements were on target, but they would have meant little without the confluence that came next. Just as Harley-Davidson straightened out its manufacturing and management deficits, the economy began to grow again. Aging baby boomers led the way back into the stores. Locked into jobs, raising families, and approaching middle age, boomers as a group were hungry for adventure and excitement. They wanted an escape from the serious responsibilities of everyday life. They were restless. They had money. Harley-Davidson was ready for them.

With a grip on its identity like never before, Harley-Davidson began to sell the sizzle along with the steak. Harleys are big, beautiful machines, the company promised, but they are also about dreams, youthfulness, freedom, recreation, and adventure. Harleys provide transportation, the company said, but they also offer a lifestyle. Buyers were invited to reclaim their individuality and connect with a whole brotherhood of riders escaping the rat race.

Next came what Beals calls "the brightest thing we ever did." In the early 1980s, with "the place falling apart," 6 of the 13 owners, Beals included, attended a retreat. "We had a consultant come in who said, 'How many Harley riders are out there? You know where they are— what're you doing with that?' " Beals recognized the flicker of a powerful idea. In 1983 his company began to sponsor Harley Owners Group (H.O.G.), a club to organize events and get people on bikes. Senior executives went to H.O.G. rallies and mixed it up. Beals went, too, and this is where he began to understand the power of the Harley-Davidson brand. "People were wearing T-shirts that said, 'I'd rather push my Harley than ride a rice-burner,' " he says. "And they had Harley tattoos. I've never seen anyone tattoo 'Chevrolet' on their body. I'd meet people whose entire being was wrapped up in their motorcycle, earning $30,000 a year and driving a junk car—but they had their Harley."

THE TURNAROUND BEGINS

Beals amplified the idea. Harley began to sell the notion that its riders were a kind of worldwide family. It began promising buyers a great bike— and a lifelong relationship. The Harley Owners Group worked wonderfully. Riders connected with each other, built the Harley culture, and got a good feeling about "their" company. H.O.G. rallies were also fine spots for conducting market research. Was there something riders particularly liked? The company wanted to know. Something not right? Suggestions welcome. "If you have top management hanging out in a parking lot for the weekend, you find out your quality problems," Beals says.

Harley-Davidson in 1983 made a very small profit. Company owners who a few years before would have been thrilled just to recoup their original investments thought they had died and gone to heaven. There was another small profit in 1984. Harley's market share began to climb, slowly. Beals took Harley-Davidson public again, and displaying public relations and political smarts, called off tariff protection in 1987 before it could expire on its own. It was a shrewd move that called attention to his company's healthy bottom line.

BUILDING A BRAND

Teerlink, already president, became Harley's chief executive officer in 1989. Sales and earnings increased steadily through the 1990s. Analysts praised the company as a Rust Belt success story and part of America's manufacturing renaissance. Teerlink rightly understood his company as consumer-driven. One would think that with his University of Chicago MBA and numbers-crunching background Teerlink would be a spreadsheet man, but Teerlink talks people first, then numbers. Staying close to the customer, a phrase Teerlink favors, practically became a religion at Harley during his tenure. "We call them family," Teerlink says. "I believe in what Harley-Davidson is: an emotional attachment. People think I'm weird talking about family, love, and emotion but that's what it is."

Harley's "family" rewards the company with fanatical loyalty. Hundreds of thousands of Harley riders belong to H.O.G. chapters around the globe. To keep the sizzle strong, H.O.G. continues to sponsor huge national rallies and tours and is gearing up for a blow-out 100th birthday party in 2003. If it's anything like Harley-Davidson's 90th birthday party, which attracted a parade of motorcycles eight miles long, Milwaukee might as well turn over the keys to the city right now.

Teerlink is particularly proud of transitioning Harley-Davidson from a relatively traditional command and control organization to a more collegial management model. "Harley-Davidson has no senior vice presidents," he states. "There's little top-down decision-making." But Teerlink made another powerful mark on Harley-Davidson by cultivating its brand. Under Teerlink, Harley-Davidson devoted itself to merchandising its image. It built up its own huge parts and accessories lines. Licensing became a cash machine. Teerlink concedes that the company made some poor choices early on. "In fact when we started out, we ended up licensing things that didn't have the right quality," he says. Including cigarettes.

These days the agreements are more sophisticated. The Harley-Davidson name is on restaurants in Las Vegas and Manhattan, not because Harley-Davidson makes money selling steak tips, but because they boost the company's image, give riders places to gather, and keep the sizzle going. The trademarked Harley-Davidson shield and bar image appears on T-shirts, men's cologne, baby clothes, shot glasses, teddy bears, and blue jeans. The company guards its name fiercely. Aftermarket dealers can't get Harley stickers without paying a fat fee. The brand is so hot—and Harley's marketing has grown so calculating— that the motorcycle maker has petitioned the U.S. Patent and Trademark Office for exclusive rights to its engine sound, which sounds like "potato-potato-potato." (The effort is half serious, half publicity stunt.)

THE NEXT GREAT LEATHER-CLAD WAVE

The still-common mental model of Harley riders as leather-clad, bearded outlaws cuts both ways for the company. The image adds a certain gritty mystique, but it also suggests a darker, edgier side to motorcycling. The Hell's Angels have selected Harley motorcycles as their vehicle of choice. Many nonriders picture one when they think of the other. Certainly at a small number of Harley-oriented events, Hell's Angels are a presence. Teerlink says only about 1 percent of Harley owners are Hell's Angels, but it is a distasteful subject. He's happier bragging about the millions of dollars that Harley owners raise annually for combating muscular dystrophy. The Hell's Angels are intriguing, but they are not the story.

In fact, more Harley owners are well-off and white-collar than ever. Between 1985 and 1997 the median age of Harley owners rose from 34 to 43. Their median household income increased from $37,000 to $70,000. Two-thirds of riders now have some college credits, and one-third have a college diploma. Most buyers are still men, although the company likes to tout the 9 percent who are women. Boomers are physically active, serious about their leisure time, affluent, and eager to feel young. For many of them a motorcycle hits the spot.

In fact, demand has far outstripped supplies for years. There are more than 1,000 dealers in Harley's worldwide network, including nearly 600 in the United States, and many plead with the company for more bikes. Would-be owners have endured waiting lists, then paid well over manufacturer suggested retail price, a fact that Teerlink does not dispute and characterizes as "just terrible." Sometimes buyers flip bikes—they purchase and then resell immediately at a higher price—for a quick profit. Year-old Harleys commonly sell for 25 percent more than the list price for a new bike. Motorcycle shipments more than quadrupled between 1986 and 1997. Sales revenues during the same period skyrocketed, and net income jumped almost 50-fold. Harley-Davidson is debt-free, and its investors are happy.

Right now the company is intensely devoted to its potential overseas market, where it is building the next great leather-clad wave. Exports account for 30 percent of Harley-Davidson's business. About a fifth of H.O.G. members live outside the United States, motoring to rallies in the Czech Republic, Germany, England, France, Norway, Canada, New Zealand, and Australia. Harley is also moving to market bikes catering to Asian and Latin American tastes.

INTO THE SUNSET

Teerlink, now retired, says his time at Harley-Davidson was "the greatest learning journey you could ask for." What's he going to do next? "Ride off into the sunset," he says in a clear quick voice. Fat chance. After passing through the storm and savoring the rainbow at Harley-Davidson, Teerlink is too interested in how companies manage rapid, radical change to stow his briefcase forever.

Beals has also moved on. There is a large oil painting in his Arizona home of three kids admiring a Harley, and his garage holds an interesting assortment of old, well-worn leathers, but Beals's house is no motorcycle museum. His retirement plan: golf. Still, Beals talks about Harleys with all the energy of a young man. He has also passed on his passion. Now his 23-year-old granddaughter wants a Harley. She's been told to save up.

CHALLENGES AHEAD

Harley-Davidson is on a sweet stretch of road, but trickier terrain lies ahead. The company must also be ready for the next recession, which will leave blood on the floor for big-ticket consumer durables producers, Harley-Davidson included. Cash could dry up quickly, and this company that prides itself so publicly on internal harmony will feel the pressure to lay off workers and cut costs. Even in good economic times, questions dangle about how long Harley can trade on its name. The company must merchandise its image with care if it wants to grow old.

For years there haven't been enough new Harleys to go around. "We've increased production every year at least 10 percent since 1987," Teerlink defends. "It is not our plan to be undersupplied." Some say the shortage has been the only way to ensure quality. But there's more to it. Harley-Davidson knows that its bikes have a mystique that is driven in part by their scarcity. Now Harley is building a new Kansas City facility that will increase output from 140,000 to 210,000 motorcycles annually. That sounds like overcapacity, particularly because Harley's market segment is aging. By the time the cake is cut at its 100th birthday party, boomers will be heading over the proverbial hill. The company needs to attract the next demographic subgroup, but gen-Xers are a different kind of consumer. They aren't nostalgic like boomers, they don't have money, and they don't consume conspicuously. "Gen-Xers are excited about our name, not our motorcycles," Teerlink confesses. "We need to find ways to bring them in." Beals chimes in, "We don't have an entry-level product, and that's an exposure."

And now, having starved the market and with margins wide enough to attract attention, Harley-Davidson has lured imitators. Domestic and offshore competitors, including Polaris, BMW, Coleman, and Japanese manufacturers have come courting. They don't have the storied brand or loyal core to dent Harley's market much, but neither did Honda when it first brought cars to the States. Japanese bikes are a generation ahead of Harley—cleaner, quieter, and more efficient. Beals sees no threat. "The Japanese are fantastic engineers, fantastic at manufacturing. They still set a goal for quality that we have to reach. But the Japanese do not understand the soft side of the business, the customers."

Teerlink? He just laughs off the competition. Harley-Davidson will never win an engine technology competition, he states, and so what? The company strategy is built on a total relationship with its family of owners. Japanese bikes are no threat, they're only about technology. "Why don't we talk about emotional design?" he asks. "Do you just own your bike for the fastest quarter-mile? If so, we don't want you."

ON A GREAT RIDE

Beals and Teerlink ran Harley-Davidson successively, but don't ask Teerlink to characterize his personal contribution. He won't do it. Ask him to rate himself as a business leader and he begs off. He even gets a little annoyed. Teerlink is the consummate team player, and part of his legacy at Harley-Davidson is the nonhierarchical company he left behind, a company where everyone down to the lowliest hourly employee is celebrated as a hero. Self-congratulatory statements apparently violate the rules, and Teerlink won't break rank. What's Teerlink's definition of leadership? "Being part of a group that makes a difference."

"I am one person that was blessed enough to be put in a position that I stumbled into," he says. "I worked with a group of people who were committed to making this thing happen together. If any of them hadn't been there, we wouldn't be here."

Teerlink's version is all good fortune, right-place-at-the-right-time stuff. Beals is more forthcoming and this makes sense, because the earlier version of Harley-Davidson that Beals ran required a different, more dominant, more visible leader. Harley-Davidson was going down the tubes, he points out. Someone had to take decisive action. "When the enemy's coming over the ramparts," he says, "you shoot."

No one who knows the Harley-Davidson story thinks the company succeeded so gloriously because of dumb luck. Beals bought Harley-Davidson from AMF not to run it, but to remake it. He threw out old methods and reached for new thinking, fished good ideas out of the muck, and prepared the company's future leaders. Teerlink supplied financial wizardry and carried consensus management to a new, unusually innovative level. Both men showed an exceptional feel for the market. They capitalized on Harley's brand power and put it to work. Both men made Harley-Davidson the well-oiled, wealth-making machine it is today, in successor Jeffrey L. Bleustein's hands.

Manufacturing high-quality hardware was a critical step, but at Harley-Davidson it was only half the job. This company is a phenomenon because it understands how to sell sizzle. Its motorcycles—the Softail, the Sportster, the Dyna Glide, the Road King—are the best-loved in the world. They promise a fantasy, and they deliver. Owners and shareholders alike are enjoying a great ride.

Andrew S. Grove

Dennis L. Carter

Andrew S. Grove and
Dennis L. Carter at Intel

"I couldn't understand how this story, almost like OJ or the Clinton stuff, kept cropping up on the front page of the newspaper day after day after day. . . . So what went wrong?"
—ANDREW S. GROVE

"I stayed up all night one night, thinking every angle through. Then I called Andy. I don't know how many hours we were on the phone."
—DENNIS L. CARTER

Intel towers over California's Silicon Valley. The world's number-one chipmaker owns between 80 and 90 percent of the worldwide microprocessor market for IBM-compatible machines and for years has dwarfed all comers. Intel's engineering brilliance and operational focus have been sung long and loud. Chairman Andrew S. Grove is that rare creature: a living legend.

But a giant, less-explored chunk of the company's success is due to astute branding. Intel for years was obsessively and almost exclusively focused on creating new technology. The semiconductor maker figured out branding, and sizzle selling, quite by accident, then used its new know-how in remarkable ways to turn microprocessors into hot consumer products. It's equally remarkable, then, that when a routine flaw popped up on the company's premium Pentium chip, Intel almost threw it all away. Intel transformed itself into a consumer product company, then realized it had to behave like one.

MR. GROVE AND MR. CARTER

Intel Chairman Andrew S. Grove is a wiry man with rings under his eyes and the mental flexibility of a much younger man. His facial expressions change quickly and with subtlety. Grove has the ability to charm you completely or dispatch you bluffly. Contrary to his popular image, he can be very funny. He is known for his stubborn, mercurial, hands-on management style and for a measure of personal obsessiveness. Grove sets a very high bar for Intel employees. The company has long been infused by his personal philosophy which states that "only the paranoid survive."

He was born Andras Grof in Budapest. Grove survived the Nazis and then fled to the States after the 1956 Soviet invasion. He waited on tables, studied at City College in New York, and then took a Ph.D. in chemical engineering at UC Berkeley. After a few years at Fairchild, Grove in 1968 joined friends Robert Noyce and Gordon Moore just after the two men founded Intel. He became president and COO of the semiconductor company in 1979, CEO in 1987, and is now by choice simply chairman.

Grove is deeply interested in marketing details, which means he is often in the same room with vice president of marketing Dennis Carter. Carter has a long mouth, sparse hair, and oversize glasses. He reveres Grove. His manner is low-key and affable, but Carter speaks with rapid precision and his thinking leans in analytical directions. As Carter speaks he regularly breaks his thoughts out loud into first, second, and third parts or points one, two, and three.

Carter plotted the day-by-day details of Intel's branding strategy. Grove calls him "Mr. Intel Inside." He was born in Louisville, Kentucky, and studied electrical engineering at Purdue. After designing airplane flight controls at Rockwell, he earned a Harvard MBA and carried it straight to Intel. Carter is modest. By his telling, he almost stumbled into branding simply by trying things and not because of any vision or gifted thinking. Carter says this attitude typifies Intel's scientific culture, where teams of highly-trained people analyze the big picture, identify objectives and obstacles, and then design rigorous outcome-oriented plans. It is a fact-based world where ideas evolve, where no one shoots from the hip. This is why Intel's branding strategy worked so well. This is also why Intel got into such a pickle with its Pentium chip.

GRABBING THE MARKET'S ATTENTION

Intel makes microprocessors, which very simply are the brains of computers. Grove's organization has supplied them for PCs since 1981. Intel also makes other computer products, but chips are king and Intel is continuously upgrading them by cramming more transistors onto ever-smaller wafers of silicon. Rivals AMD and Cyrix do what they can to keep up.

Company founders Moore, a chemist, and Noyce, a coinventor of the integrated circuit, took Intel public in 1971. Success was a round-about road. The semiconductor industry back then was in an embryonic state, and though Intel tried to read the tea leaves it struggled to antici-pate the market. Other obstacles appeared in the 1980s, including weak demand for memory chips, factory problems, and Japanese competi-tion. "Quality became an incredible mantra in this company," Carter says of that time. "Craig Barrett [now CEO] became Mr. Quality. He benchmarked everything." By the late 1980s, Intel was emerging as an industry leader. In a few more years it was offering the hands-down best microprocessor on the market. Consumer companies need a superior product to sell the sizzle. Intel was on the mark.

At roughly the same time (about 1989) the PC industry began shift-ing its focus away from computer manufacturers toward what the indus-try calls "end-users," or retail customers. Up to this point, Carter explains, "all of Intel's marketing was engineer to engineer—and we knew how to do that quite well." Intel realized that design engineers weren't making decisions anymore about which products to use. Instead, PC manufacturers were placing their orders based on what buyers were requesting of retailers. "We realized we had to start com-municating to our end-user," Carter states. "And we had no way to reach or talk to them."

"WE HAD ACCIDENTALLY DISCOVERED BRANDING"

Intel considered how to adjust its strategy. Most consumers were buying PCs by manufacturer's name, such as Compaq, for example, or IBM, and didn't think much about the components inside the box. Now Grove wanted them to think differently and ask retailers for Intel by name. Intel had a second reason to make consumers think again. The company was trying to get customers to move up from its 286 micro-processor to the 386. Buyers weren't budging.

Intel decided to try to create demand for a component, its 386 microprocessor. Grove handed the job to Carter, his technical assistant at the time. "Andy said, 'I'll budget you $5 million, but you'll have to prove first with $500,000 that this can make a difference,' " Carter says.

For the first time, Intel published an advertisement that spoke directly to retail customers. In the ad, a big red X was spray-painted graffiti-style over the number 286, and next to that, scrawled in red, was the number 386X. The ad was known around Intel as the "eating our own baby" campaign. Denver was Carter's test market, and for a few days his team "ran around town like maniacs," he recalls, collecting data on the ad's effectiveness. The results, Carter says, were electrifying. "People who had seen the ads had changed their purchasing in a meaningful way. Not only were we successful, but it was clear that something very meaningful had happened. It was an incredible moment." Shoppers had defied conventional industry wisdom. They had digested relatively technical information on a computer component, then changed their purchasing pattern. Grove, his voice still flavored by a Hungarian accent, puts it like this: "We had accidentally discovered branding."

Intel's discovery soon took on real importance. By 1990, Intel was a $3.9 billion company, the market and technology leader, with micro-processors in almost 8 out of every 10 IBM or IBM-compatible machines. "Our first components were so significant that the world had started to call computers by our component names, colloquially," Grove says. Intel went to court to protect those names, but a Federal judge dealt Intel a blow by ruling that numerical chip names could not be trademarked. Any company could call their machine a 386, no matter who supplied the chip, and regardless of differences in quality or per-formance. Intel was knocked for a loop. It had introduced the 386 and built up its brand value. "Our problem was that all our marketing equity was in that product," Carter says. "We were agonizing at the possibility of losing our ability to differentiate ourselves," Grove adds. Intel needed a new branding strategy, quickly. Other manufacturers, includ-ing AMD, were already moving products to market using the 386 desig-nation. "Grove said go figure out something," Carter says. "And do it quick."

NAILING DOWN THE EQUITY

Over the previous year, in no particular hurry, Carter had been formu-lating his thoughts on brand-building. He whipped up a proposal. Grove liked it immediately. The goal was to make Intel a well-known brand and to nail down the company's hard-won equity. The challenge, Carter says, was to make consumers care about an ingredient buried inside their computers. Intel wanted to offer their microprocessors as safe, superior products worth a premium price. And Intel had to approach marketing efforts with care. "This whole industry is an industry of change," Carter says. "Just about the time we figured out we'd branded the 386, the industry moved beyond it." Intel needed a branding strategy that wouldn't grow moldy or obsolete as products evolved over time.

While formulating his plan, Carter scrambled to come up with a company logo. "I remember sitting behind him, watching him doodle at a meeting, little symbols," Grove says. Carter eventually modified a design used by Dentsu in Japan, that wrapped the words "Intel In It" inside a curving line. Carter changed it to "Intel Inside," then asked Intel's designers to give it a polish. "They came back with a totally different look," Carter says. "I had to send them back four times." Carter wanted something friendly and casual. The designers kept offering high tech. Why casual? "It was a gut call," Carter says. "Informality was a better tone. We were trying to create positive images." Finally the designers threw up their hands. "They said, 'Show us what you want,' " Carter says. "I went to the blackboard and drew the swirl." Intel had its logo. Some at Intel liked it, some called it a mistake. "The most important thing I did at that time was I protected Dennis from the naysayers," Grove says. "A lot of people thought it was ridiculous to brand a component." Consumers were about to prove them wrong.

BE COOL, HAVE FUN, BE FASHIONABLE

Intel asked computer manufacturers to include the "Intel Inside" logo in their print ads. "We could spend a huge amount of money on branding, but if consumers couldn't ID Intel products on the shelf, it wasn't worth much," Carter explains. As an incentive, Intel offered a subsidy through a co-op advertising fund. This program didn't catch fire all at once. Third-tier computer manufacturers signed on right away because the logo gave their products a quality assurance boost, but first- and second-tier manufacturers, the ones Intel needed most, were a harder sell. Many had their own strong brand names and feared dilution. "There was a four-year period of time when they were in and out, in and out," Grove says of the upper tier. "They couldn't figure out whether they hated it or loved it." By end of 1992, however, many lower-tier manufacturers had signed on. In time, as the logo grew familiar and PC buyers began to request Intel by name, bigger manufacturers jumped aboard too.

Intel followed up with a series of its own television commercials. Some of these used special effects to give consumers a "fly through" tour around a PC that left them hovering above something they'd never touched or seen: an Intel microprocessor. Intel couldn't sort out whether to end these ads with the company name or the "Intel Inside" logo. "It seemed like a very complex decision at the time," Carter says. In the end the company chose the logo, sizzling inside what Carter calls "a real fancy swirl." The singsong four-tone "Intel Inside" sound was a later addition.

Intel had become a sizzle seller. Just a few years before, the company had been selling industrial components to consumer product manufacturers solely on the basis of a compatible, supremely well-engineered performance. The relationship had been chipmaker to manufacturer, and based upon product specifications. Now that Intel was selling to retail buyers, it was pitching much more than technical performance— it was selling excitement. Intel told retail buyers they needed Intel chips inside their computers to keep up, to stay on the cutting edge of an evolving universe, to be cool, have fun, be fashionable.

NAME GAME

Between 1990 and 1993, Intel spent more than $500 million in advertising and promotional fees to build brand equity. As the chipmaker readied its next generation microprocessor, code-named P5, its name became an issue once again. Grove, still steamed about the 386 trademark ruling, said the new chip would be called the 586 over his dead body. The chip's name had to stand on its own. It had to be trademarkable, have positive associations, work globally, and sound like an ingredient. The Intel Inside campaign had raised the company's profile, and many inside and outside the industry were waiting on this new chip and watching to see what Intel would do.

Carter's team brainstormed hundreds of names, ran a companywide naming contest, and hired a naming firm. After a protracted process, three candidates survived the next-to final cut: InteLigence, RADAR! and Pentium. At a top-level meeting just days before the name was scheduled for announcement, Grove called on each person to state a preference. It was a three-way tie. Later, alone together in Grove's office, Grove and Carter chose Pentium. "Over the weekend I had misgivings," Carter says. "Each time I picked up the phone and called Andy." It was an emotional moment, Carter explains. "There was a tremendous amount of equity to be walked away from." Grove stayed calm, Carter says. The following Monday he announced the name on live television. The "pent" came from Greek and meant five, Grove says, alluding to the fifth generation of chips. The suffix "ium" was intended to make the chip sound like an ingredient and a fundamental element. Some said the name was ridiculous, but critics and fans alike noted the milestone: It was the first time a chip had been so purposefully branded.

TRIPPED BY A TINY FLAW

Intel's branding campaign gathered steam. "It caught the fancy of PC users, and by the time we got to '94, Intel Inside was very well-known and very hot," Carter says. Intel had successfully transformed its microprocessors into consumer products. Trouble was, Intel didn't understand that it had become a consumer product company. In fact the company wouldn't understand until it had to, in 1994, when Intel's successful branding efforts rose up and smote the company on the back of the head.

Intel had known about a flaw in its Pentium microprocessor for months, but dismissed it as a small problem that didn't merit any special disclosure. By company estimates the defect caused an error only about once in every nine billion mathematical calculations. Undisclosed blemishes or bugs in microchips were common. Technical users had never made a stink about them; they just worked around them or waited for a product upgrade. Intel's engineering army planned to fix the Pentium, but quietly, as always before, during a routine upgrade. The decision was based on a rational assessment of the facts.

But Intel had spent millions of dollars making the Pentium name into a household word. Most powerful desktop computers contained the company's flagship Pentium chip, and when PC owners became aware of the defect they didn't care that the miscalculation was rare— all they registered was the word "flaw." Customers began to complain. They questioned Intel's commitment to quality. Intel responded as if its buyers were deranged. It pooh-poohed the complaints, then told customers they could have a replacement chip only if owners could prove they were affected. Intel's technical arguments made the company seem deceptive, then stubborn, then dim-witted. The company took a beating in the media.

"You know how when you were a kid and your mother or your father took you to task for something and you felt utterly and completely misunderstood?" Grove says. "Those are the feelings we had here. We couldn't understand what this was all about. As problems go with chips, this was not a problem. This was nothing." Grove, perhaps the most-admired high-tech manager in the world, was stunned. "I couldn't understand how this story, almost like OJ or the Clinton stuff, kept cropping up on the front page of the newspaper day after day after day, at a time when Intel had never made the front page of *The Wall Street Journal* or *The New York Times* before. And now it was making it every day. So what went wrong?"

What went wrong: The consumer durable goods market tolerates no defects in quality whatsoever. Nobody buys a scratched Cadillac, no matter how teensy the scratch, no matter how dreamy the ride. "Later, when we could reflect back on it," Grove says, "we could see in simplest terms that we were dealing with the people with the scratch on the Cadillac."

ABOUT-FACE

Intel came around—slowly. Its analytical engineering mindset made the corner particularly hard to turn. Intel had always poured itself almost exclusively into advancing new generations of technology. Market dominance had bred a bit of arrogance. After years of selling primarily to the business market, Intel had only the most rudimentary understanding of how to manage direct relationships with retail buyers. "The Pentium flaw episode happened over only a few weeks," Carter says, "but it felt like half my life." As the criticism flew, IBM joined the fray. It bad-mouthed Intel for hiding, then trivializing, the flaw, and then it suspended Pentium shipments.

"Finally it was really clear that we were losing equity," Carter says. "I stayed up all night one night, thinking every angle through. Then I called Andy. I don't know how many hours we were on the phone."

Grove describes this conversation as a watershed. "Dennis was ahead of me in understanding the reality of the situation. We shifted and started to see it from the outside in, rather than the inside out." Grove doesn't mince words. "Dennis at that time saved Intel's life."

So, four weeks into its crisis, Intel did an about-face. "There is an old saying that branding is a promise," Grove says. "Branding meant a different course of action." Intel offered to replace all of its flawed Pentium chips, no questions asked. Grove backed the switch fully, but he worried out loud about its ramifications. The perfection standard troubled him. Microprocessors were among the most complex manufactured products ever, he said, and probably impossible to guarantee as flawless. Such an exacting standard, he thought at the time, was sure to sandbag the pace of innovation.

The Pentium flaw episode was a defining moment at Intel. The company learned a lesson. The lesson got carved on the wall. "And in a lot of us," Carter adds. Intel understood that it was answering to a new customer. It took a $475 million pretax charge for chip replacements. In spite of the uproar, sales never suffered. In fact, Intel seemed ultimately to prosper from the incident. Most PC owners couldn't grasp the specifics of the obscure flaw, but they understood CEO Grove going the distance to back his company's product. Looking back, Grove is philosophical on the subject. "It was a very difficult incident, and probably represents some instances in which corporations have to deal with an existential issue," he says. "They have to examine who they are and what they do in ways that go way beyond words."

Almost immediately after the Pentium crisis, Grove was diagnosed with prostate cancer. By the time he publicly acknowledged his illness, radiation treatments had put the cancer into remission. It is a testament to Grove's personal strength that one after another he managed both crises so well.

INTEL INSIDE

Intel today remains far and away the industry pacesetter, but the enormous cost of developing and manufacturing successive generations of chips means the company needs a steady, roaring river of profits. Intel worries that the money stream will slow. Unless computer users upgrade, a cash drought could choke off the next round. Grove knows he has to keep the technology exciting or Intel's torrid growth rate will tail off. For some time the company has gone to great lengths to entice buyers with more sizzle. Intel backs companies developing gear and software that is cool to use and that requires huge doses of microprocessing power. Yet despite Intel's extensive efforts, PC demand is slowing. Buyers are turning to low-priced PCs, which drives down Intel's prices. The microprocessor market is also increasingly segmented. In an effort to stay hot, Intel is creating distinct chips for different applications—low-end, high-end, and consumer electronics-oriented. The Intel Inside campaign remains an important way to communicate product differences to consumers.

Once considered controversial, the Intel Inside effort is now a successful part of the high-tech landscape. Billions in advertising have spread the Intel Inside logo, and the co-op program continues. What role did the Intel Inside campaign play in propelling Intel to the top of its market? "That's a chicken-and-egg question," Carter says. "But our market segment share has risen since we launched the program." Intel closely monitors the effectiveness of its branding campaign. "We are an engineering company, so we are very quantitative," Carter says. The numbers, he continues, show that branding makes a difference.

LISTENING WELL

Carter describes his management style as collegial. "I try to approach everyone with a lot of respect," he says. "Everyone has great ideas. I try to get a lot of discussion going." As an engineer with a marketing bent, Carter makes decisions by studying the numbers and listening to his gut. "You can believe market research, but follow it exactly and you probably won't make the best possible decision. You need to use intuition, too."

What about Grove—is he a god at Intel? "There are a lot of brilliant people here," Carter says. "Andy has his special brilliance, coupled with his curiosity, coupled with his energy. I'll go to a review meeting and he'll ask insightful questions, make insightful comments, and I'll walk out and think, this guy is the most brilliant branding guy ever. Then at the next meeting we'll discuss semiconductor design. Andy asks insightful questions, makes insightful comments, and I come out thinking the same thing. Andy has a commanding presence, but also I've never known anyone who listens like him. He absolutely listens."

Intel's open culture is well known. "Dennis didn't have any problem arguing very vociferously with me and succeeded in changing my mind," Grove says about the Pentium flap. "We are very free to disagree with each other. But we also understand that once a decision is made, we don't second-guess the decision." Grove may be a god at Intel, but he is an open-minded god. "I don't have a problem with a lot of yes-men," he shrugs.

It is now standard operating procedure at Intel to disclose chip flaws as they pop up, a policy instituted after the Pentium flap. A typical chip has 30 to 50 errata, all usually pretty obscure, Grove says. "Consumers rarely take action to protect themselves, but they seem to take comfort in knowing what the flaws are." Flaw specifics are published on the company website. "If you care to know the dirty little secrets of our chips, you can look them up," Grove says. "One thing about Intel, once we decide something we implement it. To this day, we're sticking with that policy."

SEEING THE BIG PICTURE

A few years ago Grove handed off his Intel presidency to second-in-command and heir Craig Barrett. Grove attends fewer meetings these days but still works full-time. Out of a cubicle. Like everyone else at Intel. His walls are decorated with newspaper clippings. "Most of them are yellow and flopping in the wind," Grove says. "There is one where someone described me as cuddly, which I thought was funny." His window overlooks the parking lot. His desk is clean, and he's compulsive that way.

Grove believes he is successful because he excels at distilling the big picture out of rafts of smaller data. "I'm good at extracting patterns. It sounds "New Age-y," but I'm good at finding a bigger truth out of information. An associate once said that when someone dumps their little facts on the table, I reach in and pull out what it's all about. I wish it were always true." He's still passionate about his work. "I relish the same thing I dislike about it, the unrelenting change and variety. I constantly have to study. For example, five years ago I knew almost nothing about the telecommunications industry, and now I'm reasonably comfortable. I love it, and it's hard. It's overwhelming, but I'm a pretty good student."

Away from Intel, Grove teaches management at Stanford. He plays tennis, runs, swims, bikes, and skis. "I don't collect things," he says. "I don't fly planes." He does drive a convertible sports car. "Not high-end," Grove says quickly. His bout with cancer gave him a mission beyond Intel. "Someday I would like to make a difference, to get a real cure for prostate cancer," he says. "I'm working on that, and it's immensely challenging."

Intel is struggling now to figure out its role in a rapidly evolving market. The huge price spread between its low and high-end chips has staved off any scary declines in its market share, but Intel faces a greater challenge now: it must anticipate the next high-tech consumer products wave. For years the company was moving closer to being the most profitable in the world. Its earnings grew annually at an average rate of nearly 45 percent. Intel will have to sustain its paranoid vigilance into the new century to remain the industry pacesetter. Keeping its brand strong and its sizzle piping hot will be necessary parts of that effort.

C H A P T E R   7

Saviors
Virtuoso Performers

Saviors:

⇨ Believe in their mission
⇨ Deviate from standard operating procedure
⇨ Strike out in creative, new directions
⇨ Inspire the troops
⇨ Successfully juggle both worshippers and critics
⇨ Work best when time is short

Companies sometimes stumble into such trouble that nothing short of a miracle can reverse the sickening slide. The business is so far gone that its owners question the future and its top managers are paralyzed with fear. In public companies, senior executives dread the ignominy that will greet their failure. People who work for foundering firms go home at night to anxious families and pitying neighbors. The next morning they are back in the trenches. It's a brutal life.

Desperate companies searching for salvation sometimes find the real thing: a messiah who offers to heal the afflicted. When the messiah delivers, the failing company is saved and the rescuer acquires a holy aura.

Saviors inhabit a different world than everyday CEOs. They are fixed on the future. They believe in their mission and their ability to carry it out, and they frequently believe that they alone know what to do and how to do it. Saviors carry the conceit of conviction openly. Most often they are charged with the rescue not on the basis of experience, but through a convincing combination of guts and vision.

Saviors are often summoned to failing companies by frightened boards that still have the guts to fight and are willing to try something radical. They may cross over from other industries or be die-hard company insiders. There is no special breeding ground or training program. This type of manager is granted exceptional leeway to deviate from standard operating procedure and can strike out in a direction that no predecessor ever had the backing or the courage to attempt before. The typical board isn't happy about charging off in a new direction—but it knows the old one will put the company six feet under.

Most executives don't know how to respond in an emergency. They change things a little bit here, a little bit there, and their judgment may even deteriorate under pressure into half-baked ideas bathed in fear. They live in a superorganized, unvarying world called "Plan, Organize, Execute, and Follow-Up." This crusty, unimaginative approach is a poor match for a crisis.

Saviors think differently. They take a fresh, powerful slap at whatever is killing a company. They set difficult goals, then they inspire the troops. One kind of savior makes quick progress and attracts a following to help push through the rest of the results. A second, slow-but-steady type earns respect by laying one good brick on top of another and prevails over time—sometimes problems are so intractable that an executive's primary asset is persistence. The savior role requires extraordinary self-confidence and single-mindedness. Saviors are not afraid to hurt some to rescue the many. The ethic is survival. The work calls for a thick skin and the strength to endure the derision of the envious and the barbs of conventional thinkers.

Saviors must learn to work a mixed audience of worshippers and skeptics. The worshippers are relieved since, if nothing else, they will have someone to blame if the company tanks. Skeptics watch from the sidelines, waiting for proof one way or the other. A true savior wins the admiration of the watching world, particularly within his or her own industry. It's a feat to yank a company back from the grave.

There is no single spectacular formula for rescuing a failing company. Some have suffered too long from inertia. Others have over-indulged management, failed to grasp changes in the marketplace, or failed to apply new technology. A grave product design error, lousy marketing over the years, or neglectful labor relations can send a company into a danger zone. Every business runs into trouble from time to time, but not every situation calls for a savior. Messiahs are useful when the prognosis is terminal.

Many business saviors have been widely celebrated, including Lee Iacocca at Chrysler, Jack Welch at General Electric, and Louis V. Gerstner at IBM. But smaller companies have their saviors, too. They get less press, but their achievements are no less remarkable. Greyhound CEO Craig Lentzsch, a bus industry insider, knew precisely how to revive his company when it sputtered off the road. When a new strategy bombed at Federal-Mogul, CEO Dick Snell rebuilt the company in spirit and substance. RJR Nabisco CEO Steve Goldstone led the way to a historic settlement that will carry his pariah industry into the next century. US Airways Chairman Stephen Wolf turned a shrinking airline into a contender. All four of these virtuoso performers are remarkable for their persistence and vision.

Steven F. Goldstone

Steven F. Goldstone at RJR Nabisco

"In most places now, you smoke a cigar, people don't
mind it. They'll chase you down the street
and almost kill you if you light up a cigarette."

Steve Goldstone is the tobacco industry's chief strategist and would-be savior. He was the first tobacco executive to perceive that the old rules were dead and that his pariah industry had entered a new era of accountability. As the industry's most visible leader, Goldstone had the daunting task of carrying Big Tobacco into the new century, even if he had to cut a deal to do it.

LEGAL MIND AT THE TOP

Goldstone is outgoing, funny, a charmer. Even those who dislike his ethics admire his style. He often seems to be having a good time. He's a snappy dresser who favors double-breasted suits and cracks jokes about his own balding pate. Goldstone is not a big man, but he easily captures a room. One-on-one, he wins over most people on a personal level if not on the subject of smoking. Goldstone quit cigarettes years ago, but he still enjoys a cigar. "In most places now, you smoke a cigar, people don't mind it," he says. "They'll chase you down the street and almost kill you if you light up a cigarette."

The son of a factory manager, Goldstone grew up in the Westchester suburbs of New York City. He took a law degree at New York University and made a beeline for Wall Street. Before RJR Nabisco, Goldstone spent his entire career litigating at Davis, Polk and Wardwell, a New York firm specializing in mergers and acquisitions. Clients included United Airlines, General Electric, and J.P. Morgan. When he became president of RJR Nabisco in late 1995, Goldstone the executive was something of an unknown quantity, and he was not necessarily expected to last.

That doesn't mean he was a stranger. Goldstone had been lawyering for RJR for years, and was lead counsel in 1989 when Kohlberg Kravis Roberts & Co. seized control in the largest hostile takeover in business up to that time. Goldstone warned RJR chairman F. Ross Johnson that the buyout seemed half-baked. He would be proven right: When KKR in 1994 finally unloaded its 40 percent stake in RJR, investors were no more flush, and the buyout burdened RJR with $25 billion in debt, most of it junk bonds with brutally high interest rates. After the deal went through, short-term executives came and went, including Louis Gerstner Jr. and Charles Harper. They could not right the ship.

Goldstone surprised just about everyone in 1996 when in under eight months he vaulted from president to chief executive to chairman. RJR's board promoted him instead of a high-powered outsider or a juice-stained tobacco man because they saw dangerous legal crossroads ahead and recognized the value of installing an outstanding legal mind at the top. "I'm probably one of just a few CEOs in this country [who] didn't work their way up through a corporate environment," Goldstone says. Wall Street has never questioned Goldstone's legal acumen, but has on occasion expressed uncertainty about how his litigation skills translate to general operations. "My job is to run some very big businesses," Goldstone defends. "I happen to be a lawyer, and people say because he's a lawyer, his job is to take care of litigation. Not true. My main job is to strengthen our cookie, cracker, and tobacco businesses all around the world. Just because you're a lawyer does not disqualify you from leadership."

CASCADING HOSTILITY

When Goldstone took over at RJR Nabisco Holdings, Inc., it was the sixth-largest consumer product company in the world. It employed about 130,000 people worldwide and was the parent to R.J. Reynolds, the number-two U.S. cigarette maker. R.J. Reynolds sells Camel, Winston, Salem, and Doral, 4 of the 10 top-selling domestic brands. RJR Nabisco was also parent to Nabisco Holdings, one of the world's top food companies, whose well-known products include Oreos, Chips Ahoy!, Ritz crackers, Lifesavers, Grey Poupon mustards, and Planters Peanuts. RJR Nabisco's top tobacco industry rival was the much-larger Philip Morris; its top food business competitor was Keebler.

RJR's domestic cigarette business in 1996 was slowly declining, and global tobacco marketing efforts were also sliding, but Goldstone's bigger worry was the mounting public hostility against tobacco. People had called cigarettes "coffin nails" for generations but without any serious legal ramifications. Tobacco manufacturers in the 1930s had actually peddled the health benefits of smoking, then shifted over the years to a lesser "no throat irritation" pitch. The Federal Trade Commission announced in 1950 that smoking wasn't harmful, but later that year acknowledged possible links to lung cancer. Health-related ads tapered off. The 1964 surgeon general's report was a tobacco industry watershed, leading the FTC to quickly brand smoking a health risk and require ads to carry warnings. Cigarettes could no longer be marketed as healthful or even benign. They were recast as hip, sophisticated pleasures.

In the early 1990s, for a welter of reasons, antitobacco sentiment in the United States began to cascade. Lawsuits mounted. For years the tobacco industry's aggressive tactics had made suing cigarette makers expensive and burdensome. The informal industry strategy of wearing down and outlasting opponents had worked splendidly for decades. Big Tobacco could brag that it had never lost a verdict in a liability case and never paid out a red cent. Jurors always arrived at the same general conclusion: Smokers knew the risks.

Goldstone says he, personally, agrees with such thinking. "I smoked until I was about 32 years old," he says. "I believed I was increasing my risk of getting sick if I continued to smoke. That's risk-assessment. Grownups, not kids, can make that choice." Goldstone offers another personal analogy: He likes to fly small airplanes. "My hearing isn't as good as it used to be," he says. "My eyesight's not that good, and I never was that coordinated. I still like flying planes. My life insurance has gone way up, my wife and friends think I'm insane. Have I increased my risk of dying?—you bet I have—but I'm a grownup and I can make that choice. There are a lot of people who enjoy smoking. They make the judgment that it's a risk they want to bear, and if they do it as adults, for me, I have no problem selling the product."

PRESSURE MOUNTS

Early court victories aside, investors in the early 1990s grew extremely nervous about the tobacco industry's potential legal liabilities. RJR Nabisco shares were depressed by as much as 50 percent, and the company came under pressure to spin off its food unit to unlock its share value. In 1994, RJR did offer the public a 19.5 percent stake in its fast-growing food operations. A further spin-off seemed to make sense, and RJR's board announced that it would act when the time was right.

That timetable didn't suit Bennett S. LeBow. LeBow, a leveraged buyout artist and the head of Liggett, a small tobacco company, joined forces with corporate raider Carl Icahn to try to force an immediate food and tobacco split at RJR. LeBow sought an edge. Perhaps he planned to merge his small, stumbling company with RJR, or maybe he was just after cash. Either way, RJR fought back. The company by this point was fending off a torrent of liability lawsuits, and company directors could face fraudulent conveyance charges if assets were sold off improperly. We will not rush a further spin-off, RJR said, even if shareholders beg for one. LeBow conceded the round.

But the $45 billion tobacco industry faced a rising tide of assaults from regulators, health industry advocates, and the amassed power of a fraternity of trial lawyers. Food and Drug Administration chief Dr. David Kessler urged stricter tobacco regulations, and criminal probes were under way after three former Philip Morris employees, contradicting sworn testimony, told FDA officials that their company manipulated nicotine levels. At hearings led by California senator Henry Waxman, seven tobacco executives, one after another, swore under oath before the U.S. Senate that they believed nicotine was not addictive, and then secret documents showed the industry may have known otherwise. Contingency fee lawyers went on attack. A massive class-action suit threatened, and sick smokers filed hundreds of private lawsuits.

There was more bad news. Mississippi attorney general Michael Moore sued the industry on his state's behalf to recover hundreds of millions of Medicaid dollars spent treating sick smokers. The way Moore figured it, taxpayers had not chosen to smoke but now they were paying for the consequences. Moore was assisted by millionaire Mississippi attorney Dick Scruggs, who had made his name and fortune suing the asbestos industry. The Mississippi lawsuit offered up a blueprint for every other state attorney general in the country.

Then LeBow reappeared, this time in a dangerous form. Breaking rank, Liggett settled its piece of a huge class-action lawsuit against tobacco manufacturers. Just as bad, LeBow promised to turn over key documents expected to show that the tobacco industry had knowingly hoodwinked the public about the dangers of smoking. Liggett's settlement was a huge victory for antitobacco forces. It proved that Big Tobacco was not impenetrable. A few days later, LeBow settled Liggett's state Medicaid lawsuits. Frightened investors dumped tobacco shares.

THE JUNE 1997 AGREEMENT

At RJR, domestic cigarette sales were slumping, and share prices were deeply depressed. Litigation was siphoning away management attention and hundreds of millions in legal payments, money RJR Nabisco would have preferred to use to pay down its crushing debt. Big tobacco was heading toward a cliff, and Goldstone could see from his vantage point that R.J. Reynolds would be one of the first to fall.

Breaking with the past, Goldstone proposed a brave, alternative course. He suggested that the industry reverse its aggressive stance and negotiate. He said the tobacco industry couldn't continue in public as "kind of an outlaw industry," then floated the idea of a massive settlement. Antitobacco interests liked what they heard, but the rest of the industry needed persuading. The odds against reaching a settlement were staggering. Rival tobacco companies would have to agree to terms. Plaintiff's attorneys would oppose future legal protection. State attorneys general and federal regulators would have their say, and health advocates would play hardball. Each party was sure to fight for its own agenda, but as Goldstone saw it, Big Tobacco could either cut a deal or die in court.

Three landmark events followed, each historic, each shaping in different ways the tobacco industry's future.

First came the June 1997 agreement, hammered out in private by 5 tobacco company CEOs and 42 state attorneys general. It proposed a $368.5 billion industry-wide settlement over 25 years in new cigarette taxes and other antismoking measures. Tobacco industry leaders— Philip Morris, RJR Nabisco, B.A.T. Industries, Loews, and UST Inc.— agreed to submit to new FDA oversight. New cigarette labeling and voluntary advertising restrictions were part of the package. The tentative agreement also settled state lawsuits and barred class action suits, including the awarding of punitive damages. Big tobacco left the bargaining table hoping the worst was over.

THE FLAWED MCCAIN BILL

The June 1997 agreement made regulators and politicians suspicious. If tobacco was for it, something must be wrong with it.

Goldstone watched the critics descend. FDA chief Kessler and other public health advocates were outraged by the immunity request. President Bill Clinton called it the most important public health measure in years, but then he said it wasn't tough enough. Congress, in response, began grinding out its own legislation. In April 1998, the Senate Commerce Committee overwhelmingly approved Arizona Republican senator John McCain's bill, a piece of lawmaking that raised the price of peace and was more punitive.

The McCain bill, landmark event number two, offered Big Tobacco no legal immunity from class-action lawsuits or punitive damages. It doubled the price hikes proposed in the June 1997 settlement. The revenue-raising bill would cost the tobacco industry more than $500 billion and raise the cap on what the tobacco industry could be forced to pay in annual legal damages. The FDA won extensive regulatory powers. The McCain bill also stated that if teen smoking rates didn't fall, the tobacco industry would pay the penalty.

Goldstone threw in the towel. Washington had played "the politics of punishment," Goldstone said in a speech to the National Press Club. The McCain bill would create a huge black market in smuggled cigarettes, he warned, and would drive his company into bankruptcy. No deal, Goldstone said. No more conciliatory negotiations. RJR Nabisco would rather fight it out the old-fashioned way, case by case, in court. Goldstone had very much wanted a negotiated solution. His frustration was intense.

He left Washington without a plan. Shortly after Goldstone's speech, the rest of the tobacco industry pulled out, too. The tobacco industry had miscalculated and Goldstone admits as much. Neither he nor any other tobacco CEO had fully appreciated how deeply hated and distrusted their industry was. They were grossly out of touch with common sentiment and they had seriously misconstrued the political climate. For most outside observers, even for many who defended the industry's right to exist, Big Tobacco had an unsettling history of dissembling about the risks of smoking, denying nicotine's addictive qualities, and marketing to children. Lawmakers had been afraid to look like tobacco industry friends. Clinton had endorsed the June 1997 negotiations but then backed down. Goldstone found Clinton's partisan positioning particularly galling, even if it was in character.

Goldstone had envisioned the original overall settlement as an escape from endless litigation, as an immunization, as an industry stabilizer. State attorneys general viewed it as a way to cut through the risky, expensive process of putting tobacco on trial. However, congressional leaders saw political opportunity. Public health officials saw an opportunity to leverage the tobacco industry's help in cutting underage smoking rates. Kessler, former surgeon general C. Everett Koop, and the antitobacco lobby saw something else: a chance to maim or kill what they believed was an immoral industry. In the end, the tobacco negotiations died trying to satisfy too many conflicting, highly charged agendas.

TOBACCO FIGHTS BACK

Goldstone's righteous retreat made him an industry hero. Tobacco country interests greeted his pullout with relief. They had been nervous about "caving," and now they went on the attack. A $50 million advertising campaign was launched to persuade Americans that the McCain bill was nothing but a tax-and-spend scheme. Tobacco industry commercials showed average people, smokers, who said they would be unfairly punished by higher cigarette taxes. "I'm no millionaire," a waitress asserted in one effective ad. "I work hard. Why single me out?" Tobacco interests called the bill an assault on hardworking Americans who would have to pony up even more taxes to enjoy a simple cigarette. The tobacco lobby also warned that the bill would create a huge black market, cost thousands of jobs, and drive the domestic tobacco industry into the ground.

Tobacco's expensive public relations campaign was effective. The McCain bill, overwhelmingly approved by the Senate in April, had no heartbeat three months later. Congress showed no interest in resuscitation.

GETTING KILLED IN COURT

Goldstone left Washington with a profound personal sense of missed opportunity. RJR Nabisco was back to square one and just as vulnerable.

It still carried about $9 billion in debt and paid hundreds of millions a year in service. Enormous legal cases loomed and distracted attention from operational issues. Even just one large jury verdict in a state or class-action case might do serious damage to RJR.

And damage looked likely. Washington politicians and regulators had failed to maim Big Tobacco, if that was their intent, but the states were proving capable of doing a bang-up job all on their own. Lawsuits filed by 37 state attorneys general were pending. Mississippi, Florida, and Texas had already settled for payouts totaling $30 billion. A flood of once-secret tobacco industry documents, disclosed in the course of state litigations, detailed decades of damaging information about the health risks of cigarette smoke that allegedly had been deliberately concealed from the public. Other incriminating documents were brought to light by industry whistleblowers. They offered damning evidence of a tobacco industry conspiracy to hook and keep smokers, and to keep their efforts looking clean in court.

Goldstone says that these documents—and there were millions of them—mean little. Scientists who work for RJR, he says, are free to reach their own conclusions about their research. "Is it surprising that you might find a document over the last four years from a scientist who says, 'You know what, I've read all the material, and I think cigarettes cause cancer'?" he asks. "That to me is free speech and a good mind working." There is nothing in those documents, he says, that the public hasn't known for years. "When I was a kid, they were called 'cancer sticks,' when I was a kid they were called 'coffin nails,' did anybody not know that? So what did these tobacco companies know that we didn't know?"

In June 1998, the Tobacco Institute's Committee of Counsel, a virtually unknown group of high-powered tobacco lawyers, was accused of crafting a deceptive industry-wide strategy to fight off antitobacco efforts. Committee members were accused of suppressing unfavorable research and hiding the truth about smoking. Cigarette companies sniffed at these charges. They said comparable attorneys' groups existed in other industries, and that 40 years of litigation more than justified the committee's activities.

SEEKING SALVATION

Tobacco did win one important round when the FDA was denied the authority to regulate cigarettes or smokeless tobacco. But throughout

1998, Goldstone was under tremendous pressure. RJR share prices were way down. Philip Morris, with its super Marlboro brand, superior financial flexibility, and well-funded marketing program, was steadily siphoning off RJR's customers. Profits were slumping. Overseas it was worse: Mismanagement and economic misfortune in important markets like Asia and Russia began showing up in scary ways on R.J. Reynolds' bottom line. Add to RJR's woes hundreds of millions a year in debt service and hundreds more to settle state lawsuits. Philip Morris was settling lawsuits, too, but it was triple RJR's size and on firm financial footing.

As if these troubles weren't enough, Goldstone also faced a cracker and cookie crisis. Instead of producing the usual profits, Nabisco was now struggling to keep up with the competition. RJR's operational weakness raised questions on Wall Street about Goldstone's management know-how. Sure, he was an ace lawyer with financial expertise, but if operations were in a slow death spiral, so what?

THE LANDMARK 1998 SETTLEMENT

Goldstone still hoped for salvation. It would come in both predictable and unexpected form.

In 1998, the tobacco industry finally put its Medicaid troubles behind it with landmark event number three: the biggest civil settlement in United States history. Every state with an outstanding Medicaid suit signed on, wiping out Big Tobacco's most potent financial and legal threat. Big Tobacco talked its way into a national settlement that was actually far less restrictive than the original June 1997 agreement.

It also came at a bargain price. This final November 1998 settlement would cost the tobacco industry $206 billion, spread in payments across 25 years—far less than the $368.5 billion written into the June 1997 agreement. Cigarette makers agreed to foot the bill for smoking-cessation programs and pledged not to market to the under-18 crowd. There was no onerous "look-back clause" to penalize tobacco if youth smoking didn't decline. The agreement standardized many marketing and advertising restrictions the tobacco industry had already accepted in previous state lawsuit settlements. Advertising was widely banned. Much tougher restrictions from the 1997 agreement were gone.

Some legal protections for the tobacco industry were also missing, apparently traded away. The November 1998 settlement didn't shield tobacco companies from individual suits resulting in punitive damages and class-action liability lawsuits. Masses of individual and trade union lawsuits stayed alive. The Justice Department continued investigating whether cigarette makers had conspired to conceal health risks or mislead Congress or federal regulators.

But the worst was over. R.J. Reynolds signed the historic agreement with allies and competitors Philip Morris, Lorillard Tobacco (a subsidiary of the Loews Corporation), and Brown & Williamson Tobacco (a subsidiary of B.A.T. Industries P.L.C.). No Congressional approval was required. President Clinton hailed it as a milestone and asked Congress to "finish the job" by granting the FDA regulatory rights. (Congress didn't.)

Health activists blasted the November 1998 settlement as a sellout, too soft on public health measures and not aggressive enough about rising teenage smoking rates. Others criticized the rushed, take-it-or-leave it settlement deadline imposed on the states.

These weren't the only criticisms. Smokers will ultimately pay for most of the damages, passed on by tobacco companies as an additional sales tax. In addition, attorneys who worked on the settlement took home obscene contingency fees totaling billions of dollars, easily the largest in United States history, all paid for by consumers.

The tobacco industry breathed a sigh of relief. RJR wasn't completely out of the woods, but a tobacco industry future looked possible. Bankruptcy talk at RJR Nabisco died down.

But practically as soon as the settlement was inked, Goldstone made his next move. Early in 1999 RJR Nabisco separated its food business and cigarette operations and sold its struggling international tobacco business for a hefty $8 billion to Japan Tobacco Inc. Shareholders expecting a food business spin-off were taken by surprise when Goldstone spun off the tobacco business instead. The breakup was aimed at boosting the company's depressed stock price, but it will take time to assess the gain. The company's food division still shares the same corporate parent's umbrella, and could feel a sharp sting if there is a huge antitobacco verdict.

RJR Nabisco is now a holding company, renamed Nabisco Group Holdings. Its single asset is the 80.6 percent stake it owns in Nabisco Holdings Corporation, which makes food. Fundamentals at the now-

separated cookie and cracker business are slowly improving under president and CEO James M. Kilts. As for the domestic tobacco business,
the news is all good. The now-freestanding company is known once
again as R.J. Reynolds. Proceeds from the foreign tobacco business sale
have been used to cut the company's debt, down now from $6.5 billion
to about $1 billion. For the first time in at least a decade, R.J. Reynolds
isn't looking rival Philip Morris in the knees. They are not eye-to-eye
yet, but thanks to Goldstone's maneuverings, R.J. Reynolds now has the
financial strength to at least call itself a competitor.

STANDING UP FOR A "ROGUE INDUSTRY"

Goldstone has his own theory about why, in the 1990s, the tobacco
industry became a legal target, as compared to the alcoholic beverages
industry, for example. "In the United States, there is a holy trilogy of
plaintiffs' lawyers, the media, and special interest groups. The plaintiffs'
lawyers have become very powerful; they're better at public relations
than anybody else," he says. "Alcohol has never been very attractive to
them. With alcohol, you get a disability, you can't work, you can't function in society. Alcohol causes societal problems that don't necessarily
result in something you can sue for." Because it's a regulated industry,
Goldstone implies, lawsuits against the producers are negligible.
"Tobacco is a wealthy industry whose product is known to have health
consequences." And compared to alcohol, tobacco is largely unregulated. That, Goldstone says, makes it a "tremendous target for plaintiffs'
lawyers."

Goldstone says he would willingly put up with regulation if it would
end tobacco's legal troubles. "I'm quite willing to have people come into
our plant, look at how we supply ourselves, look at how we manufacture
our product, watch how we distribute our product, and I'm quite willing
to have significant restrictions on the marketing of our product. But
here's the key," he continues. "If you're going to tell us how buy the
tobacco, how to manufacture the product, how to distribute it, market
it, in my mind it's lunacy then for us to put that legal product out in commerce and have the attorney general of every other state and every city
and county suing us. If we distribute it, market it, and pay taxes on it the
way you tell us to do it, don't sue us when we sell it!" And if you don't
like it, ban it, Goldstone says, but ban it through Congress. Nobody's

going to do that, Goldstone says. The tax revenues are too good. "Also, Americans do believe in the end—and polls show this—that adults have the right to choose."

That said, Goldstone is not a big believer in federal regulation. "In most ways it kills American business," he says. "But I can say with some perspective that I think this industry may have been better off if it had been regulated a long time ago. I think you wouldn't have seen some of the claims about tobacco manipulation. Because tobacco hasn't been regulated, it's been easier for people to argue that it is a rogue industry." Goldstone adds, not entirely tongue in cheek, that perhaps the ultimate solution would be a government buyout. Let Washington run the tobacco industry, as governments do the world over. The government would have total control over pricing, youth purchasing, health management issues, and advertising. A buyout would also, by the way, bail out RJR from its debt and operational shortcomings.

Goldstone defends his company's Joe Camel campaign, now retired, as a First Amendment issue. The campaign was criticized for allegedly pitching cigarettes to kids. If the government hadn't been "screaming" as much as it did about the campaign, Goldstone says, he probably would have retired it sooner. Camel smokers loved Joe, Goldstone says, and expected RJR Nabisco to stand tall against government meddling. "We did a study," Goldstone says. "We found out that 70 percent of underage kids recognized Joe Camel. That quote has been in every newspaper. But the next line of the study said that 97 percent of the 70 percent who recognized Joe Camel had negative views of smoking. That's never quoted."

Goldstone has nothing nice to say about the media, which he seems to consider a vexing, monolithic source of misinformation. "When people say, 'What have you been surprised about?' one of the things that has surprised me is how overwhelmingly negative the press is on our industry," he states.

What if cigarettes are proven to cause cancer? "Is anyone going to be very surprised?" Goldstone counters. "Is anyone who smokes cigarettes today going to be very surprised? I don't think so. I don't think it changes the dynamics of this industry." Goldstone claims to believe, as incredible as it sounds, that proof might even be of benefit to the tobacco industry. Perhaps the carcinogenic agent could be identified. "Maybe we could start working on getting that [constituent] out," he proposes. "It could be the greatest breakthrough in the tobacco industry that ever happened." No one else in the tobacco industry would ever breathe such a thought.

SAVIOR

This is the kind of breakthrough thinking that makes Goldstone a maverick. He deserves credit for saving RJR and perhaps his entire industry from slow extinction. Old-line tobacco companies would never have proposed settling with their archenemies. Philip Morris, with all its clout and eleemosynary activity, felt less need to settle because it would have whipped the competition just by waiting out the storm of litigation. The irony is that without the 1998 settlement, litigious antitobacco forces like Mississippi attorney general Michael Moore would likely have become Philip Morris's best friend by killing off the company's smaller, less wealthy competitors.

Goldstone is a savior. For antitobacco forces, the November 1998 settlement was a letdown after years of fist-shaking. For R.J. Reynolds, and for the tobacco industry, it was a stabilizer. Goldstone broke with the past to save his industry from a slow legal death. A Justice Department civil suit filed in 1999 and seeking to recover government expenses for Medicare recipients and veterans harmed by tobacco looks weak. After all, the U.S. government has taxed tobacco manufacturers, subsidized growers, and regulated tobacco advertising for many years. Nabisco Group Holdings continues on. Now Goldstone gets a chance to show Wall Street what he can do to rev up a consumer products company. He is a good bet.

Craig R. Lentzsch

Craig R. Lentzsch at Greyhound

"I don't even know how to drive a bus. I couldn't
fix a diesel engine if my life depended on it.
But I have 800 guys who can."

When Craig Lentzsch took over sputtering Greyhound Bus Lines, he had just three options: Fix it, sell it, or liquidate it. Lentzsch fixed and sold. Liquidation was for losers, and at Greyhound that option became unacceptable. Lentzsch gave Greyhound the tune-up of its life. He may be rightly considered the secular saint of bus travel. What's more, he actually wanted the unglamorous job of hauling Greyhound out of the ditch.

Lentzsch is a precise, highly analytical thinker with a tightly organized mind. He never answers questions halfway, and if he doesn't like the topic he says so rather gruffly. There isn't a bit of bombast or self-promotion in Lentzsch. He's an unpretentious meat-and-potatoes operator who gets the job done, minus the bells and whistles. He characterizes his management style as numbers-driven but people-sensitive. "If you don't care about people, you can't be effective," Lentzsch says. "I don't even know how to drive a bus. I couldn't fix a diesel engine if my life depended on it. But I have 800 guys who can."

Lentzsch doesn't drive Greyhound buses but he does ride them once in a while. "They know it's me—I don't believe in being the world's highest paid mystery rider," he says. "The drivers are great, but sometimes they're quiet and then I have to drag out of them what's wrong. I usually learn something out in the field. I can't afford to be out all the time, but I can't sit in my office disconnected from the world, either."

EMPTYING SEATS

Lentzsch was born on Long Island, then grew up in Charlottesville, Virginia, where his father worked for an aircraft company. He studied applied mathematics at Georgia Tech, then finance and marketing at Wharton. His bus industry career started in strategic planning at Trailways Lines, Inc. Lentzsch joined Greyhound as vice chairman after a leveraged buyout in 1987, but left two years for another bus industry job. He would be back, with a better grip on the bus business than anyone else around.

In the early 1980s the Phoenix, Arizona–based Greyhound Corporation was running more than just a big bus line. Operations ranged from duty-free shops to mortgage insurance to canned meat. The original company running Greyhound long ago changed its name to Dial Corporation and has since exited the bus industry, but back then it was the bus business that gave the company grief.

Trouble began in 1982, when bus industry deregulation near-tripled the number of bus companies plying American roads, up from 1,100 to more than 3,000. Airline industry deregulation four years earlier had already encouraged a fleet of low-cost air carriers with fares low enough to snare intercity bus passengers. All this new competition zapped about half of Greyhound's customers.

A labor dispute in 1983 led to a bitter strike. CEO John W. Teets took a hard line. He was looking at distressing numbers that would only worsen. Intercity bus service fell from 64 million passengers in 1980 to about 34 million in 1985. Industry profits tumbled from $132 million in 1980 to $40 million in 1984. Small discount bus outfits and low-cost air carriers were picking off Greyhound's passengers. Others were simply choosing to drive instead. To stay afloat, Teets cut 17 percent of his workforce, scaled back routes, sold off terminals, and franchised routes to other operators.

CURREY VERSUS LABOR

New CEO Fred Currey arrived in 1987, leading a $270 million leveraged buyout. Lentzsch was a buyout investor, and Currey named him executive vice president and vice chairman. A few months in, Currey paid $80 million to acquire the assets of competitor Trailways, Inc. Now, with links between 12,000 communities in 48 states, 8,500 employees, and 2,800 buses, Greyhound could brag that it was the nation's only nationwide intercity bus carrier.

Currey was an intellectual, a passionate man, an evangelist. He promised Greyhound passengers better service, lower fares, and a computerized fare system. He made plans to pay down $373 million in acquisitional debt. But Currey went wrong with labor. He cruised around the country in a private jet. He extracted wage concessions from resistant employees. Currey eliminated some drivers, then tried to install a new seniority plan. Labor relations grew testy.

Ridership and revenues did rise. By June 1989 the company was reporting a small profit, the first since 1985. Then Currey's good start skidded into a wall. Greyhound was making money, and workers who had accepted concessions wanted their due. When Currey refused, arguing back that Greyhound still owed $350 million in LBO debt and $80 million from its Trailways purchase, labor revolted. Some 6,300 drivers walked off the job.

Then the violence began. Snipers fired at buses and heaved rocks through windows, injuring passengers and scaring off what was left of business. A driver was accidentally killed during a protest when he was crushed against a wall. Dozens of violent incidents followed, including bomb threats. Currey was tough, but his unions were determined to see him fail.

IN A BIND

Currey fought back. He drew on a massive $50 million strike fund to replace union members with new hires. He built back operations and vowed to make the strike irrelevant, and the strike soon became a war of attrition. Even so, Greyhound's financials were in ruins. The company lost $195 million in 1990, then missed a big debt repayment, then another. Curry had mistakenly believed that Greyhound could fight off a strike and simultaneously pay off its whopping debt. The company filed under Chapter 11.

Greyhound sued its unions for allegedly trying to extort wages and benefits through violence. The National Labor Relations Board in turn weighed an unfair labor practice complaint against Greyhound, which if it succeeded could force the bus line to pay tens of millions in back wages. Greyhound was in a terrible bind: Currey had declared the strike long over and picketers had dispersed, but creditors wouldn't approve a reorganization plan because of dangling backpay liabilities.

Currey resigned in 1991 at the behest of creditors. New president and CEO Frank J. Schmieder quickly won approval for a reorganization plan by the end of the year, and Greyhound emerged from bankruptcy.

STRANDING PASSENGERS

But three rough years later, Schmieder was out, too. Schmieder, a former investment banker, was fine at finance and ran Greyhound by watching the bottom line, but it was the equivalent of trying to play basketball while gazing at the scoreboard. He impressed Wall Street early on by cutting costs, improving buses and terminals, and clearing out the labor dispute, but Schmieder didn't understand the bus industry. He cut, cut, cut—workers, routes, telephone operators, the size of Greyhound's fleet. On-time departures and arrivals became a joke. Customer service was abysmal. Travelers phoning for scheduling information rarely got through the first time, or the second, or the third. Poorly paid employees were pressured for greater efficiencies while Schmieder had his office expensively redecorated, and Greyhound executives rode around in limos.

Schmieder admired the airlines' reservation, seat assignment, and baggage handling systems. Why not copy success? But Schmieder didn't understand that Greyhound customers wanted something entirely different—boarding on the run, no reservations required, and real people on the phone and behind the counter. Schmieder's much-touted computerized reservation system was introduced while it was still full of bugs and went down in flames, leaving passengers furious, stranded, or both, and defecting in droves.

Shareholders fretting about mounting losses were glad to see Schmieder go. Board member and former Pan Am CEO Thomas Plaskett became acting CEO, but management was in turmoil. From bus drivers to board members, morale was terrible. Adding pain to punishment, the Interstate Commerce Commission reported that the bus industry's share of long-distance travel in the United States was way down. Intercity bus travel was also taking a bath. The Greyhound era seemed finished.

PLEASE COME BACK

In late 1994, searching for a savior, Greyhound directors invited Lentzsch back. Lentzsch had left Greyhound just before its first bankruptcy filing to take the CFO job at Motor Coach Industries, Greyhound's largest bus source. Now, with a second Greyhound bankruptcy threatening, Lentzsch took the job. He explains his return in high-minded terms, as an opportunity to preserve an essential first rung in the transportation ladder. "We're not big," he says of Greyhound, "but we're important. If we don't have that first step into transportation, a lot of people tend to stay at home and don't look for opportunities. We were about to lose that national infrastructure in 1994." It was an opportunity, Lentzsch summarizes, to do something "socially relevant."

By now a seasoned bus transportation executive, Lentzsch found few surprises back at Greyhound. "I had my arms pretty well around what needed to be done," he says. "The only surprise was the extent to which parts of this business were truly screwed up." For example, Greyhound wasn't answering its telephone, Lentzsch says. In June 1994, the average customer had to call the company 4.4 times to get through once. The budget as written made customer service a very low priority, Lentzsch says disgustedly. "Also, there was a belief in a captive customer. Captive is one of worst words in business. People who use that word should be taken out and shot."

DODGING A BULLET

But before Lentzsch could address operating issues, he had to get the banks off his back. A restructuring agreement was worked out with debtholders who were threatening to force the company into Chapter 11 once more. Lentzsch waved a prepackaged filing under shareholders' noses but never had to use it. Debtholders swapped $98.8 million in convertible debentures for a 45 percent equity stake in the reorganized company and the right to choose two of nine company directors. The rest of the company was split between current shareholders and $35 million in new stock.

Lentzsch had dodged the bankruptcy bullet and snagged a capital infusion along the way. Now he could rebuild. But he needed nothing short of a brilliant strategy. Greyhound had just reported its fourth consecutive quarterly loss. Ridership was down through 1994; the first quarter in 1995 was also a big loss; and Greyhound felt the constant chill of $188 million in lingering long-term debt.

BACK TO BASICS

Lentzsch got busy. "Sure, we had a BHAG," he jokes, referring to the popular notion that a company ought to adopt a Big Hairy Aggressive Goal to optimize success. "It was to survive another 60 days."

Fortunately for Greyhound, which was in chaos, Lentzsch had a pretty good idea of what needed to be done and didn't need much time to get his bearings. He hit the ground running. There were enough competent people in place, he says, to execute basic changes immediately. "Also, I came back and told everyone to do what they [had] wanted to do all along. There was almost instantaneous understanding of the objectives; almost instantaneous agreement about what to do. People in the company knew all along what to do, but they had not had the ability to execute."

Lentzsch understood the nature of the bus industry better than any of his predecessors. He knew Greyhound would die if it continued to offer a steady diet of delays, late arrivals, lost luggage, and lousy service. So Lentzsch refocused his company on bus industry basics—enough buses, everyday low prices, and reliable service. Lentzsch is a realist. Most people ride buses because they have to. Riders tend to be senior citizens, minorities, immigrants, and young people short on cash. Budget considerations rather than speed of travel are the top priority, although passengers do expect to depart and arrive on time. Bus riders need a reliable way to get from here to there on the cheap. In 1998, the median income for a Greyhound passenger was $22,500—not poverty level in the United States, but not a fortune, either. Unlike his predecessors, Lentzsch understood that his job was to provide basic, affordable transportation at a profit.

So Lentzsch rebuilt Greyhound with customer needs in mind. He discarded airline routing practices and dumped the hub-and-spoke model. Routes and schedules were fine-tuned to improve convenience. Lentzsch understood that Greyhound passengers paid cash for tickets on the day of departure. He junked the computerized reservation system. Lentzsch knew most customers didn't plan their travel far in advance, so he replaced promotions and deep discounts with everyday low prices, and always below the transportation competition. He hired enough operators to answer the phone—not a brilliant decision, just good common sense when you understand your market.

DETERMINED TO GROW

By 1996 the back-to-basics approach was bearing fruit. Core customers as well as discretionary customers were returning. Revenues were up, operations were running smoothly, and customers were more satisfied.

Despite the dramatic turnaround, Wall Street stayed guarded. It saw the bus travel industry as a dinosaur, once big stuff but now past its prime. Lentzsch was determined to make Greyhound grow anyway. He signed agreements to coordinate service with other bus lines. Lentzsch set up joint agreements with Mexican bus companies, to offer cross-border and direct trips deep into Mexico, a country where buses are primary transportation. When Amtrak announced cutbacks, Greyhound moved its terminals to train stations to scoop up the traffic. It joined ValuJet Airlines to offer ground transportation under a new FlightLink program. In November 1996, Greyhound enjoyed its best Thanksgiving in seven years.

DANGER, AND A SOLUTION

Lentzsch had carried Greyhound a long way in just four years. In addition to assembling the debt restructuring and installing the back-to-basics policy, the Greyhound CEO had built up his route system and beefed up his fleet. Earnings were better and ticket sales were rising. Labor had rejected his proposal but hadn't rejected Lentzsch. Labor relations were better than they'd been in years.

Lentzsch had brought Greyhound farther than any predecessor—but it still wasn't far enough. The company in 1997 lost $16.9 million on revenues of $771 million and still had $208 million in long-term debt. Labor worries lingered. Lentzsch needed only to flip back a few chapters in company history to see Greyhound's vulnerability. In 1998 the company turned a profit for the first time in five years, but Lentzsch still sensed danger. Then he spotted a solution. In 1999, Lentzsch sold

Greyhound to Laidlaw Inc., the Burlington, Ontario, bus and ambulance giant that already owned Greyhound's Canadian bus lines. Laidlaw paid $465 million and assumed another $185 million in Greyhound debt.

Lentzsch, who remains CEO at Greyhound's Dallas headquarters, believes the sale was Greyhound's best option. The company sacrificed its independence, but now it doesn't have to choose between investing in growth areas or upgrading its fleet. It can borrow money as needed, at lower rates. With investment-grade partner Laidlaw, Lentzsch says, his company can grow without gaps and compete more effectively. In five years, Lentzsch says, Greyhound will be a $2 billion Laidlaw subsidiary. "On our own we'd be damn lucky to get to $1.2 or $1.3 billion."

"I DON'T DO DESSERT"

Greyhound continues to negotiate its position relative to the airline industry. Do airlines steal much business? "Clearly there is an overlap," Lentzsch says. "Some 50 percent of our customers have flown in the last year. Then again, 50 percent haven't. We do have a core customer base that can't be accessed by the airlines, but for 750-mile trip lengths and up, there is a reasonable amount of overlap." Interestingly, Lentzsch says that when competitor Southwest Airlines enters a Greyhound market, it creates so much positive interest in travel that it improves the market for everyone.

Lentzsch says he still has work to do at Greyhound. Unlike a turnaround artist, he says he is in it for the long haul. Greyhound still has its critics. Customers say service is much improved, though sanitation and equipment issues sometimes pop up. Still, compared to its position just a few years ago, Greyhound is thriving.

Lentzsch, an intense man, has a hard time remembering what he does to relax. "I go to sporting events," he says finally. "The Cowboys, the Rangers. I get Stars tickets." He pauses. "I like fancy restaurants. I collect wine." He thinks some more. "Oh, I like to cook," he says, at last sounding excited. "I'm a grilling or sautéing person. I don't do dessert."

Sometimes a business in decline can't be saved, or shouldn't be saved. Big cross-country bus travel, however, is a vital industry and basic transportation for many Americans. If the industry ever truly tanked, the federal government would have to step in and save it. If it didn't exist, we'd have to invent it.

Greyhound today is the largest bus company in the United States. More than 20 million passengers ride the company's 2,500 buses each year, between major cities and to rural outposts. Greyhound's workforce has expanded to handle higher passenger volumes and to keep the customer service coming. Lentzsch saved a half-dead national transportation system under the worst of circumstances. He is nothing short of a hero.

Richard A. Snell

Richard A. Snell at Federal-Mogul

"You have to say, here's how we're going to do it, WHAM!
We're going to change this place from losers to winners."

Dick Snell is the ultimate BHAG disciple. If there were a commission to promote the Big Hairy Aggressive Goal, Federal-Mogul CEO Snell would be its smiling poster boy.

Snell saved Federal-Mogul when it was a sinking ship. Company directors only came to their senses at the last moment, and they understood that they would have to bet it all on finding the right manager the first time around. Fortunately, they found Snell.

A salesman, and by his own reckoning a "damn good" one, Snell has an easy manner that softens even skeptics. He wears dark suits but yanks off his tie when he feels like it. In conversation he switches smoothly between the conceptual and the quantitative. Snell's hands sweep generously through the air as he speaks. He is not above the occasional football analogy.

But what Snell most enjoys is instilling values, helping employees feel good and work well, and building a culture that promotes a kind of corporate self-esteem. A brilliant manager, Snell understands the importance of "bringing people along." Visions are terrific stuff, he says, but they never get off the ground if others don't believe. "I think the soft stuff is way more important than the numbers," he says. "I'm a marketing guy. I don't know how to make a muffler or a bearing. I depend on good people, and the soft stuff counts enormously." Snell makes statements like this: "I've never had one person work for me who didn't want to do a good job." His sincerity is impressive.

LEANED ON

Snell's journey to Federal-Mogul didn't take a straight road. First he attended "about 95 undergrad schools, fighting my way through." He discovered a taste for management as an artillery officer. "I was in charge of 250 people in the field, with $8 billion in equipment following behind us," he remembers. "Suddenly I realized I was the only one in the whole place worried about what we were doing and how we were going to get there." Snell studied marketing at Wharton, then held a series of jobs at Procter & Gamble, SmithKlineBeecham, Quaker State, and Tenneco. "I fell in love with the automotive business," Snell states. "I realized I could make a huge impact." At Tenneco's Walker division he was a tin bender supplying exhaust equipment to auto manufacturers. Dull stuff, but Lentzsch made it exciting. He caught the attention of directors at Federal-Mogul.

Federal-Mogul for more than a century has been a major automotive industry parts supplier. The Southfield, Michigan–based company started off producing engine bearings, then added oil and grease seals, pistons, ball bearings, and an array of engine, fuel system, and transmission parts. By the late 1980s its manufacturing core was parts for cars, trucks, and farm and construction vehicles.

In the late 1980s the automotive industry began switching over to "systems engineering," and Snell and other big automotive parts suppliers faced a profound market shift. Automakers no longer wanted to assign brake drums, brake pads, and connecting hydraulic lines to three different suppliers—now they wanted to buy the entire prebuilt combination from a single company. Automakers began demanding more design and engineering work from their suppliers, produced to world-class quality standards, and all guaranteed, of course. At the same time they leaned on suppliers to reduce prices.

Most big-parts suppliers responded by trying to grow as big as they could, as fast as they could. Some cozied up to automakers, hoping for an edge. Not Federal-Mogul. CEO Dennis J. Gormley had long disliked his company's exposure to the rising and falling fortunes of the car industry, and he resented the narrow margins his company had to live on. Gormley decided to ease his company out of the Big Three supplier game. He was sure that he had a better idea.

OVERSEAS AMBITIONS

By 1993, Federal-Mogul was thumbing its nose at the Big Three and raising prices. Gormley began phasing his company out of its core manufacturing business. He envisioned instead a chain of auto parts after-market supply stores in developing countries, with much higher profit margins. Federal-Mogul directors were enthusiastic and so was Wall Street. Shares trading in January 1992 for $14.50 were by February 1994 trading at $37.50.

Federal-Mogul continued throughout 1994 to build its overseas aftermarket business. It entered a joint venture to distribute parts in Spain, and acquired a retail distributor in Venezuela. Gormley said his company would hit earnings projections for all of 1994 and predicted record earnings in 1995. Sales, he said, would rise about 12 percent a year for the rest of the decade.

These predictions blew to bits in the wind. Federal-Mogul's earnings fell short for 1994. Then a steep drop in the Mexican peso stung Federal-Mogul badly, ensuring that 1995 earnings would also disappoint. Shares plunged 23 percent on the news. Gormley scolded that the market was overreacting and pushed on. He signed more joint ventures and shed several "nonstrategic" businesses. By this time Federal-Mogul was earning 70 percent of its revenues from aftermarket sales. Gormley called this a far more reliable market than the one for new car parts and predicted that Federal-Mogul's financials would soon show improvement.

FOLLOWING A FAULTY VISION

But Federal-Mogul's performance worsened. Big Three parts buyers saw their old supplier pouring resources into international retailing and concluded that manufacturing premium auto parts was no longer a Federal-Mogul priority. Several important retail customers like Pep Boys and NAPA felt threatened. They canceled their Federal-Mogul contracts because they thought the company was positioning itself as a future competitor.

Federal-Mogul lost $9.7 million in 1995. A debt level of $125 million in 1989 zigzagged up over $500 million. Gormley continued to believe in his strategy. The board backed him up. Facing financial hardship, Federal-Mogul began a restructuring that eliminated 500 jobs and initiated a series of divestitures. CEO Gormley, always bullish, announced that earnings in 1996 would improve by more than 50 percent. Instead, Federal-Mogul lost $211 million more.

Gormley's overseas retailing plan was three years in and failing spectacularly. Federal-Mogul was an expert at making and shipping parts, but it knew little about creating a chain of retail stores in far-flung locations. The company was dying bit by bit, and no one was doing anything to stop it. "My predecessor was a good, hard-working honest man, very smart, who had a vision that didn't work," Snell says. "It's very difficult for CEOs to say, 'We're wrong, we gotta try something else.'"

MASOCHIST OR JUST NUTS?

Something had to give and it did, finally, in September 1996. Federal-Mogul's board awakened from its deep sleep and asked for Gormley's resignation. It was a blow for Gormley, who got the news while at home in bed recovering from coronary bypass surgery. Federal-Mogul stock jumped 6 percent on the news. With Gormley gone, board member Robert S. "Steve" Miller Jr., a seasoned manager with Chrysler and Morrison Knudsen experience, agreed to take over until the company could install a new leader. There was a sense of terrible urgency. The board knew it needed nothing short of a savior.

Enter Snell, the exceedingly successful 55-year-old president of Tenneco Automotive. When people heard he was going to be the new boss at Federal-Mogul, Snell says, they asked him what kind of a kook was he—a masochist or just nuts? Snell thought he understood the problems at Federal-Mogul and could fix them. He asked the board for a free hand and got it. Time was short and cash was running out, employees and investors were worn down after years of dashed expectations, and now the company had no clear direction.

By this point Federal-Mogul was operating more than 80 parts distribution centers around the world and 132 retail parts stores outside the United States, primarily in Latin America. The company also produced engine, transmission, steering, and suspension parts. Snell concluded quickly that there was more wrong at Federal-Mogul than just poor execution. He saw a tangle of related but different businesses.

There were, however, some pleasant surprises. "Federal-Mogul still had some very good manufacturing technology," he says. "There was still a really good bearings business. We had good, high-quality, efficient manufacturing plants, and we had core competencies that were still competitive and world-class."

TRUST ME

After two months on the job, in February 1997, Snell met with his board. "I made it my goal to lay out at that meeting everything that was going to change," he recalls. "I said here's what we're going to do, here's the core we're going to build on, here's how we're going to act from a cultural standpoint, here's how we're going to do it." Snell said he wanted to can the company's overseas aftermarket strategy. He lobbied strongly for a return to the company's manufacturing core. "The board thought the old strategy was right and the execution was [just] slow," Snell recalls. "I said, 'Come on, fellows, you got it wrong, the strategy is wrong, and I've got to fix it fast and take no prisoners.'" Snell kept talking until the board gave in. He calls this moment a turning point. "It was just me, Dick Snell, standing up there saying, 'I've been here 60 days, trust me.' It was very satisfying, because for the most part, people did."

To save a company heading for a smashup, Snell says, you've got to move quickly. "If you are going to sit around and refine things, you will lose the hearts and minds of the people you need. You have to say, here's how we're going to do it, WHAM! We're going to change this place from losers to winners!" A good CEO can get about 80 percent of the way like this, Snell believes. "Then if people can see the seas parting, the sun coming up, and hear birds singing, if you are at 70 or 80 percent already, you can pick up the other 20 percent on the fly."

So Snell launched a massive restructuring plan. He moved in broad, decisive strokes. Federal-Mogul cut its worldwide workforce by 2,900 jobs, or nearly one-fifth. Thirty wholesale operations in 10 countries went on the market. Snell shuttered a U.S. factory and two warehouses, and relocated product lines around the world to cut costs. Unprofitable overseas retail stores were sold, too. They were good businesses, Snell explains, but Federal-Mogul didn't have the expertise or infrastructure to realize their potential.

RESTORING

Snell also had to refocus his manufacturing workforce. "I told them they were the foundation for the company's future," he explains. "Once I did that, it let out enormous energy. You could almost hear a sigh of relief. People knew viscerally that the company [had not been] going in the right direction." Part of the job was restoring morale. "It's hard to come to work every day and think you're going to fail, your company's going to fail. These are talented people," he says of his workforce. "We wanted them to have a slight swagger. We didn't want arrogance, but if you feel you can kick butt, you'll work much better because you feel you are going to win the game."

Snell's efforts to restore his company in both spirit and operations also required sacrifices by management. In a show of solidarity, the office art collection went. Ditto the company condo in Florida. No more free executive car washes or gas-ups. Snell attacked the lard that had thickened the midsection of Federal-Mogul and its executives, meta-phorically and even literally. He actually challenged company managers to lose two pounds a week, then fined them at weigh-ins if they fell short. The program was dubbed "Dump the Plump," and it was a silly symbol, but it signaled the rest of the workforce that visible results were expected of every employee.

People began to realize that Snell was a different kind of leader. Costs went down at Federal-Mogul. Sales went up—and quickly. Strained relations with the company's Big Three automotive customers evened out. Federal-Mogul was making a dramatic recovery, and Wall Street expressed its optimism. Snell is secure enough to poke fun at the dramatic reversal of opinion. "This was the most condemned company management in the history of American business," he says. "It was crazy. Within three months on the job, analysts were saying we're the greatest management in the nation."

BHAG TIME

Another CEO at this moment might have settled back to enjoy the suc-cess. Not Dick Snell. He invoked the mantra of the BHAG: the "Big

Hairy Aggressive Goal." No more small steps. Be aggressive. Do something bold. Build something big. Break the mold. Become a force for the future. Take a risk. Strike out in an unexpected direction, and set your sights high.

Snell's BHAG was to shape Federal-Mogul into a world-class manufacturer providing exactly the kind of systems engineering components its customers wanted most and would pay a premium for. To accomplish this, Snell began searching for a global partner. He found one in T&N PLC, a British manufacturer almost twice the size of his own company, whose auto parts were complementary for systems engineering purposes. In late 1997 Federal-Mogul, already the world's largest maker of engine bearings, swallowed the world's largest maker of engine and transmission products.

The meal cost Federal-Mogul $2.4 billion, which also assumed the British company's $600 million debt. But overnight Federal-Mogul became the largest automotive engine parts supplier on the planet and more than doubled its workforce and revenues. It was a big, hairy, aggressive move: an attention-grabber. Stock values soared. Snell became an instant deity.

Snell wasn't done. Instead of stopping to savor his company's transformation into a $5 billion behemoth, he announced another big goal. By now 80 percent of Federal-Mogul's retail stores had been unloaded, and debt reduction was ahead of schedule. Snell said he would increase sales fivefold, to $10 billion, by 2002. The T&N acquisition had already boosted Federal-Mogul more than halfway there. Snell struck again. In 1998, Federal-Mogul bought Fel-Pro Inc., a leading gasket maker based in Skokie, Illinois, for $720 million. The shopping spree continued with several additional acquisitions.

TURNING A HORSE INTO A THOROUGHBRED

Federal-Mogul is now in an enviable position. Stock prices are extremely healthy and climbing, and earnings are well into the black. "The noncore businesses dragging us down are now pretty much off our plate," Snell says. "We can focus on our core competencies; we've got a good cash machine; and we can keep our eye on future growth, too."

Snell talks like a CEO stalking further acquisitions. He has rules about those. "Number one, no matter how small the acquired company, they always have some people better than us," he says. "If we do it right, we can upgrade our management every time." Rule two: "Acquisitions always have some processes better than ours. We have to identify them, lock 'em in, and upgrade." And the most important Snell rule of acquisition: "Each time, bring everyone into our culture. We spend a lot of time on purpose, core values, and how we have to conduct ourselves to be successful here."

Snell is superb at conveying a mission to employees. How does he do it? Snell laughs, then answers, "Sheer terror. I don't know, it's one of the things a CEO must do. Employees want to do a good job—this is where people are spending most of their lives. They need a common view. They need to be able to see clearly where the company is going, how it will get there, and how it will conduct itself. If you haven't done this as CEO, you haven't done the most basic, fundamental thing."

BHAGs sound deceptively simple, but very few soar like Snell's. It's worth noting that Snell's predecessor, Gormley, also had a BHAG—but he chose the wrong one. Gormley abandoned Federal-Mogul's basic strengths and tried to shape a manufacturing company into a global retailer—that is, into a fundamentally different kind of company. It was the equivalent of trying to change a horse into a llama. Snell's BHAG succeeded because he began with Federal Mogul's strengths and matched that competency to customer needs. He changed a horse of a company into a thoroughbred.

THRIVING

What's Snell's personal BHAG? "This sounds bad," he says, laughing. "From a career standpoint, I'm having more fun than ever in life. I don't need to go anywhere. We can make this company as big or customer-serving as we want. We've gone from a bunch of people in jeopardy to a thriving place, up from 13,000 to 56,000 people. It's exciting to be here."

Federal-Mogul employees agree. They've swapped their stoic resignation for cheery optimism, and they no longer think in survival terms. Federal-Mogul has become a powerful, profitable global company operating more than 150 manufacturing facilities around the world, with annual sales totaling $7 billion. Getting there required a savior. Dick Snell proved himself that person.

Stephen M. Wolf

Stephen M. Wolf at US Airways

*"I don't pay attention to characterization.
I have a view of me and I know precisely
what I am doing. That's what counts."*

Stephen M. Wolf knows the airline business cold. He has held nearly every airline position and worked at nearly every major carrier. Wolf tried to resist the offer to save struggling US Air because he knew it would be a bitch. He couldn't help himself. That is US Air's good fortune.

THE PATH TO US AIRWAYS

Wolf is an imposing six feet six inches tall. He has straight brown hair, a bristling mustache, and huge hands. He is known for wearing impeccably tailored suits over trademark red suspenders. Wolf's authority seems to come naturally and can be intimidating. His delightfully dry wit invites you in, but everything else says mind your distance. People may disagree about Wolf's personal style, but no one disputes his brilliance.

He grew up very modestly in East Oakland, California. Wolf's father left when the boy was 15, and he became the family breadwinner. After working his way through San Francisco State he joined American Airlines and rose through the ranks until there were only five executives ahead of him, including future CEO Robert Crandall. "I was waiting for one of them to die or get hit by a truck," Wolf jokes. Impatient and ambitious, he left for brief turns at Pan Am, then Continental. Next, as CEO at struggling Republic Airlines, Wolf threatened bankruptcy unless his pilots took a hefty pay cut. When they did, he restored Republic to profitability, then sold it to Northwest. Then Wolf took on Flying Tiger, a California-based cargo carrier on the verge of collapse. He squeezed out labor concessions worth $50 million; the company perked up; and Wolf sold this one off to Federal Express.

Wolf's expertise at tightening operations and extracting labor concessions was well-known by 1987, when he arrived at troubled UAL and United Airlines. Wolf made United a global player, but most significantly he transformed it into the largest employee-owned company in the nation and dragged $4.9 billion in wages and benefits out of his unions in the process. Labor demanded his departure as a condition of the buyout agreement. Wolf hit the ejection button in 1994 and parachuted to earth with a hefty severance package.

He decided to get off the fast track. Wolf says he had worked every day of his adult life. "I'd made more money than I thought was reasonably possible, I had no economic reason to work, and thus why work?" he asks. "Why do push-ups for the sake of doing push-ups?" Lazard Frères took him on as a consultant. Wolf says he "dabbled." At the end of a year he was sure he would never work full-time again. "I couldn't even dream up a job I would take," Wolf states. The US Air position was offered several times, and Wolf says he was "not at all interested." US Air had performed so poorly for so long. The problems were so hardened, the odds were so unfavorable, the revival process would be so all-consuming. But as time passed, Wolf grew intrigued in spite of himself.

DISTRESS CALL

US Air, the largest carrier on the East Coast, was created by the mergers of six airlines: Allegheny, Lake Central, Mohawk, Empire, PSA, and Piedmont. The Washington, D.C.–based company flew profitably before deregulation in 1978, then began losing staggering sums of money. The airline ended the 1980s with an unforgettable fatal accident at LaGuardia that left a 737 in the water. During the early 1990s, US Air was ravaged along with the rest of the industry. Cash-starved and eager for an overseas alliance, it cut a deal. "British Air bought a large preferred holding that gave our company $400 million," Wolf says of a transaction that took place before his arrival. "One could argue correctly that had they not done that we would have filed for bankruptcy." British Air got three board seats in return, but it was most pleased about US Air's agreement to supply a steady feed of passengers.

Despite the cash infusion, US Air continued to fail. Its costs were the highest in the industry, and losses simply mounted. "Between 1990 and 1994 we distinguished ourselves by losing $3 billion," Wolf says. "On our revenue base, that was a significant accomplishment." Market share shrank. No-frills operators feasted on US Air passengers, and fare wars ruined revenues. In 1994 CEO Seth E. Schofield announced plans to cut costs by $1 billion a year, with half that to come from labor concessions. But labor refused to line up. Adding pain to pressure, US Air suddenly found itself trying to explain its fifth fatal crash in five years. At the end of a routine flight from Chicago to Pittsburgh, a plane had taken a mysterious and catastrophic nosedive 6,000 feet to the ground. Schofield begged the public to believe that US Air's crash record was just bad luck. Many travelers ignored him and took their dollars elsewhere.

WOLF TAKES CHARGE

Schofield, a lifelong US Air employee who had begun as a baggage handler, pleaded with labor for concessions. He could not break the labor-management stalemate. In 1995 he stepped down. Frustrated investor Warren E. Buffett was forced to write down his Berkshire Hathaway Corp. stake in US Air by $270 million. Buffett resigned from the board and called his investment a huge mistake. The airline went on the auction block. There were no takers. It was during this extremely bleak period at US Air that Wolf's fascination got the best of him. For an airline expert seeking part-time work, Wolf says, US Air had to be the very worst option. He hired on anyway. US Air's grateful board gave their new chair and CEO complete control and, as usual, Wolf chose stock and options instead of a princely salary. In January 1996 Wolf moved from his farm in Middleburg, Virginia, into a hotel in Georgetown. For the next two and a half years, whatever time remained after his 12-hour workdays, he would spend there.

US Air's outlook brightened just as Wolf arrived. Earlier restructuring efforts began to pay off and, most important, the economy collected itself. Blessed by a bit of blue sky, Wolf took a deep breath and looked around. "I've joined new airlines many times," he says. "I've learned that no matter how comprehensively I've analyzed a company, until you move into their living room you don't know what you're getting into." US Air's unions didn't know what to expect, either. Some people respected Wolf for having made United a champ. Most, however, were apprehensive. They knew Wolf's track record and they expected him to come after concessions, with pliers in hand.

ELEVATING EXPECTATIONS

Wolf saw US Air as a product of multiple mergers that had never been effectively integrated, operationally or culturally. Quality and service were second-rate. Costs were out of line. The fleet of aircraft was old, flew predominantly short hauls, and was probably the most complex in the industry. "Also, somewhat disturbingly, between 1990 and 1995 our competitors on average had grown by 24 percent," Wolf adds. "US Air had shrunk by 4 percent."

One of Wolf's first moves was to recruit Rakesh Gangwal, a talented airline strategist Wolf had plucked from a low rung during his time at United. "There are some number of good people and there are those who move the needle," Wolf says, referring to Gangwal. "You want to find those who move the needle." Wolf made Gangwal president and began grooming him as US Air's future CEO. In fact, Wolf had told US Air's board he wouldn't take the job without just such an arrangement with Gangwal.

Wolf spent much of his first year at US Air defining strategy and maneuvering into position. He threw himself into raising expectations. Wolf went on the road with a slide show and spoke to dejected employees. "I said I'm going to do my job, but you gotta do your job," he says. "What I want you to do is this: When you get up in the morning or for midnight shift or whatever it is [and] get in your Volkswagen and go to work—as long as you're going to do that, give it your all. It really doesn't consume any more energy, and you'll feel much better about yourself. It will not cost a dime, and the quality of the product will go like this. . . ." Wolf's left hand takes off toward the ceiling. "All of which is true," Wolf says. "And all of which they did."

PROFITS AND PRESSURES

In mid-1996, US Air's relationship with British Air went downhill. Wolf was frustrated by the terms of the alliance, which he describes as "heavily, heavily weighted in British Air's favor." British Air was frustrated, too, by the rapid decline of its American partner. It had already written off half its $400 million investment. US Air's biggest shareholder began a series of quiet discussions with a more viable partner, American Airlines, even as three BA representatives sat on US Air's board. Wolf filed an antitrust suit, and some said his goal was to jettison the alliance altogether.

At home, Wolf kicked his strategy into gear. He changed the name from US Air to US Airways to give the company a more integrated, international image. The company repainted its planes in more conservative colors, went after business travelers, and moved to expand internationally. Wolf and Gangwal also sharpened the airline's focus on quality. US Airways was infamous for being second-rate, and Wolf was determined to turn that around. He spent a lot of time, he says, "dreaming up service measurement criteria." For example, Wolf decreed a maximum number of seconds that an arriving aircraft could sit at the gate before employees popped the cabin door. He pressed hard for on-time arrivals and fewer lost suitcases. "If you lose a person's bag, he or she only remembers it for the balance of their natural life," he quips. Airlines don't have much in the way of product, Wolf says. What they sell is service. Get it wrong and say so long to your customer.

But Wolf knew all the fresh paint and on-time luggage in the world meant little without lower operating costs. US Airways needed a new labor agreement to survive as a stand-alone airline. Competitors old and new, all lower-cost, were expanding into US Airways' lucrative East Coast territory and pressuring Wolf to do what he had done well so many times before: extract those concessions. But for the first time in years, US Airways was profitable, and labor wasn't in the mood for givebacks.

TO SHRINK OR TO GROW

Ever since his arrival at US Airways, Wolf had taken extra effort to cultivate his unions. Formerly adversarial labor-management relations had improved greatly. Communications were better. Morale was higher. Organized labor and management sat side by side on task forces set up to solve company problems. Wolf had even permitted a union representative to take the microphone at an analysts' meeting, a gesture that was not lost on labor. Wolf was aiming for an atmosphere of trust and respect. This was unexpected, given his track record, but it was hardly by happenstance.

Early in 1997, Wolf made his move. He told organized labor he was ready to place a record order for 400 Airbus jets and call back hundreds of furloughed pilots. Wolf wanted those planes to expand US Airways and to simplify his fleet, which was costing the company a bundle on training and spare parts. In exchange, Wolf asked labor's permission to create a low-cost airline within an airline to compete with no-frills carriers. He also asked for sizable concessions from pilots who would continue to fly for the main airline. US Airways' costs were still the highest in the industry. "I couldn't find a drunk to borrow the money from to make the capital expenditure," Wolf says, "without a competitive cost structure."

Without labor's cooperation, Wolf said, he would be forced to cancel the jet order, lay off thousands of employees, park planes, and eliminate unprofitable routes. The airline would shrink and become, once more, a regional carrier. These are the options, he told labor. We must shrink or grow. "My strong preference was to grow the business," Wolf says. "I'm a growth junkie, but I would do what was right for the shareholders." Did his unions hear a threat? "Some characterized it that way," Wolf acknowledges. "Others understood it as a forthright description of the opportunities." Airlines all around US Airways were celebrating record profits, and other unions were demanding pay raises. Wolf, on the other hand, was asking his unions to take a pay cut. Wolf said he would not fight his unions. They could decide their own future.

STRIKING A MIDNIGHT DEAL

Contract talks did not take off. "One of things that made making changes difficult was the question, 'Why do we have to do anything? We're producing record profits,'" Wolf says. "But we were making record profits relative to us, not record profits relative to our competitors." It's true that in the months that followed, US Airways enjoyed the industry-wide travel boom. Airfares and ticket sales rose, and fortunately for US Airways, the good times alleviated some of the financial emergency. One deadline, however, continued to loom closer: Wolf had to commit to those 400 Airbus jets or lose the option to buy them at the negotiated price. In September 1997, with just minutes to spare on a midnight deadline, labor and management struck a deal. The five-year pact gave Wolf his low-cost airline. His pilots got pay and job protections. Wolf placed his $20 billion Airbus order, and for the first time in a decade, US Airways readied for a growth spurt.

Early in 1998, US Airways Group redeemed investor Buffett's preferred stock to the tune of $358 million. Buffett had tried earlier and unsuccessfully to unload his stake, and now the price was up from about $15 a share when Wolf arrived to above $70 a share. "Buffett had once said US Airways was the most frustrating investment experience of his life," Wolf recalls. "But when we got it turned around, he became a very happy camper."

INTO THE FUTURE

Wolf believes he revived US Airways by instilling a very high level of expectation. "If I were a football coach and I had just finished the season with a team that had won 11 and lost 1, I would say, 'We have very, very serious problem,'" he says by way of analogy to describe his style. "I expect planes on time, bags on board, courteous service. I try to convey that expectation to people. There is no sense in getting up in the morning and your lifelong aspiration is to work for the second- or third-best airline. We want to be the best. We won't become the biggest, but we can become the best and the carrier of choice."

Wolf declines to reflect on his image. "I don't pay attention to characterization. I have a view of me and I know precisely what I am doing. That's what counts." US Airways shareholders are very happy, Wolf says. "And from the perspective of our employees, they work for a much more aggressive, progressive, successful airline today than they have at any time in their career history. And they feel very good about it."

Things are going well at US Airways, now the eighth-largest airline in the world. They have some new jets and have implemented a new Sabre reservations system. The low-cost Metrojet line is profitable and exceeding expectations. Sooner or later, Wolf and Gangwal will have to establish a fruitful transatlantic alliance, but Wolf doesn't sound worried. His airline is smaller but it is also "the big gorilla on the East Coast," he says, and will one day be a very significant transatlantic player. British Airways and US Airways are no longer feuding. Is there life yet in a possible American Airlines–British Air–US Airways alliance? "We're hopeful," Wolf says.

US Airways is growing now after shrinking for years. "There are new jobs, new hirings, career opportunities, we're entering new markets, and this is a much more exciting environment. There's something in it for everyone in growth mode."

PASSING THE BATON

Wolf at the end of 1998 passed the CEO baton to Gangwal. As a command-and-control type, Wolf releases power to key executives only when he reaches a personal comfort level. "I do micromanage," he says. "I believe if you don't do little things right, the big things don't happen." Wolf remains, somewhat extraordinarily, a working chairman at US Airways. He devotes himself full-time to shareholder value, strategic direction, and keeping employees engaged. The company's most recent stock slide has undoubtedly concerned him. Wolf says he plans to stay on at the airline for some time.

But not forever. Unlike most other workaholics, Wolf has passions beyond his day job. He is exceedingly serious about the pleasures of buying and eating good food. He owns homes in Paris and Provence, and has a farm in the States where he likes to "fiddle around." Wolf restores old Jaguars. Asked what he drives, Wolf says, "I just bought five cars in the past four or five weeks. There was an XJR supercharged Jaguar sedan, a new BMW, two Renault Kangaroos, and . . . I can't think of the fifth. . . . oh yeah, I took delivery of a Jeep Grand Cherokee." Wolf plans to spend the balance of his life soaking up adventures beyond the workplace. "Life is a sum of glorious experiences, and I think an endgame," he says. "Those who experience most of them win."

Steve Wolf saved US Airways. He arrived when the carrier was half-dead, and its frightened board of directors understood that Wolf was their last chance. It was a surprise when Wolf stepped away from formula and saved the airline without selling it. If US Airways is his last hurrah, this rescue is a fine cap to his career.

CHAPTER 8

>—◇—<

Master Managers
Courage Meets Chaos

The stories in this book are pulled from the real world of business success. The executives here experienced what every ambitious businessperson waits for and hopes for: Challenged by exceedingly difficult circumstances and under tremendous pressure, they performed at their peak. Uncommon opportunity offered them a chance to demonstrate uncommon talent. In some cases the circumstances uncovered latent talent that surprised even the executive himself. All of these executives rose to the occasion and showed the way for others.

These business leaders share some similarities. They enjoy talking about their experiences. They know who they are and feel comfortable in their own skins, which is to say nobody is reading a book about General Electric CEO Jack Welch and trying to be Jack Welch, as much as they may admire him. In many ways these executives are like anybody else: They guard their privacy, hope they will be remembered for doing good, and can laugh at their mistakes. If there were any second-guessers in the bunch, they didn't admit to it or don't remember it. They are wealthy—without exception these people have earned a fortune through salaries and stock options. All of them live well, but few are living the high life.

Of course there are differences, too. Some resent being recognized; others relish recognition and drive around town in a splashy car. Some are self-involved; others are more modest and, given half a chance, spread the credit for their achievements. Many of these people are unflappable during a crisis, while others admit they ride an emotional rollercoaster. Some are political beasts, liberal or conservative. Some are affable—but not all exhibited this trait. There are also different kinds of intelligence in this bunch: Some were cerebral, some earthy, a few erudite, others very narrow. One couldn't remember what kind of food he liked to eat. Another lives in a house surrounded by a fortresslike wall. A third speaks gently and slowly enough to lower your heart rate.

There seems to be no single success profile for handling a crisis. There is no single, right way to operate. In fact, many current ideas about how to be a good manager—gotta be a team player, gotta be open to diversity, gotta be well-rounded, gotta be nice—become irrelevant during a crisis. What is clear, however, is that the odds of success improve when an executive is well-matched to the challenge. Each of the people in this book did it their way, the way that fit them best, and part of their success was that their style was such a good match for the circumstances. This match can come about either through good fortune or by design. It doesn't matter how it occurs.

Differences aside, there are some meaningful leadership traits or qualities common to all the successful executives in this book. Call it a master manager's skill set. These qualities are important for executives aspiring to manage a company in an emergency, when time is short and the circumstances call for fast, fresh thinking:

- Master managers embrace the risk—in fact most relish it. Instead of being destroyed by the crisis, by the walk across hot coals, they are edified by it. Each of the executives in this book would say, "I wouldn't want to go through it again—but I wouldn't give it up for a million dollars!"

- Master managers can size up the situation with unusual insight and speed, then reach a rapid conclusion that might take somebody else months and months, not just to arrive at but also to act upon. They read their organizations well, sometimes using intuition, sometimes analysis, sometimes experience, sometimes luck, most often a combination. Whatever the way, they are acutely perceptive about what is happening, and furthermore, what can be done about it. They intuitively know how to move in on the trouble and steer their companies to safety.

- Master managers are deeply involved in the details of their business and understand operations at every level, not just top-down—which defies the notion that strategy is everything. They know every nut and bolt, every movement and mechanism. They can reach across and down to anywhere in the organization, and they do to stay informed.

- Master managers realize that a crisis calls for doing the necessary today if there is to be a tomorrow at all. Leadership in a crisis is not long-range planning. Master managers live in the present.
- Master managers completely immerse themselves in their work. Their dedication borders on obsession. They are willing to put everything else aside, including family, health, friends, clubs. None of the executives in this book delegated the task, went part-time, or headed off to the ballgame because they had season tickets. Nobody got distracted. They stayed totally devoted and focused on the needs of the moment and nothing else.
- Master managers take charge. This sounds obvious, but it is the number-one priority in a crisis and it doesn't always happen. The executives in this book presented themselves as the company leader and made themselves worthy of following. By establishing clear values and goals they inspired employees, supporters, and doubters—the dedicated but disappointed, the angry, and the puzzled—to fight for the outfit, too.

Three or four executives claimed another special quality—in fact it came up independently too many times to be ignored. These executives called themselves chameleons. They had no special style, they said, but instead became whatever the circumstances required. The chameleon quality is not universal. Clearly there are executives whose style is a good fit for a narrow set of circumstances, and while they may perform magnificently in those circumstances, it isn't clear whether they would do just as well in another situation. But chameleons do exist. They can morph from one style to another to best suit the circumstances. They are, however, rare.

In a related observation, many executives carry their companies out of a crisis and then switch leadership styles. With the crisis under control they ease into a more collegial, consensus-seeking mode. Part of what makes them good is the way they adjust their style as conditions evolve.

All of the executives in this book possess important transferable skills, tools they can apply to any situation. They can get along with a wide range of people, spot a problem and fix it, articulate their thinking, handle ambiguity, live with competing ideas without jumping to conclusions prematurely, and resist being overcome by downside fears.

THE GROUPINGS

The groupings in this book are not intended to define hard and fast categories, like red, green, or blue, nor are they intended to be conclusive or exhaustive. They are suggested as concepts, as a useful framework for thinking about successful problem-solving styles. In fact many of these categories overlap, and some of these extraordinary executives fit into more than one grouping. Most, however, have a signature style. They are a good example of that category. Someone else might define these groupings differently. This way made the most sense to us.

The groupings are useful in other ways. They offer a shorthand way of thinking about leadership styles, and the attributes in each category help distinguish between different kinds of leaders. They offer a guide for evaluating and slotting talent and are of practical value for rising executives looking for ways to size up superiors, peers, and subordinates. These profiles offer suggestions on how to deal with a crisis; what kind of person to put in. Executives dealing with crises of their own may find role models. Finally, it is worth considering what kind of a person you are. Chances are that you are no single type, but that you will have strong tendencies toward one or another.

THE FUTURE

The stories in this book show that one person, slotted correctly, can change a big organization quickly and dramatically. The most skilled managers will not only clear away the crisis, but will rebuild their outfit to prevent it from sliding back into the drink.

The types of people described in this book are steadily assuming even more importance. It's a different business world as we start a new century. The pace of change has quickened. The business world prefers certainty, and like the rest of us resists anything new or strange, but that's just what's coming in the electronic, information-rich age ahead. The transformation under way echoes back weirdly to the nineteenth century, when the steam engine, railroads, and electricity transformed our agrarian economy into an industrial powerhouse. The business leaders who will lead us through this current transformation are those who cope well with—even enjoy—rapid, radical change. They are comfortable in a dynamic business world, recognize it as a place of flow, are extremely good at reading the subtle roadsigns, and have an appetite for risk. The people who will manage the coming discontinuities are the glue between the old business world and the emerging new one. These executives will guide us through the transitional gaps and make the difference. They will be the next generation of dealers, healers, brutes, and saviors.

INDEX

ABOUT THE AUTHORS

>—◆—◁

Gerald C. Meyers, former chairman and chief executive officer of American Motors Corporation, is currently a professor at the University of Michigan Business School in Ann Arbor. Mr. Meyers also taught for more than a decade at the Graduate School of Industrial Administration at Carnegie Mellon University in Pittsburgh. He is a well-known expert in the field of crisis management in business. Mr. Meyers is president of his own crisis management firm, headquartered in Michigan. His first book, *When It Hits the Fan, Managing the Nine Crises of Business,* sold around the world in five languages.

Susan Meyers, the daughter of Gerald C. Meyers, is a writer and former newspaper editor. She holds a Master of Science in Journalism degree from Northwestern University and a Bachelor of Arts degree from Brown University. She currently lives in Brookline, Massachusetts, raising a family and teaching writing.